Woodworking
The Indispensable Guide

Woodworking

The Indispensable Guide

Chris Tribe

FIREFLY BOOKS

A FIREFLY BOOK

Published by Firefly Books Ltd. 2017

First printing

Publisher Cataloging-in-Publication Data (U.S.)

Names: Tribe, Chris, author.
Title: Woodworking : the indispensable guide / author, Chris Tribe.
Description: Richmond Hill, Ontario, Canada : Firefly Books, 2017. | Includes index. | Summary: "A comprehensive step-by-step introduction to woodworking. Guides the reader through starting a workshop, using hand tools and power tools, routing, jointing, and finishing wood projects" — Provided by publisher.
Identifiers: ISBN 978-1-77085-990-6 (soft cover)
Subjects: LCSH: Woodwork – Handbooks and manuals. | Woodwork – Equipment and supplies. | BISAC: CRAFTS & HOBBIES / Woodwork.
Classification: LCC TT180.T753 |DDC 684.08 – dc23

Library and Archives Canada Cataloguing in Publication

Tribe, Chris, author
   Woodworking : the indispensable guide / Chris Tribe
Includes index.
978-1-77085-990-6 (soft cover)
   1. Woodwork--Amateurs' manuals. I. Title. TT185
T75 2017   684'.08   C2017-901380-7

Published in the United States by
Firefly Books (U.S.) Inc.
P.O. Box 1338, Ellicott Station
Buffalo, New York 14205

Published in Canada by
Firefly Books Ltd.
50 Staples Avenue, Unit 1
Richmond Hill, Ontario L4B 0A7

Printed in China

Conceived, edited and designed by
Quarto Press
The Old Brewery
6 Blundell Street, London N7 9BH

MIX
Paper from
responsible sources
FSC® C017606
www.fsc.org

Contents

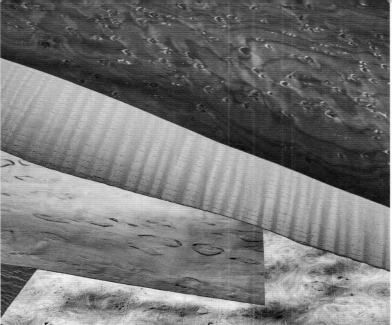

Introduction

For 30 years, designing and making contemporary furniture has been my business, but I have also taught woodwork and furniture making. In recent years, the emphasis of the business has changed, and I have increasingly enjoyed passing on my skills to others. Nowadays, most people spend much of their life at a desk with little opportunity to actually work with "stuff," so it's a real joy to introduce students to the physical pleasure of working wood. My intention with this book is to give you the skills to set out on your own woodworking journey.

The most difficult part of writing the book has been deciding what to include and what to leave out; it could easily have been twice as long. The initial chapters are the preparation for the journey, looking at wood as a material and the various tools you will use to work it. Then we set off with chapters about method and technique for both hand and power tools. Finally, there are five projects that are designed to help you hone the skills learned in the earlier chapters.

One of the things I have learned from my own practice, and from my students, is how easily things can go wrong, so rather than pretending that mistakes don't happen, you will find "clinics" throughout the book, where I explore what can go wrong and how to put it right. Experience has also taught me that there is rarely only one way of doing a task. I have, therefore, tried not to be too pedantic in describing techniques, and have tried to offer alternatives, depending on whether you prefer hand tools or power tools.

I'm glad I set out on the journey. I still enjoy working wood (especially planing!), and it's given me great pleasure over the years. I hope it will give you a similar satisfaction.

Updates and resources
Updates and resources to supplement the book are available at:
www.christribefurniturecourses.com/complete-woodworking.

CHRIS TRIBE

WORKSHOP SAFETY

Health and safety is a key consideration in the home workshop. On this page are pointers for a safe workshop. Safety issues arising from using specific tools are dealt with in the appropriate chapters.

Electrics
Make sure that you have a residual current device (RCD) fitted to your circuit, as this cuts the power instantaneously should you receive a shock. Also try to keep appliance cables tidy to avoid a tripping hazard.

Fire
A dusty, shaving-strewn workshop is a major fire hazard, so workshop hygiene is essential. Invest in a fire extinguisher, preferably a dry powder one that will cope with both wood and electrical fires, and have it serviced annually.

Dust
Ways of dealing with dust are discussed on page 19. Protect your eyes when appropriate, even if you wear spectacles. Goggles give the best protection.

Noise
Many people don't bother with ear defenders, but I now suffer from deafness because I did not wear defenders earlier in my career. Always wear earmuffs or plugs when working with machinery or power tools.

Chemicals
You may occasionally come into contact with corrosive chemicals such as paint stripper or mild acids in the workshop. Protect your hands with rubber gloves. Disposable latex gloves can also be useful when handling messy adhesives, or finishes such as shellac polishes or polyurethane glue.

Splinters
Sawn timber is splintery, so make sure you wear protective leather gloves when handling unprepared timber.

First aid
Always keep a stocked first aid kit in the workshop.

Wood and the Workshop

The best place to start with a book on woodwork is to look at the raw material and the tools that you use to work it. Wood is a beautiful material to work with — it appeals to all the senses. However, it can also be treacherous, splitting, warping and tearing unexpectedly. It is these contradictions that make woodwork so fascinating. Then there are the tools, of course. It is having mastery of finely tuned tools that allows us to cope with the idiosyncrasies of the material. In this chapter, we will look at how a tree becomes wood and the tools that you need to work it.

From tree to wood

Wood comes from trees, specifically the trunk of the tree, and for most furniture making the rest of the tree is of little interest. It is the cellular composition of the trunk, or log, that defines the strength, bendability, color, figure and more of the wood derived from it.

The trunk is composed of longitudinal cellulose cells bonded with lignin, and it is these cells that give the tree its strength, circulate sap, store sugars and define the appearance of the wood. In softwoods (needle-leaved trees), the cells are arranged in concentric circles; in hardwoods (broad-leaved trees), the cells have a more complex organization, with additional radiating cells or rays. Looking at a section cut through the trunk of a hardwood tree can tell us the story of how it functioned as a living organism and also how the wood will behave when we work it.

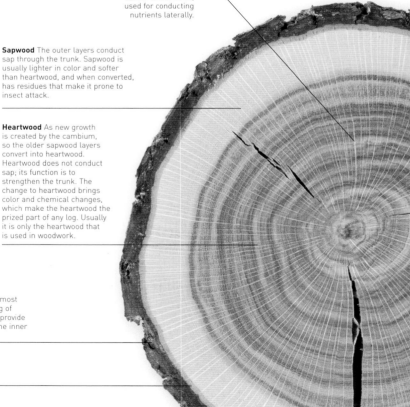

Figure Figuring occurs where the annual rings intersect with the cut surface when the trunk is cut into boards. Figure should not be confused with grain, which is the direction of the tree's fibers in relation to the cut surface.

Ray fleck On certain woods the medullary rays are pronounced. Where these rays intersect the surface obliquely, they show as flecking on the surface. When they intersect acutely, they show as fine lines in the surface.

Medullary rays These are cells that radiate out from the center of the trunk, used for conducting nutrients laterally.

Sapwood The outer layers conduct sap through the trunk. Sapwood is usually lighter in color and softer than heartwood, and when converted, has residues that make it prone to insect attack.

Heartwood As new growth is created by the cambium, so the older sapwood layers convert into heartwood. Heartwood does not conduct sap; its function is to strengthen the trunk. The change to heartwood brings color and chemical changes, which make the heartwood the prized part of any log. Usually it is only the heartwood that is used in woodwork.

Bark The outermost layer, consisting of dead cells that provide protection for the inner living layers.

Cambium layer A thin layer of tissue just below the bark. It consists of phloem, a layer that is used for transporting sugar-laden sap from the tree canopy, and xylem, a layer for transporting water and nutrients up to the tree canopy. Both bark and phloem are usually considered waste products and are discarded during processing.

Annual rings The creation of new cells in the cambium is faster in the spring/summer season than fall/winter. This difference creates annual rings of harder and softer growth.

A good stand of beech and oak. The long, clean trunks will give strong, knot-free wood.

From log to board

It is in converting the log into boards that many of the characteristics of the resulting wood are defined. The success of this process rests with the skill of the sawyer and the kiln operator — a quality log can be spoiled by bad sawing or drying.

Oak stacked for drying. The boards are kept in the order they were cut from the log.

CUTTING

The figure and quality of the wood from a trunk depends on the way in which it is cut.

Plain-sawn wood is cut with the faces almost parallel to the annual rings. This gives a characteristic "cathedral window" arch-shaped figure, and it is prone to warping if not dried carefully.

Rift-sawn wood has annual rings running at an angle (30-60°) to the cut face. The figure is usually fairly uniform on all surfaces.

Quarter-sawn wood has the annual rings running at a right angle to the cut face. This makes for a very straight figure, some ray fleck on the wide face and also great stability.

DRYING

When the tree is cut down, the wood is saturated with water (especially the sapwood), sometimes with an astounding 100% moisture content (MC). In order to use the wood, we need to reduce the MC to around 10–12%. When the wood initially loses water, there is little significant shrinkage, but as it drops past the fiber saturation point (FSP) at around 28–30% MC, the shrinkage starts to become more pronounced.

There are two ways that wet, or green, wood can be dried. The simplest method is to stack the wood in a position that provides free air flow. The stack should

At the mill, the trunk is cut into boards using large gang saws; the line of the cut determines the figure that shows on the faces. The three main commercial types of cut are:

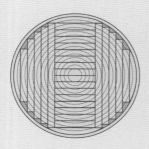

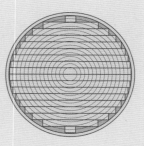

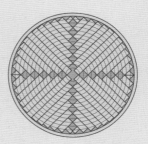

PLAIN SAWN

The log is partly cut through and through, but the center is turned before cutting through and through again. This produces mainly plain- and rift-sawn wood, with more sapwood on all except the central rift-sawn boards.

THROUGH AND THROUGH

The simplest and most economical method. The boards cut nearest to the top and bottom of the log will be narrowest, showing a plain-sawn figure, and will contain a lot of sapwood. Toward the outer edge of the plain-sawn boards, you can find some areas of rift-sawn wood where the annual rings sweep down diagonally. The widest boards will be at the center. They will be quarter sawn and probably have a split in the middle where the central pith occurs.

QUARTER SAWN

The log is cut into quarters and then tilted to cut boards with the annual rings perpendicular to the face. This method is less economical but produces the best boards, with little sapwood on each board.

Stacks of cut wood are loaded into kilns.

be raised about 2 in. (50 mm) from firm, level ground, and individual boards should be separated by cross bearers at intervals of around 39 in. (1,000 mm). The stack should be protected from rain and left for one year for every 1 in. (25 mm) board thickness for hardwoods, and six months for softwoods. This will bring the MC down to approximately 18%. However, this is not low enough for furniture making. To reduce the MC further, the wood can either be brought inside to a lower relative humidity (RH) for a few months, or kiln dried for a short period (see below). Air dried wood is usually easier to work and responds well to hand tools.

The other method is kiln drying. The boards are stacked as with air drying and then placed in a kiln, where the temperature and humidity are controlled carefully to a schedule to match the properties of the wood. The color of some species — steamed beech, for example — can also be controlled in the kilning process. Poor kilning can lead to defects that should be looked for when selecting wood.

WHAT TO LOOK FOR WHEN SELECTING WOOD

There are various considerations that you should keep in mind when selecting the wood for your project. First, you must find a woodyard that allows you to choose. This can be difficult for the woodworker who only wants to buy small quantities, but try to find a yard that will bring a pack for you to select from.

CUT ISSUES

Different parts of your project may need different figuring — perhaps rift sawn for table legs so that the figure is uniform on all faces, and quarter sawn for the top. The best way of finding this is by looking at the end of the stack to see the direction of the annual rings in the ends of the boards — this will indicate the type of figure you will find on the faces.

Sapwood can be a problem, especially in cherry and walnut because it is not easy to spot in these woods. Often you can search through a whole pack and not find a board without sapwood on one face. Look out for sapwood on the face to the outside of the annual ring curve.

DRYING ISSUES

Bad kilning or seasoning can lead to a number of problems that you should look out for.

Cupping
The board is curved across its width. This is not an issue if you plan to cut it into narrower pieces, but you need to allow for some loss of thickness (and hard work!) when you plane a wide board flat.

Bow, spring and twist
In other words, when boards are bending all over the place! They could be used if you are cutting into shorter pieces, but often it is a sign that the boards have hidden stresses that will cause further movement if they are ripped lengthwise. Best avoided.

Sticking marks
Stains at regular intervals on the board surface, left by the sticks used in kilning.

These may look like surface marks, but they often penetrate deep into the board. Best discarded.

End checking and surface checking
These are common and usually accepted as part of the kilning process, to be cut or planed away when processing the board. If they are pronounced, perhaps avoid them.

Honeycombing
Internal cracking along the grain, often aligned with medullary rays, caused by drying too fast. This is usually only exposed when the board is cut and planed.

Insect infestation
Usually found in the sapwood and often occurs pre-kilning, meaning that the insects will be dead. However, it can occur post-kilning, which is more serious. Post-kilning holes are usually cleaner and lighter in color inside than pre-kilning holes. This is sometimes difficult to spot in the sawn surface. It is best to avoid both!

High moisture content
This is difficult to spot without a meter. If you have one, you could take it to the yard with you. If the board feels damp to the touch, ask the yard assistant if they could test it for you.

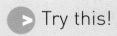 Try this!

> A friendly woodyard will cut up long lengths for ease of transport, but take a crosscut handsaw so that you can do it yourself, if not. A roof rack is useful, too.

> Woodyard etiquette is that you should help to restack the pack after you have finished picking through. Doing this means that you are more likely to get a good reception on your next visit.

> When buying woods such as walnut and cherry, where the sapwood is difficult to spot, take a plane with you to the woodyard to plane the face of boards to expose sapwood.

My 10 favorite woods

In recent years I have worked entirely in temperate hardwoods (mainly from Europe and North America), because of the environmental issues around logging in the tropics. This may limit my palette of color and textures a little, but there is still plenty to choose from.

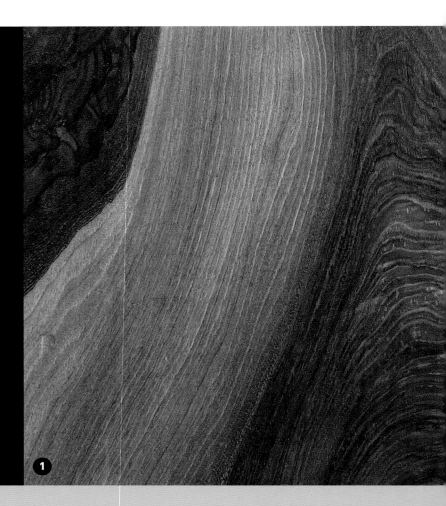

Hardwoods can be divided between those with an open grain and those with a closed grain. Open-grain wood has a textured grain that can be felt when you draw a finger across the board. The texture is caused by the wide pores in the wood intersecting the surface. Closed-grain woods have small pores, so the surface is smooth. Open-grain woods need filling if you want to achieve a highly polished finish, but some people appreciate the textured finish of an open-grain such as oak.

Wood is a beautiful medium to work with. It appeals to all the senses — the silky smooth touch of a newly planed piece of maple, the peppery aroma of worked English walnut, the swish of a sharp plane through oak, the intricate patterns in an oak burl. But it can be tricky to handle — wood will move depending on the humidity, cracks can appear when you plane a board, it may allow you to plane in only one direction or it will not accept finish well. These all add to the challenge of working the material, and understanding the qualities of different woods is an important part of the craft.

ENGLISH WALNUT [1]
Juglans regia

Origin: England, although European walnut is the same.

Grain: Open

Appearance: Brown, often with attractive darker streaking with the grain.

Comments: This really is my all-time favorite, especially air dried (see "Drying," page 12). It planes and chisels beautifully, leaving a wonderful burnished surface, plus it has a beautiful peppery smell when being worked. It works well with both hand and machine tools. When oiled or polished, the color deepens and the complex grain and black streaking become more evident.

AMERICAN BLACK CHERRY [2]
Prunus serotina

Origin: North America

Grain: Closed

Appearance: Heartwood is a rich honey to brown/red color, sometimes with dark-brown resin pockets. The sapwood is pinkish-white. Relatively straight grained and smooth textured.

Comments: Watch out for the sapwood when purchasing — it is often difficult to spot, so take a plane with you to the woodyard. Cherry will darken down nicely on finishing (avoid acrylic finishes on cherry as they kill the color) and will continue to darken to a mahogany color over the years. I often get the fragrance of cherries when working it as I cut through a resin pocket.

EUROPEAN OAK [3]
Quercus robur, Quercus petraea

Origin: Mainly Western and Central Europe

Grain: Open

Appearance: The heartwood is light brown with white- or cream-colored sapwood. Crown-cut boards (see "Cutting," page 12) often have an attractive "cathedral window" figure (repeated arch-shaped pattern). Quarter-sawn boards (see "Cutting," page 12) have a flecking that looks a little like stretch marks! Sapwood is prone to insect attack.

Comments: Black staining occurs if oak comes into contact with ferrous metals in damp conditions, so brass hardware is usually used with it. It turns a beautiful honey-brown color when fumed (exposed to ammonia vapor). It works well, but can have areas of difficult grain. It also responds well to an oil finish.

EUROPEAN ASH [4]
Fraxinus excelsior

Origin: Europe

Grain: Open

Appearance: Ash can vary a great deal in color and grain. Generally it is creamy colored, sometimes with a hint of pink. However, it can be dark brown with black streaks in it, known as olive ash. Occasionally it can exhibit a rippled figure.

Comments: If you want the lighter color, ask for white ash at the woodyard. It's easy to work and can be planed to a fine luster. It is also good for both steam and laminate bending.

HARD MAPLE (5)
Acer saccharum

Origin: North America

Grain: Closed

Appearance: A dense, cream-colored wood, often with a pinkish hue in the grain. Sometimes there are brown patches or dark staining streaks along the grain.

Comments: Maple can be difficult to work because of areas of erratic grain. However, with sharp tools and sanding, a good surface can be produced; the quality of the figure and color makes this worth it. I prefer an acrylic finish on maple, because oils can spoil the light color.

CEDAR OF LEBANON (6)
Cedrus libani

Origin: Middle East, but often sourced from local park-grown trees.

Grain: Closed

Appearance: Heartwood is light brown in color, similar to cherry, while the sapwood is lighter. Soft and smooth textured, it has a lovely aroma.

Comments: This is the only softwood (wood derived from a cone-bearing tree) on my list. I like to use it for drawers and cabinet backs because the cedar fragrance wafts out as you open them. Sometimes it can be a little resinous, which may be a problem in drawers used for storing paper or clothes. It works easily with hand and machine tools.

POPLAR, ALSO KNOWN AS TULIPWOOD (7)
Liriodendron tulipifera

Origin: North America

Grain: Closed

Appearance: A soft, low-density wood with pale sapwood and darker brown or greenish heartwood, often with blackish/blue streaks.

Comments: Although the appearance is less exciting than other woods (I usually paint over it), poplar works very easily and sands to a texture similar to medium-density fiberboard. This means it is good for painted kitchens and other painted, fitted furniture.

UNSTEAMED BEECH

STEAMED BEECH

ELM (8)
Ulmus glabra, Ulmus hollandica, Ulmus procera

Origin: Europe

Grain: Closed

Appearance: The sapwood is creamy, with a brown heartwood that can have deeper brown or greenish streaks. Quarter-sawn boards have a checked flecking, while crown-cut figure is irregular.

Comments: The texture can be coarse, sometimes with stringy areas that are difficult to plane. It takes an oil finish well, if the surface is sanded well. Dutch elm is considered to be superior to English. Although elm has been ravaged by Dutch elm disease in recent decades, it is still available.

AMERICAN BLACK WALNUT (9)
Juglans nigra

Origin: North America

Grain: Closed

Appearance: I have included the walnuts in open-grained woods, although they are on the margin. Black walnut is dark brown, often with a purple tint and occasional ripple. The sapwood is light brown.

Comments: It's usually steamed (see "Drying," page 12) in production, making the sapwood difficult to spot. When visiting the woodyard, it's worth taking a plane with you to plane the surface and check for sapwood, which can extend the whole face of a board. It works and takes a finish well, especially French polish.

EUROPEAN BEECH (10)
Fagus sylvatica

Origin: Western Europe

Grain: Closed

Appearance: Can be steamed when drying. Unsteamed beech is light brown, almost white, while steamed beech is a deeper honey color. Grain is usually even, with slight "freckles"; these become more checkered on quarter sawn. Texture is smooth and even.

Comments: I find beech a little boring in appearance, but I like it for its easy working properties. It is good for painted kitchens, if you don't want to use the softer poplar. It's also good for steam and laminate bending.

Man-made boards

We have already mentioned that solid wood can be difficult to work with. It can also present problems with movement years after a piece of furniture was made. Various man-made boards have been developed that overcome this problem.

Most man-made boards are usually supplied as 8 x 4 ft. (2440 x 1220 mm) sheets. In the thinner sizes they are light enough to carry, if a little difficult to maneuver. Anything over ¾ in. (18 mm) becomes too heavy and should be cut down or moved with an assistant.

There are three main types of board you are likely to come across:

PLYWOOD (1 & 2) AND BLOCKBOARD (3)

Plywood is made from thin laminations (plies) that are bonded together, usually with the grain at right angles to each other, to form a single board. There is always an odd number of plies to ensure balance around the central ply and so that the grain is the same direction on both sides. Plywood comes in varying thicknesses and with varying resistance to moisture. It can also be obtained pre-veneered. Blockboard is similar to plywood, but the central core is made from rectangular strips of softwood with one or two plies overlaid. It is less commonly available than plywood.

CHIPBOARD (not shown)

This is the form of particle board that you are most likely to encounter. It is made from a mixture of chipped soft- and hardwoods that have been formed under pressure with adhesive in a heated press. Chipboard is not often used in fine furniture making, because it is liable to break up if you try to nail or screw into the side of the board. It also seriously blunts tools due to the amount of ground-up metal in the composition.

MEDIUM-DENSITY FIBERBOARD (MDF) (4 & 5)

MDF is formed in a similar manner to chipboard, but the wood composite is broken down into wood fibers, rather than chips, and then formed into a mat that is compressed with adhesive. This produces a smooth board with a uniform texture that cuts and machines well. MDF will edge-joint more easily than chipboard, but still does not hold screws or nails very well on the edges. It takes paint easily and is an excellent substrate for veneering. Moisture-resistant MDF is often used for painted work because the edge takes paint more easily. Pre-veneered MDF is commonly used in furniture making. The adhesive used in manufacture contains formaldehyde, which has some health concerns as a possible carcinogen. Dust created from cutting and machining MDF is quite noxious, so good extraction and a face mask should be used.

The workshop

For the woodworking hobbyist, the workshop should be an environment to do good work, but it should also be a space in which you feel comfortable — a sanctuary, almost! The layout should allow you easy access to your most used tools and materials, and the environment should allow you to relax and concentrate on the craft. However, it is difficult to be prescriptive about how to organize your workshop, because everyone's space and what they want to do in it will vary.

Here are a few factors that you should keep in mind when setting up your workspace.

Light
Good natural light is best, but fluorescent lighting with "daylight" tubes provides the best alternative if natural light isn't available. A spotlight is useful for local illumination when doing close work. Be careful with natural light, because wood can fade or darken if left in strong light.

Damp
Furniture made in a damp shed is likely to move when taken into a centrally heated house. Tools will also rust in a damp atmosphere. You can avoid this issue by applying a damp-proof membrane to the walls and floor. The membrane should be on the interior side of the insulation. If damp remains a problem, you may have to bring the wood you are working on into the house between sessions. Tools can be protected by wiping with WD-40 or camellia oil (which is better as it doesn't mark the wood). Condensation will also lead to damp, so some heating may be required.

Heat
Your workspace needs to be warm in the winter and cool in the summer. If you use a shed or garage, it may be worth considering some insulation, such as a polyisocyanurate (PIR) insulation, fixed inside the walls and then covered with a damp-proof membrane and finished with chip or oriented strand board (OSB) panels. The main area of heat loss in a garage is the large door. If you do not keep your car in the garage, you could even think about bricking this over. To avoid degrading your materials, it is good to keep the workshop above freezing at all times. If it is an attached garage, you could plumb it in with central heating. However, most people will not have this option. Other possibilities for heating the space may be a small wood-burning stove, which could be economical, or electrical heating, such as an oil-filled radiator or fan heater. You could use a thermostatically controlled radiator to keep the chill off 24/7, but this could prove expensive. Avoid calor gas or paraffin heaters, as these generate moisture and will lead to condensation.

Electrics
If you are planning to use power tools, you will need an adequate number of sockets: at least a double by the bench and a few elsewhere — perhaps one near the router table, if you have one. Place the sockets as high as is convenient, as this makes cable management easier. If you are setting up a workshop with machinery, it might be worth installing a 16-amp circuit for larger machines.

Dust
This can be a nuisance if it gets into your lungs or in the house! Dust is best controlled at the point of creation, so good vacuum extraction is essential. Vacuum extractors with an integrated appliance socket are useful, as switching the appliance on also turns on the vacuum. Additionally, make sure that you use an efficient, comfortable half-face dust mask with at least an FFP2 rating. Unless you have larger free-standing machines, such as a jointer/planer, you do not need a large chip-extractor.

Organization
Keeping a workshop tidy is important. Cupboards are better for storage than shelves because, even with good extraction, you will find that dust settles on shelves. Wood storage may be an issue. Sometimes it is worth keeping wood outside the workshop in some form of lean-to. Sheet material is best stored vertically on edge in a rack to prevent warping.

Tip: In some areas, your local building control officer will give advice about damp proofing and insulation.

Introducing hand tools

Many beginners are seduced into thinking that they need lots of expensive, special tools to do the job right, but it's not the number of tools that is important — it's the skill and competence in using a small set of quality tools that leads to good work and satisfaction with the craft. The tool set outlined here is a good starting point; work on developing skill with using these tools before you consider extending the kit. Here, I've grouped the kit by function.

MEASURING AND MARKING

Accuracy in woodworking is crucial, and this starts with measuring and marking. You will need:

Engineer's squares [1]

(Two sizes shown: 4 in./100 mm and 12 in./300 mm) Make sure they are square by marking a line from an edge you know is straight and then reversing the square. If it lines up with the previous line, it is square. If it does not, send it back.

Sliding bevel [2]

Those with a locking lever rather than a screw are easier to use.

Steel rules [3]

(Three sizes shown: 6 in./150 mm, 12 in./300 mm and 39 in./1,000 mm) These have two functions: measuring and checking for flatness. Rules made in spring steel are better than stainless steel because they stay straight, making it easier to check for flatness.

Steel tape measure [4]

Preferably 16 ft. (5 m). A hook at the end moves to allow measurement of internal and external dimensions. Check its accuracy by comparison with a steel rule.

Marking knife [5]

A hardened steel knife, sharpened with a bevel on one side. The ambidextrous knife shown here is preferable to the left-/right-handed type.

Awl [6]

This is a pointed instrument useful for emphasizing a point prior to drilling.

Gauges

These are composed of a sliding shaft in a stock, which can be locked with a turn knob. A pin or knife on the end of the shaft is used for marking. There are a number of different types:

Marking gauge and cutting gauge [7]

A marking gauge has a single pin that is used to mark a line parallel to an edge. A cutting gauge (shown here) is used to give a crisp line when marking across the grain. The pin is replaced with a knife that is beveled on one side like a marking knife; usually the flat faces out. This is very useful when dovetailing.

Mortise gauge [8] — has two pins, one of which can be adjusted in relation to a fixed pin. Those with a turn knob for adjusting the pin are easier to use. Often there is a single pin on the reverse side, so the mortise gauge can double up as a marking gauge.

Wheel gauge [9] — you may want to try this all-metal gauge, which replaces the pin with a sharpened wheel for marking.

Vernier gauge [10] — often you will need a very precise measurement and a rule will not be accurate enough. In this case, a vernier gauge is useful; I find the digital version easiest to use.

Pencil [11]

Use an "H" pencil for marking out and an "HB" for general notation. Needless to say, the "H" must always be very sharp.

Combination square [12]

Can be used for marking both 90° and 45°, but also has many other uses, such as checking mortise ends, depth stop and quick pencil gauge.

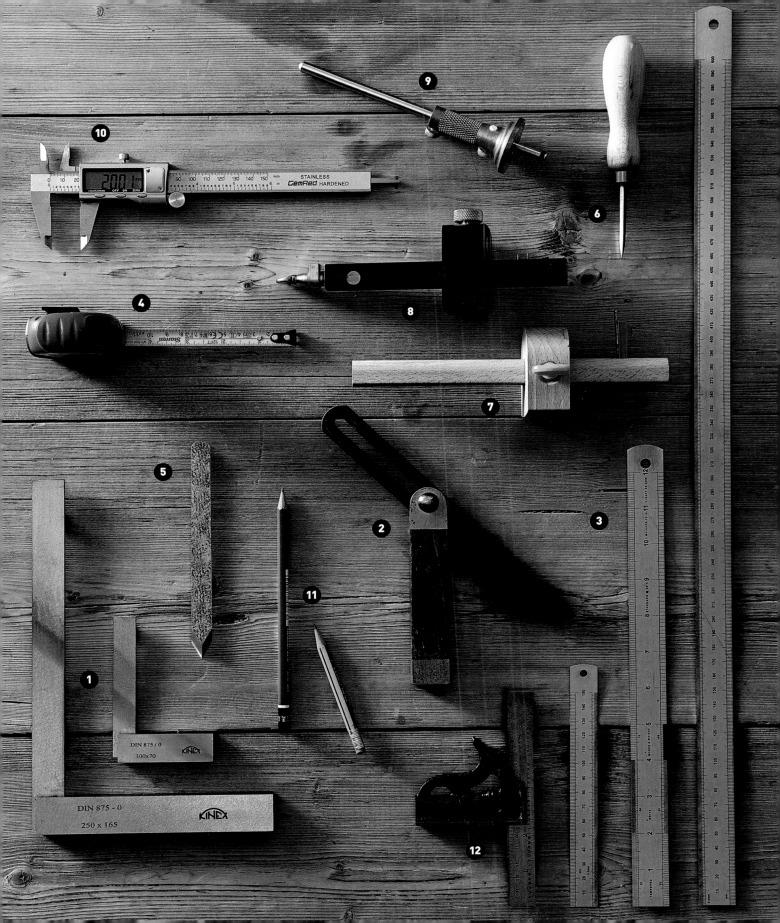

SAWING

For basic work you will only need two saws — a handsaw and a backsaw. However, as you take on new projects that are more challenging, you may wish to extend your armory with more specialized tools, especially if you prefer not to use machinery.

Choosing a saw

A saw works through the action of its teeth severing the wood fibers as you push it backward and forward. On most saws the teeth will have a set, whereby alternate teeth are bent either side of the center line — this means that the saw does not bind in the groove, or kerf, formed by the teeth. The number of teeth — measured as teeth per inch (TPI) — and the set affect the quality of the cut; the higher the TPI, the less the set and the finer the cut.

Traditional Western-style saws are usually sharpened crosscut or rip:

Crosscut sharpened saws cut best across the grain. The teeth are sharpened to form knife-like points so that they sever the fibers. This is achieved by filing the teeth at an angle of about 30°. Crosscut saws have a slope on the front of the tooth, about 15°.

Rip-sharpened saws cut best with the grain. The teeth are sharpened to form chisel-like points so that they pare away the ends of the grain fibers during the cut. This is achieved by filing the teeth at 90°. They can be recognized by the steep front to the tooth, about 8°.

Western-style saws cut on the push stroke. Recently, Japanese saws and their derivatives have become popular in the West. Japanese saws have a more complex tooth geometry and a thinner blade, and they cut on the pull stroke. Many of the cheap hard-point saws available today have borrowed Japanese tooth profiles so that they can cut on both strokes.

Hard-point saws are now almost ubiquitous for general DIY. The teeth on these saws are induction hardened and very sharp when new. They stay sharp for longer but cannot be re-sharpened, so are disposed of when blunt. As they are very cheap, this may not be a problem for the pocket, but some may see it as a sustainability issue. Hard-point handsaws are usually sharpened for crosscutting, often cutting on both the forward and backward strokes.

Crosscut saws can cut with the grain and ripsaws can cut across the grain, but not as efficiently as using a dedicated saw.

THE BASIC SAWS

The two essentials that you will need are a handsaw and a backsaw.

Handsaw

This is used for all your rough cutting. Nowadays, there is a choice between tradition and innovation.

The traditional handsaw has a large wooden handle with a long flexible blade, often ground to a taper across its width to ease the passage of the blade in the kerf. For ripping, use a 26 in. (650 mm) rip-sharpened 4–5 TPI saw [1]; for crosscutting, use a 26 in. (650 mm) 7–8 TPI crosscut sharpened saw. However, if you only want to buy one saw, then make it a crosscut because this will also rip adequately. Innovation comes in the form of a cheaper alternative — the plastic-handled hard-point saw. A 22 in. (560 mm) 8 TPI would suffice [2].

Backsaw

These are used for more refined work. They are smaller than a handsaw, with a smaller handle and a steel or brass back that keeps the blade rigid and gives weight to the saw to aid the cut. Backsaws can range from a weighty tenon saw with a 18 x 5 in. (450 x 125 mm) blade with 9–12 TPI sharpened rip style, to a small, dovetail saw of 8 x 2 in. (200 x 50 mm) with 20 TPI sharpened rip style [3].

A good backsaw for beginners would be a 12 x 2½ in. (300 x 65 mm) carcass saw with 13–15 TPI sharpened crosscut style. This would be your workhorse saw and could cope with most detail sawing operations, such as tenon and dovetail cutting. As you progress, you may wish

Saw teeth

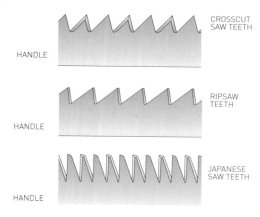

CROSSCUT SAW TEETH

HANDLE

RIPSAW TEETH

HANDLE

JAPANESE SAW TEETH

HANDLE

In crosscut and ripsaws, the teeth point away from the handle. For Japanese saws, the teeth point toward the handle.

②

to buy a larger, dedicated rip-style tenon saw and a smaller rip-style dovetail saw.

Other saws to add as the need arises
Various curve-cutting saws — these have a narrow blade stretched by a metal or wooden frame. They include:

The delicate **fret saw** [4], used for shaping veneer for marquetry and for removing waste between dovetails when the kerf is too narrow for a coping saw.

A **coping saw** [5], which is similar to the fret saw but larger in size. The blade is thicker, so it is used for less delicate work in thicker wood that the fret saw could not handle.

A **bow saw** [6], which is the most coarse of the curve-cutting saws and usually consists of a blade stretched in a wooden frame, tensioned by a windlass.

You may wish to try **Japanese saws** [7], which come in various sizes, with or without backs. A good starter is a *dozuki* — this small, fine saw is good for dovetailing. Japanese saws usually have replaceable blades.

> ## Try this!

> The nomenclature of backsaws can be confusing. Don't get hung up on the names — it's easier to just look for the size and tooth style you want.

CHOPPING AND PARING

A set of six bevel-edged chisels would be a good start for the beginner, perhaps adding a couple of paring chisels later.

Bevel-edged chisels [1] are a good workhorse tool, but for furniture making, look for those with a narrow edge. Some are quite chunky with wide edges, making them difficult for use in tight corners. For a good range, choose sizes ¼, ⅜, ½, ⅝, ¾ and 1 in. (6, 9, 12, 16, 20 and 25 mm).

Paring chisels [2] are very long, fairly thin-section, bevel-edged chisels. The extra length gives more control and allows work into long dadoes. ¾ and 1¼ in. (20 and 32 mm) would be a good pair.

The price of a chisel is often reflective of the steel it is made from. Although you can get a good edge on most chisels, cheaper ones will blunt more quickly.

As with plane blades, new or secondhand chisels will most likely need the backs flattened (lapped). This is partly because it aids sharpening and also because it is difficult to pare horizontally using a chisel with a convex back, because it tends to ride up the slope formed by the back.

New chisels will also have machining marks on the back. (See "Lapping edge tools," opposite.)

Mortise chisels (not shown) If you are planning on doing a lot of hand mortising, then consider buying a set of mortise chisels. They are much thicker in section, making them more robust and able to stand the hammering and levering when chopping a mortise.

Tool preparation

Lapping edge tools

Barring unfortunate mistakes, you should only need to lap (or flatten) the back of a chisel or plane iron once in its lifetime. The easiest and most low-cost lapping method is to use abrasive strips about 2¾ in. (60 mm) wide, stuck to ⅜ in. (8–10 mm) float glass. This could be 3M microfinishing (MF) film, which is available with a pressure-sensitive adhesive backing, or silicon carbide wet-and-dry (WD) abrasive strips, fixed to the glass using a sprayed contact adhesive such as Spray Mount. It is important that the abrasive is perfectly flat, so be careful to exclude any dust, larger particles or air bubbles from under the sheet or film.

MF and WD use different abrasive grading systems (see comparison chart, page 35). Which grade you start with depends on the state of the back surface: for very out-of-true plane blades, you need to start with a coarser grade, such as 60- or 80-grit WD; for reasonable plane blades and new, fairly flat chisels, progress through WD grades 120, 180, 220, 400 and 600 or MF grades of 100, 80, 60, 40 and then 30 microns. The final lapping can be completed on your preferred sharpening medium.

Beginning with the coarsest grade necessary, spray the abrasive with water to lubricate it, place the blade flat on the abrasive and rub using moderate pressure.

It is vital that you keep the back flat on the abrasive, because the slightest lifting of the handle (if it's a chisel) will quickly round the end. For plane irons, it can be useful to stick a block on the back of the blade using double-sided tape. For chisels, have only your little finger hooked around the handle to steady it. All your intent should be on keeping the blade flat on the abrasive. You only need to work on the front 1⅜–2 in. (35–50 mm). Many new chisels are ground slightly concave; this is good, because it ensures two points of contact. You only need to work a short flat on the end —

Add a block of wood to the back of a plane blade to aid holding.

don't worry if there is a slightly lower area back from the edge. On old chisels you may have the reverse, a convex back; with just one point of contact, this can be very difficult to correct, and it is often better to discard the chisel.

You should be able to see where abrasion is happening from the scratch patterns, and you can enhance this by applying marker pen — where the marking remains is a low spot.

Keep working the blade on the coarse grit until it is flat. You can then work your way through the grades. This now becomes a polishing exercise, removing the scratch marks from the previous grade until you have a shiny surface. Changing the angle of presentation between grades helps to highlight scratches from previous grades.

Grinding marks on new chisel blade.

Change the angle of blade between abrasive grades. The blade is kept flat on the surface, with only the little finger crooked underneath to steady the handle.

A mirror finish.

PREPARING AND SMOOTHING

For a beginner's kit, you only need a jack plane, block plane and scraper. If you decide not to use an electric router, you may need a hand router and a rabbet plane. A plane is essentially a jig for holding a blade in an optimal position for cutting. Planes are defined as being bevel up or bevel down. Bevel-down planes usually have the blade fixed at an angle of 45°, with a back iron or chip breaker fixed on top of the blade. Bevel-up planes have the blade at an angle of 15–20° and no back iron.

Jack plane [1]

This is usually a bevel-down plane of the Bailey pattern (although bevel-up jack planes are available). The Bailey pattern is the ubiquitous plane style found in most workshops in a range of sizes, from a miniscule no. 1 at 5½ in. (140 mm) to the mighty no. 8 at 24 in. (610 mm). A good jack plane is a no. 5 or no. 5½ at 14 in. (355 mm) and 15 in. (381 mm).

The no. 5½ is better, because it is slightly wider and weightier, giving it more momentum.

Block plane [2]

This is a bevel-up plane. Smaller than the jack plane, it is useful for end-grain planing and small tidying jobs, such as chamfering or rounding sharp edges or corners. A block plane is usually used one handed, fitting nicely into the hand.

Hand router [3]

Used for removing the waste in dadoes, the blade is "L" shaped to allow it to cut along the bottom of the dado. Hand routing is falling out of use, being replaced by the electric router.

Rabbet plane [4]

Used for working a rabbet on the edge of a workpiece, the rabbet plane is difficult to master and, like the router plane, most of its functions can be done more effectively with an electric router.

Card scraper [5]

A very simple tool, this is a piece of spring steel about 5 x 2⅜ x 0.02 in. (125 x 60 x 0.6 mm), with a burr worked on the edges. The burr is used for removing fine shavings in areas of planing breakout.

Scraper plane [6]

This is similar to a card scraper, but the steel is held in a plane body. Some scraper planes have a thicker blade, similar to an ordinary plane blade. In both, the blade is angled forward.

Spoke shave [7]

This is used for shaping curved forms and consists of a blade between two handles. For forming concave curves, the sole is convex; a flat sole is used for convex curves.

Sanding block [8]

The final tool for smoothing is sandpaper wrapped around a cork sanding block.

PLANE PARTS

The illustration shows the parts of a standard Bailey-pattern bedrock plane, but not how they work together, so we'll break this down to get an understanding of how it works.

The blade assembly is retained by the cap iron. To remove the blade, lift the cam lever and lift away the cap iron. You should now be able to remove the blade assembly.

The blade assembly consists of the blade and the back iron or chip breaker. The back iron must be removed if you want to sharpen the blade; use a wide-bladed screwdriver to loosen the retaining screw, slide the chip breaker back, then turn it 90° and move it forward so that the retaining screw can pass through the hole. This ensures that the chip breaker will not rub on the blade edge and damage it.

Removing the blade exposes the frog and the adjusting parts. The lever at the top provides lateral adjustment, while the round button at the bottom of the lever engages with the long slot in the blade. Moving the lever to the left tilts the blade

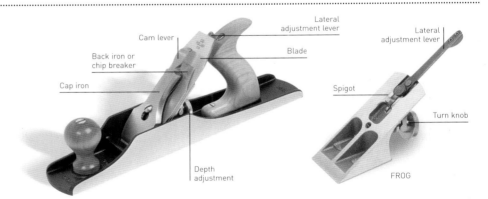

to cut deeper on the right, and vice versa. The spigot sticking up in the middle of the frog engages via a pivoting yoke with the turn knob below the frog. The spigot fits into a slot in the chip breaker, and turning the knob adjusts the depth of cut (clockwise deeper, and vice versa).

On most common planes, the frog can be removed by unscrewing the two screws at the bottom. This shows how the frog engages with the sole with four flat points of contact. On more expensive bedrock planes (shown here), the frog seating is different, with a large contact area between frog and seating.

The position of the frog can be altered by loosening the retaining screws and adjusting via the screw at the back of the frog. This moves the frog backward and forward, changing the distance between the blade and the front of the mouth. You should aim for about 1/32 in. (1 mm) for most uses. Once set, this adjustment is only changed very occasionally.

Tool preparation

Fettling your plane

Fettling is a term originating from the North of England, which means to make ready or prepare. Most new planes and those bought secondhand will require some fettling. Here we look at three main areas to consider:

Is the back of the blade flat?

Check using a short, straight edge. This should not be an issue on good-quality, new planes, although it is worth removing the machine marks from where it was flattened in manufacture. The back may not be flat on cheap or secondhand planes, in which case it needs lapping in the same way as chisels (see page 25). Drawing with a marker pen on the back can highlight where the high and low spots are.

Mark the back of the blade with a marker pen.

Grinding marks from the factory

Rub the blade on your lapping medium. It's vital to keep it flat.

The lighter area shows the high spot where the marker pen has rubbed off.

Does the chip breaker fit correctly?

Once you have lapped the blade, sharpen it and try out the plane. If the shavings jam up in the mouth even though it is adjusted correctly, or come out in an accordion shape, it's probably because the chip breaker is not seated onto the back of the blade correctly. To correct this, hone the flat on the end of the breaker so that it sits cleanly on the back of the blade. This is best done on a diamond stone or abrasive on glass, because soft stones may get grooved. Sometimes breakers have a negative angled part at the very end in which the shavings clog — work this off on the stone. On quality bedrock planes, the breaker is different to that shown, being more like a reversed blade.

Shavings jammed in the mouth

Hone the flat area at the end of the breaker so that it sits flat on the back of the blade.

Accordion-shaped shaving

Then work the end if there is a negative angle.

Is the sole flat? The plane should be cutting fairly well now, but if the sole of the plane is not flat, the cut can be a little erratic — the plane tends to "skitter" over the surface. Check if the sole is flat by backing off the blade, wiping the sole and placing it on a known flat surface (⅜ in./10 mm float glass works well). Use a .002 in. (0.1 mm) feeler gauge to feel under the sole to test for flatness. If it's not flat, use 60-grit aluminum oxide abrasive paper stuck to ⅜ in. (10 mm) float glass as an abrasive plate to flatten the sole. The sole does not need to be perfectly flat as long as four points — the front end, in front of the mouth, behind the mouth and the back end — are in line (coplanar). When a sole is nearly flat, you should feel a slight suction when you lift it off the glass test plate.

Tip: Use a magnet in a yogurt pot to clean the filings off the abrasive when it clogs. With the pot over a trash can, lift the magnet out, and the swarf will drop off into the can.

Checking for flatness with a feeler gauge.

Marking the plane with marker pen makes it easier to see the high spots.

With the blade backed off, work the plane sole on the abrasive.

An even wear shows the plane is flat. This is almost there.

SHARPENING EQUIPMENT

To maintain your edge tools at their peak, you will need to grind them occasionally and hone them frequently. Grinding gives a wide primary bevel at 25°, while honing gives a smaller 30° bevel at the tip of the tool. It's important to have a system that will give you a good edge quickly and easily.

Grinding tools

Grinding can be done using either a dry grindstone [2] or a water stone [1].

The modern **water stone** is an aluminum oxide wheel, 8–10 in. (200–250 mm) in diameter, that turns slowly in water so that the tool steel is never in danger of overheating. A leather stropping wheel is often fitted to the other end of the arbor. Jigs and guides are usually available to assist holding the tool at the correct angle. The cutting action is quite slow.

The **dry grindstone** is usually a smaller, fast-running silicon carbide (carborundum) wheel. This leads to heat buildup that can burn the tool, indicated by blue or black spots on the edge. A replacement cool-running ceramic wheel can help to prevent this. Jigs and guides are often available to aid tool holding.

Honing media

There are various media available for honing. Different abrasive grades are discussed here (see conversion chart, page 35, for further details). For the beginner, I would recommend starting with the scary sharp system using 3M micro finishing (MF) film, perhaps progressing to water stones at a later stage.

Oil stones [1] — usually made from graded aluminum oxide or silicon carbide, although natural stones, such as Arkansas and Washita, are available. The surface is lubricated with mineral oil. Oil stones are usually harder than water stones but do not cut as quickly. Grading is usually not very specific — simply coarse, medium and fine. An 8 x 3 in. (200 x 75 mm) combination medium/fine is a good stone for a beginner.

Water stones [2] — usually made from graded aluminum oxide, but natural stones are available. The cutting fluid is water. These are softer than oil stones, so they need flattening regularly, but they cut quickly. The cutting action comes from a slurry of particles built up on the stone surface. On fine stones, a small Nagura stone [3] is used to develop this slurry. All but the finest stones should be kept in a water bath. An 8 x 3 in. (200 x 75 mm) combination 1,000/6,000-grit stone would be a good start.

Diamond stones [4] — a steel plate coated with graded diamond particles. Diamond stones do not need a cutting fluid (although most people use oil or water). An 8 x 2⅝ in. (200 x 68 mm) combination 325/1,200-grit would be useful.

Scary sharp [5] — abrasive sheets stuck to float glass (preferably ⅜ in./8–10 mm). This can be PSA-backed plastic impregnated with aluminum oxide (3M MF film), or silicon carbide wet-and-dry paper sheets, stuck to the glass with

Comparing honing media		
	Advantages	**Disadvantages**
Oil stones	Cheap; moderate wearing	Slow cutting; oil can get on wood
Water stones	Fast cutting; available in very fine grades	Needs flattening regularly; has to be kept in water bath
Diamond stones	Stays flat; clean to use; good for sharpening narrow tools	Good stones are expensive
Scary sharp	Very cheap initially; clean; fast cutting	Film tears easily; needs replacing regularly

Spray Mount; the MF film is more durable. MF film is graded in microns, and a good selection for a scary sharp is 60, 40, 30, 15, 9 and 3 micron grades.

Honing guides

It can be hard for a beginner to get the hang of freehand honing, especially with plane irons. Instead, try using a honing guide. There are many different guides available, but here we compare two — one fairly simple, the other less so.

Simple guide [6] — a very basic guide from Stanley that runs on two plastic wheels. The blade is clamped in the guide by two finger screws, and a plastic flap drops down to indicate the appropriate blade protrusion for 25°, 30° and 35° honing.

Advantages: Cheap; simple to set up; low center of gravity makes it easy to use.

Disadvantages: Problems getting the blade square in the guide (a workshop-made template can help here); plastic wheels can wear; blade has a tendency to slip in the guide.

Complicated guide [7] — the Veritas MKII guide is very robustly made and consists of a brass wheel, with an alloy mounting assembly above. A setting piece is clamped to the front with a stop, positioned to give the required honing angle. The blade is clamped in the jig against the stop before the setting piece is removed and the blade is ready for honing.

Advantages: Great variety of angle settings available for honing; robust construction; micro-bevel facility.

Disadvantages: Quite expensive; complicated initially for the beginner; the setting stop can damage the blade edge if you are not careful.

CLAMPING AND HOLDING

Clamps act as holding devices, providing an extra hand to steady a piece while you are working or helping to exert pressure when gluing. It is important to choose a tool that can deliver the appropriate amount of pressure — for example, gluing together the top of a dining table would require robust bar clamps that can exert considerable force, but it may be possible to apply a piece of thin lipping using only masking tape.

Here, we discuss a limited selection of the many clamps available.

Bar clamp [1]

A flat or "T"-section steel bar with a sliding tail piece and an adjustable jaw that can be tightened via a threaded handle. Generally available from 18 to 48 in. (450 to 1,200 mm), longer "T"-section clamps are available up to 72 in. (1,800 mm). Separate clamp heads are available that can be used on wooden bars. You can also get aluminum bar clamps, but they are usually of low quality. Used mostly for gluing up, bar clamps can exert considerable pressure.

Tip: If your flat bar clamps are not long enough, it may be possible to join them end to end to clamp over longer distances.

"C" clamp [2]

A "C"-shaped frame that forms a jaw, tightened using the threaded handle. Used for gluing up and holding work in place, this is especially useful for clamping your work to a bench top. Available from 2 to 12 in. (50 to 300 mm).

"F" clamp [3]

Often performing a similar task to the "C" clamp, this consists of wide jaws on a flat steel bar. One end is fixed, the other can slide and tightening the screw on the sliding end onto the workpiece locks it against the bar so that it can no longer move. "F" clamps have a greater capacity than "C" clamps, up to a 78 in. (2,000 mm) opening and a 5 in. (120 mm) throat.

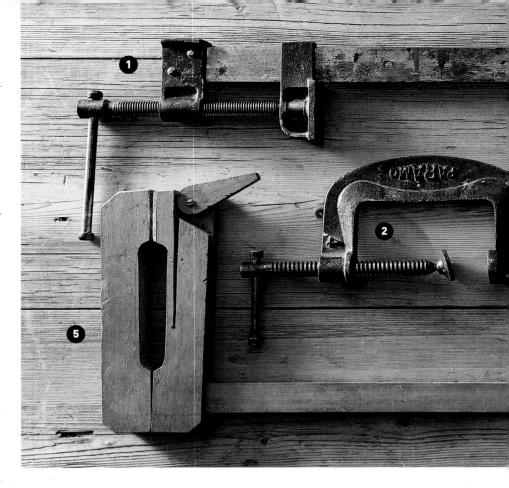

Quick clamp [4]

Has a squeeze-and-release ratchet clamping action that is similar to that on a caulk gun. Quick clamps do not exert as much pressure as the screw-action clamps, but they have the advantage of one-handed use. The jaws also include built-in plastic protection, so there is no need for fiddly clamping blocks. Some models can be reversed so that they can be used for forcing frames, etc., apart.

Cam clamp [5]

Also called a guitar maker's clamp, this is mainly used for light holding. The sliding head is engaged and then pressure is exerted using a cam leaver.

Spring clamp/clamping peg [6]

Plastic pegs of varying sizes. Useful for very light clamping and holding.

Web clamp [below]

Essentially a ratchet strap that can be used to tighten up a mitered or more complex-shaped frame.

WEB CLAMP

Comparing clamps				
Clamp type	**Clamping weight**	**Uses**	**Approximate sizes available**	**Remarks**
Bar clamp	Heavy	Assembly and gluing	18–72 in. (450–1,800 mm)	Sometimes can be joined for longer distances
"C" clamp	Heavy/Light	Assembly, gluing and holding	2–12 in. (50–30 mm)	
"F" clamp	Heavy/Light	Assembly, gluing and holding	6–78 in. (150–2,000 mm)	More versatile than "C" clamp but more expensive
Quick clamp	Light	Light assembly, gluing and holding	6–50 in. (150–1,270 mm)	One-handed operation — good for tricky gluing together
Cam clamp	Light	Mainly holding	12–24 in. (300–600 mm)	
Web clamp	Heavy	Gluing	N/A	
Sliding wedges	Light	Light gluing	N/A	Good for light panels
Masking tape	Light	Light gluing and general holding	N/A	Good for edging and lipping
Toggle clamps	Mainly just holding	Holding	N/A	Indispensable for machining jigs, etc.
Clamping pegs	Light	Mainly holding	1–3⅛ in. (25–80 mm)	Very useful for general holding of work

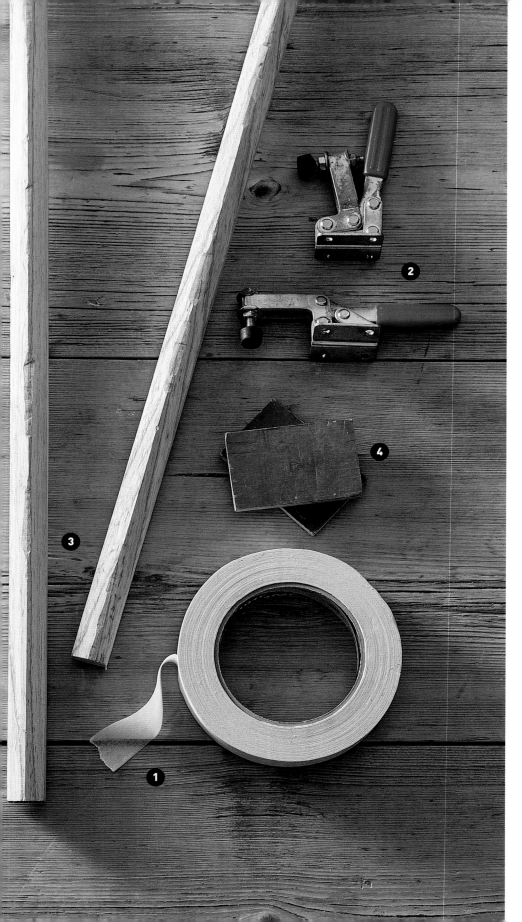

CLAMPING AND HOLDING CONT.

Sliding wedges [not shown]

If you don't have the clamps available to glue together a panel, you could consider sliding wedges. Two battens are screwed to a board a little wider than the panel and pairs of gently tapered wedges tapped home to exert pressure. A weight on the panel prevents it from lifting. This arrangement is good for gluing thin panels.

Masking tape [1]

This is one of the most useful tools in the workshop. It can be used for many different light gluing jobs, such as applying lipping to panel edges or gluing together thin panels.

Toggle clamps [2]

Toggle clamps are excellent holding tools, especially useful for holding a workpiece onto a jig for machining. The clamp is adjusted until the handle can be pressed down into the locked position while holding the work. Various sizes and configurations are available.

Clamping and holding aids

When clamping and holding, you need to protect your work from compression damage. The following tools are useful for this:

Clamping strips [3] — long clamping strips

easily stay in place compared to separate blocks, and if you shape them to an apex on the outside edge, the clamping force will be through the center rather than low down.

Magnetic or bar-holding clamping blocks

[4] — useful for general gluing operations when standard clamping blocks can easily fall out of place. Make your own magnetic clamping blocks by drilling and positioning a 3/16 x 5/16 in. (5 x 8 mm) rare earth magnet into a piece of 3/8 in. (9 mm) MDF or plywood, then glue a piece of leather, rubber or thin plywood on the surface on the hole side. A bar-holding block (not shown) has a slot cut into it in order to fit over the bar on a bar clamp. The magnetic block is more versatile but more complicated to make.

Workshop materials

As well as tools and wood, you will need some additional materials to complete your woodworking kit. These are the indispensable workshop consumables.

ABRASIVE PAPER

Nowadays it is a misnomer to call this sandpaper because the sand has been replaced by various man-made abrasives, particularly aluminum oxide. Abrasive paper is not an accurate tool for actually working wood, so its use should be limited to blending surfaces, smoothing prior to applying a finish and rubbing down between finishes. You should need only three grades:

- 120 grit for working curved surfaces that need blending after initial work with cutting tools.
- 180 grit to follow the 120 grit or used immediately on hand-planed surfaces. This grit prepares the surface for finish application.
- 400 grit for rubbing down or de-nibbing between coats of varnish.

ABRASIVE PADS

These are used to rub down moldings or other shaped parts for finishing. 0000 grade steel wool can be used for this, but can cause contamination problems in tannin-rich woods such as oak and chestnut. Webrax abrasive-impregnated nylon fiber pads are a good substitute. They are color coded, and gray is the grade required.

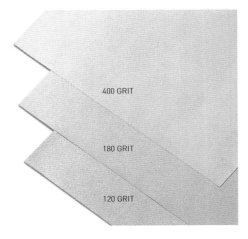

400 GRIT

180 GRIT

120 GRIT

ABRASIVE GRADING

There are two main systems of grading for abrasive sheets: the US Coated Abrasive Manufacturers Institute (CAMI) system, and the Federation of European Producers of Abrasives (FEPA) system, usually prefixed "P." Both systems are based on the number of holes in the mesh through which the abrasive is filtered; hence the larger the number, the finer the abrasive. Microfinishing film is measured by the average size in microns of the abrasive particles, so the smaller the number, the finer the particles. The chart (right) shows a comparison of the most common grits.

Abrasive grading chart		
CAMI	**FEPA**	**Microns**
60		265
	P60	269
	P80	201
80		190
	P120	125
120		115
180	P180	82
	P240	58.5
240		53
	P320	46.2
320		36
	P400	35
400		23
	P600	25.8
600		16
	P1200	15.3
800	P1500	12.6
	P3000	6
	P6000	4

Aliphatic resin glue [4]

A water-based yellow glue. Almost as commonly used as PVA, it dries more quickly and is less prone to creep.

Urea-formaldehyde (UF) resin glue [5]

Usually a powder that is mixed with water, resin glue sets glass hard. It is good for marquetry and laminating. It is also waterproof, so is often used in external joinery. It is the only commonly available glue with gap-filling properties, so it is useful if your joints are loose! Always follow the mixing instructions on the product packaging.

Polyurethane glue [6]

A strong, water-resistant glue that cures by absorbing moisture. Be frugal when applying, because it foams as it cures. Wear latex gloves because it is impossible to remove from skin. It is more expensive than PVA and UF.

Cyanoacrylate glue [7]

Superglue is not very useful for construction because of its short open time of less than two minutes and high cost. However, it is very useful for fixing minor cracks, dings and splinters. Use sparingly straight from the bottle.

MASKING TAPE [1]

Useful for all kinds of small jobs around the workshop, such as:

- Wrapping around a drill bit to set drilling depth.
- Holding edges together when edge-jointing thin boards.
- Putting on the ends of clamps to stop them getting stuck to the workpiece.
- Helping with notation when you don't want to write on the workpiece.

The possibilities are endless!

DOUBLE-SIDED TAPE [2]

Less versatile than masking tape, but still quite useful for:

- Holding a thin piece while planing it on the bench top.
- Retaining a sacrifice piece in place when machining a workpiece.
- Various temporary positioning jobs.

ADHESIVES

The most useful adhesives are:

Polyvinyl acetate (PVA) [3]

A water-based white wood glue. It cures through water evaporation and clamping pressure, but will not cure at very low temperatures. It is subject to creep, a slight movement due to its elasticity when set, so do not use in lamination.

Adhesives						
	Approx. open time	Approx. clamping time	Approx. cure time	Shelf life once opened	Creep	Comments
PVA	20 mins	3–4 hours	12 hours	Long if not allowed to freeze	Yes	Dries clear; the "go to" adhesive; does not cure below 5°C
Aliphatic resin	15 mins	2 hours	24 hours	Long	Yes, but less than PVA	
Urea formaldehyde	30 mins	5 hours	24 hours	12 months — keep container sealed	No	Waterproof; dries white but can be colored; gap filling; will not work below 10°C
Polyurethane	10 mins	Varies, but short	24 hours	6 months	No	Good if in a hurry, but very messy if care not taken
Cyanoacrylate	Seconds	5 mins	24 hours	Short	No	Good for little jobs around the workshop; too expensive for anything else

HARDWARE

To describe the full range of hardware would require a book in itself, so I will limit myself to the two items you are most likely to use: screws and hinges.

Screws

For most work, you will need either steel or brass screws.

For general work, you need steel posidrive screws — these have a cross slot in the head and are driven by a cross-point screwdriver. Steel screws are usually bright zinc-plated (BZP) to prevent corrosion. Steel screws should not be used in oak and other tannin-rich woods, because the steel will stain the wood — it's better to use brass for these woods.

Brass screws are used when steel is not suitable or when fitting brass hardware. They are more aesthetically pleasing, but not as strong as steel screws, so precautions should be taken to prevent the head from shearing off when inserting them. Brass screws commonly have a slotted head.

There are several different patterns of screw head, but you are most likely to use either countersunk or round head. A countersunk head is conical, so that the screw sits level with or just below the surface. Round-head screws are used for fitting fixtures, often where adjustability is required.

Wood screws are sized by length and diameter. The length specification is straightforward, but there are two methods of sizing for diameter. One is a numbering system based on shaft and head size — the larger the number, the thicker the screw — and the other is a measure of gauge or thread diameter. You are most likely to need numbers from 4 to 10.

Posidrive/Phillips

There are two types of cross-point screw — posidrive and Phillips. Phillips screws are usually machine screws and not used in woodwork. Although a posidrive and a Phillips screw look the same, they are not interchangeable. A posidrive screw head is indicated by little lines in the corners of the slot; these are copied as little ridges in the corners of the screwdriver.

There are three sizes of posidrive screwdriver, designated PZ numbers, used for different size screws:
PZ1 for screw sizes 2–5
PZ2 for screw sizes 6–10
PZ3 for screw sizes 11–14

Hinges

There are many different patterns of hinge, but here I'll discuss one traditional pattern and one modern design.

Butt hinges

The standard butt hinge consists of two leaves that are interlinked to fit around a pin; the interlinking and pin are known as the knuckle. Butt hinges are sized by the length of the leaves. The hinges most commonly available are steel or brass, ranging in size from 4 in. (100 mm) to 1 in. (25 mm). Brass hinges are used in fine woodwork and where steel would stain the wood.

It is important to use the correct screw size for the hinge. You want the head to sit just below the surface of the leaf, but not too low — otherwise too much of the countersinking will show. A head sitting above the surface will prevent the hinge from closing fully.

Butt hinges should be housed into the wood surface and should be fitted with precision — shoddy fitting can spoil a piece. For details on fitting butt hinges, see the memory box project, page 248.

Concealed hinges

Concealed hinges are the hinges that are now ubiquitous in contemporary kitchen cabinets. The hinge is fitted to the door with a surface plate and a boss that fits into a hole (usually 1⅜ in./35 mm drilled into the back of the door); when closed, the hinge mechanism closes into the hollow boss. The other end of the hinge is fitted to a plate screwed to the wall of the cabinet; the plate usually allows for limited adjustment in three dimensions.

Concealed hinge types

There are many different configurations of concealed hinge, and the fitting of the hinge onto the plate can vary.

- **Slide-on fitting** where a screw at the back of the plate is slackened to allow the hinge to slide on and off.

- **Clip-on fitting** where the hinge clips onto the plate and a small lever at the back of the hinge flap is pressed to release it. I find the clip-on more convenient.

The way the hinge and plate are attached to the cabinet can also vary. Some are designed for mounting with ordinary wood screws; others use Euro-screws, which are thick parallel-sided screws that self-tap into 3/16 in. (5 mm) diameter holes. Dowel fitting hinges use plastic dowels that fit into 5/16 in. (8 mm) holes. The wood screw fittings are easiest to fit.

The configuration of the hinge and plate will vary depending on whether the door is inset into the cabinet or frame, or overlays the front of the cabinet either the full width of the cabinet side or half width. The hinge may be cranked for inset fitting; different thickness plates are used, depending on whether it is full or half overlay.

Some hinges now have an integral soft-close feature, or a soft-close mechanism can be clipped on.

Some suppliers provide a specification that gives the drilling positions, but often you will need to do this by experimentation. See the workshop cabinet project, page 242, for details on this.

Once the door is fitted, the position can be adjusted using various adjusting screws:

- The vertical position can be adjusted by slackening the screws holding the plate on the cabinet side and manually shifting the door up or down. Some plates have a built-in adjusting screw.

- The side-to-side position of the door can be adjusted using the screw on the hinge flap closest to the door.

- The gap between the door and cabinet front can be adjusted by slackening the back screw on the hinge flap and manually shifting the door in or out.

Introducing power tools

When correctly used, power tools can help with accuracy and also speed up the work. However, for the woodworking hobbyist, speed is not always an important factor, and the journey is as interesting as the destination. So for the beginner, it may be worth really getting to know your hand tools and learning how wood reacts to these, before buying power tools. Only then will you have an understanding of tool quality and be able to decide which power tools, if any, are for you. When you're ready, these are the key power tools you might consider as an investment.

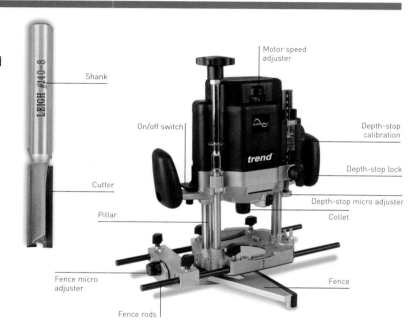

Shank

Cutter

Motor speed adjuster

On/off switch

Depth-stop calibration

Depth-stop lock

Depth-stop micro adjuster

Collet

Pillar

Fence micro adjuster

Fence

Fence rods

ROUTER

The router can perform a vast range of tasks, from simple grooving, rabetting and molding to forming complex shapes and joint cutting. This versatility makes the router possibly the single most important power tool for the hobby woodworker, and fitting it to a router table increases this versatility further.

The tool consists of a shaft driven by a powerful motor running up to 24,000 RPM. At the end of this shaft is a collet that can receive a myriad different, shaped cutters — and it's this variety of cutters that makes the router so versatile. Routers vary in collet size and motor power, but the two are interdependent. Smaller machines will have a ¼ in. or ⁵⁄₁₆ in. (approximately 6 mm or 8 mm) collet with a motor of around 1 KW, while larger machines

have a ½ in. (12 mm) collet and a motor up to 2 KW. The larger machines are more flexible because they can take smaller collets, but small machines cannot take larger collets.

Most routers are plunging, meaning that the motor and shaft are mounted on pillars that allow them to be moved vertically, with stops in place to control the depth of cut. The router sits on a base with an adjustable fence fitted to rods that controls its lateral position.

Router cutters consist of a shank that fits into the collet and the cutting end, which usually has a number of tungsten carbide (TC) tips.

Tip: Make sure your cutter shank is the correct size for the collet. A 6 mm cutter will not work in a ¼ in. (6.34 mm) collet, and vice versa.

Due to the forces involved, large diameter cutters should only be used in a router table. You can purchase router tables of varying quality, or you can make a table using a kitchen worktop and a purchased insert plate. Inverting a router under a table, so that the cutter protrudes through a hole in the top, changes the way that you use the machine. Instead of passing the cutter over the wood, the wood is passed over the cutter. This allows you to make cleaner and more accurate cuts, but there are also safety implications, because your fingers can come into contact with the cutters. This will be dealt with in the section on using the router table (see page 116).

Cutter

Workshop-made adjustable fence

Insert plate

Machine screws secure router underneath.

Router fixed to insert plate. In this case, the height of the cut is adjusted using a car jack.

Cabinet holds cutters, collets, jigs and other accessories.

Table accessories

WORKSHOP-MADE ROUTER TABLE

Router cutters

Cutters come in various patterns and configurations:

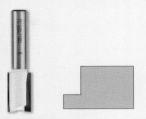

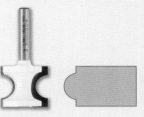

STRAIGHT FLUTE

Smaller cutters can be single or double flute, while larger cutters (over about ¼ in./6 mm) are double flute. Some larger cutters may not allow plunging cutting.

MOLDING

Molding cutters come in many different shapes, and within each shape there are a number of sizes. It is possible to combine different molding bits to produce more complex shapes.

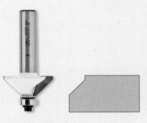

SIDE-CUTTING GROOVERS AND SLITTERS

These give a very clean cut. Different cutters and shims can be stacked on the same arbor to give different cutting widths.

BEARING GUIDED

Most cutters also come as bearing-guided versions. This enables the cutter to follow an irregular shape, either a template used to form the shape or an already created shape, to form a molding.

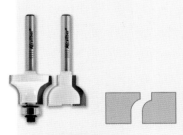

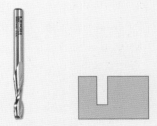

SCRIBING SETS

Used when making doors and frames with a decorative molding. The molding is carried through the joint, so that the shoulder of the rail is shaped to fit over the molding on the stile.

SPIRAL CUTTERS

These are either downward or upward cutting, depending on the spiral direction. Downward cutting gives a clean cut in inlay work, while upward cutting gives a good finish at the bottom of the cut.

DRILL

Most DIYers will already have an electric drill lying around — either corded or battery operated — and this will be adequate for many woodworking tasks. When you require precision drilling at the correct angle, then either a drill stand that you can fit your drill into or a dedicated drill press will be useful — preferably with a ½ in. (13 mm) keyless chuck.

Speed selector switch

Torque collar

Chuck

Forward/reverse button

Speed control trigger

Battery

A drill is only as good as the bit fitted in the chuck, and the bits must always be sharp. Here is a selection of the most useful woodworking bits suitable for using in a power drill or drill press:

Twist bit [1]
This will work in wood, but often leaves a ragged hole. Ranges from around 0.02 to ⁹/₁₆ in. (0.5 to 14 mm).

Lip and spur, or brad point [2]
These have a central point, and the two flutes of the drill are sharpened to spurs at the end. The action of the spurs gives a very clean hole (if kept sharp). The point makes for accurate location. Range from about ³/₁₆ to ⅝ in. (4 to 16 mm).

Flat bit [3]
A spade-like bit with a central point. The point locates the bit, while the flat area cuts the hole. It leaves a flat-bottomed hole but with a fairly deep hole in the center. Ranges from about ⁵/₁₆ to 1¼ in. (8 to 32 mm).

Forstner bit [4]
This has a small central pin with a cutting edge around the circumference. It gives a very clean cut and can be used close to another hole without dropping into the adjacent hole. The hole is virtually flat bottomed. Ranges from ¼ to 1 in. (6 to 25 mm).

Saw tooth bit (not shown)
Forstners do not work as well at wide diameters. For these sizes, the outer edge is sharpened to give saw-like teeth. Saw tooth bits have similar qualities to forstner bits. Ranges from 1 to 2½ in. (25 to 65 mm).

Countersink bits [5]
Not really a drill bit, countersinks form a conical hole above the clearance hole for the screw head to sit in. Combined bits are available that can drill the clearance hole and countersink in one.

Drill bits
Drill bits come in various patterns and configurations:

SANDERS

You can smooth wood using a plane, scraper and sanding block, but sanding machines will speed up the process. There are two main types: the belt sander and the orbital sander. A random orbital sander gives the best finish, but is not as good as the belt sander for leveling a surface. If you only buy one sander, I would recommend a random orbital. Whichever you have, be sure to connect it to a vacuum when in use.

Belt sander [1]

This is a loop of sandpaper running over a graphite-impregnated pad between two rollers. It will leave longitudinal scratches in the surface of the wood, so it is mainly used for rough sanding.

The orbital sander (not shown)

An abrasive sheet fitted to an oscillating flat pad. This tends to leave lots of small circular scratches on the surface. The random orbital sander [2] has an additional rotation that prevents scratching. Abrasive mesh pads [3] are now available that allow good dust extraction and also do not clog as much.

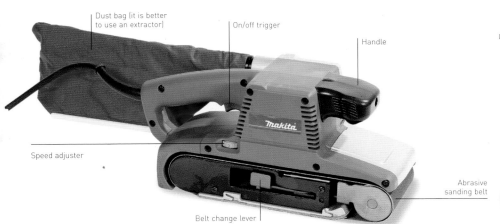

Dust bag (it is better to use an extractor)

On/off trigger

Handle

Speed adjuster

Belt change lever

Abrasive sanding belt

On/off trigger

Dust extractor port

Speed dial

A selection of saw blades — with 80 teeth for fine and crosscutting work, 40 teeth for general purpose and 24 teeth for ripping.

POWER SAWS

Circular saw [1]

A portable circular saw can be handy for rough cutting, and if used with a track, can cut panels accurately. The important features to look for in a circular saw are as follows:

Build quality This is key. Are the adjustment facilities accurate and steady so that the blade stays as set? Does the blade return to 90° every time it is reset? Is the blade cutting parallel to the edge of the baseplate? (This is important if you want to cut a straight line against a straight edge.) Many of these issues will arise with cheaper saws.

Power If the speed of the blade drops when taking deep cuts, it loses efficiency, making the speed decrease even further until the saw binds in the kerf or, worse still, rides up in the cut. In corded saws, power is indicated by wattage, while in cordless, it is indicated by voltage.

Depth of cut If you are likely to only be cutting sheet material, then a small depth of cut and a less powerful machine would be suitable. If you are thinking of

crosscutting 3 in. (75 mm) hardwood, then a larger depth of cut and a higher-rated motor would be better.

Tilt A blade tilt to 45° will allow you to cut miters.

Extraction A circular saw can make lots of dust! Being able to connect a vacuum is essential.

Blade configuration Most wood-cutting blades have tungsten carbide teeth. For making clean cuts in plywood or MDF, a blade with many teeth will give a fine cut. For rough cutting of thicker material, a coarser blade with fewer teeth is required.

Track saw In recent years, the track saw has become available. This is essentially a circular saw that can clip onto and slide along a track laid on the workpiece. Track saws have a plunging facility, allowing the saw to easily enter the work at a central point. This allows quick and accurate cutting of sheet material. If you plan to work with sheet material, such as plywood or MDF, a track saw would be useful.

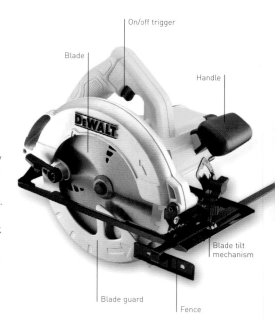

On/off trigger

Blade

Handle

Blade tilt mechanism

Blade guard

Fence

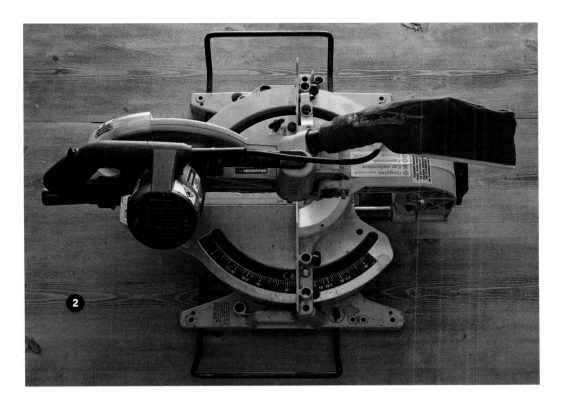

2

Chop or miter saw [2]

This is a useful tool to cut pieces to length quickly and accurately, as well as to cut miters. It consists of a circular saw, fixed to a base with a fence. The saw is tilted down to cut the workpiece, and a safety housing slides away as it is tilted. On miter saws, there is the added facility to pull the saw toward you to cut wider pieces. Although usually well guarded, these saws are not the safest of tools, so they should be used with due care. Consider these factors when purchasing a chop/miter saw:

The blade and quality of cut The same issues apply as for the circular saw (see opposite), regarding number of teeth and quality of cut.

Tilting Most allow the blade to be tilted up to 45° from vertical, and on better saws this tilt can be either to the left or to the right.

Rotation The blade can be turned in the horizontal plane up to 45°. Again, better quality saws allow this turn either to the left or to the right. By setting the appropriate angle in both directions,

compound angles can be cut. Being able to adjust either to the left or right means that, depending on the orientation of the angle, you may not need to turn the wood. However, the accuracy of the cut depends on the build quality — cheaper saws may take a long time to set accurately and may not hold that setting.

Laser guide — some chop/miter saws feature a useful laser guide that shines on the workpiece to indicate where the cut will fall.

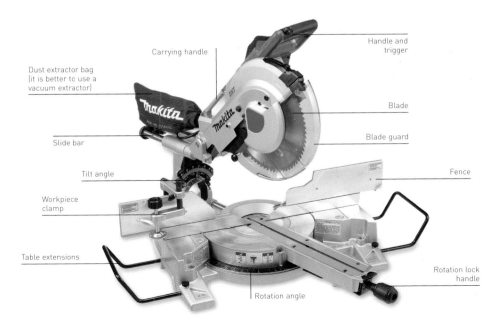

Dust extractor bag (it is better to use a vacuum extractor)

Carrying handle

Handle and trigger

Blade

Slide bar

Blade guard

Tilt angle

Fence

Workpiece clamp

Table extensions

Rotation lock handle

Rotation angle

Jigsaw

The jigsaw is particularly useful for cutting curves and for cutting sections from a panel when the blade can be dropped into pre-drilled holes. However, it is quite slow cutting and leaves a rather untidy edge. Consider these factors when buying a jigsaw:

Blade action The saw has a sword-shaped blade that moves vertically. Some have an added pendulum or orbital action, causing the blades to swing back slightly on the downstroke (most blades are sharpened to cut on the upstroke). This feature is useful when cutting thicker pieces.

Blade tilt Many models have the ability to tilt the blade on the base up to 45°. Because the cut is fairly rough, this feature is not useful in furniture making.

Blade type There are many different tooth patterns for jigsaws. Those with very fine teeth are usually used for metal cutting.

Dust removal Clearing dust away from the blade is important so that you can steer the cut. Most saws use the draft from the cooling fan to blow dust from this area. Additional dust removal should be available via a vacuum.

Laser guide Some have a laser line to guide the cut. This does not work well with dust or strong light.

JOINTERS

Although they look similar, domino and biscuit jointers have slightly different functions. The domino is a more robust jointing system that is used in many jointing situations, while the biscuit is essentially an edge-jointing tool, the joint requiring additional support through the design. However, a domino jointer is more expensive.

Biscuit jointer [1]

Biscuit jointing is an excellent way to joint man-made boards. It is also useful for edge-jointing solid boards. A biscuit is a thin wafer of wood, usually beech, that is slightly compressed in manufacture. The jointer consists of a motor driving a small circular saw. The saw remains inside a protective housing until you push it forward into the wood. The saw kerf forms a slot into which the biscuit fits snugly. A fence controls the position of cut, and a stop controls the depth of cut, depending on the biscuit size used.

Domino jointer [2]

This looks very similar to a biscuit jointer, but instead of a moving saw blade, it has an oscillating milling cutter. This cuts a slot into which wooden splines, dominoes, can be fitted. By changing the size of the cutter and the depth stop, different-sized dominoes can be catered for. A number of accessories can be fitted to the jointer.

Lock-on button

On/off switch

Orbital action switch

Base plate

Blade

Cutters and dominoes

Cutters and dominoes come in various lengths and diameters. Here's a selection:

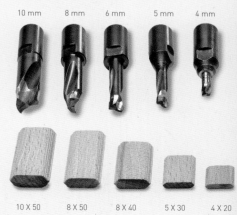

10 mm 8 mm 6 mm 5 mm 4 mm

10 X 50 8 X 50 8 X 40 5 X 30 4 X 20

1

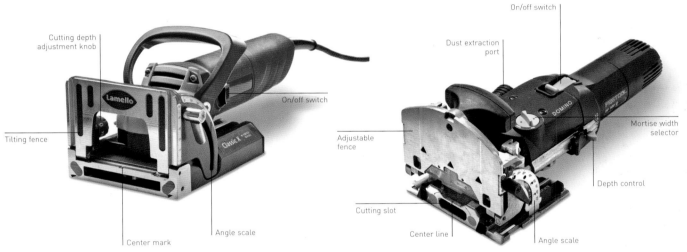

Cutting depth
adjustment knob

On/off switch

Tilting fence

Adjustable
fence

On/off switch

Dust extraction
port

Mortise width
selector

Center mark

Angle scale

Cutting slot

Center line

Angle scale

Depth control

2

The workbench

The workbench is the focal point of the workshop, and is the place where you will spend most of your time when there, so it needs to be fit for purpose. A good workbench should have mass and stability. Here's what you should look for in this, the most important tool in your workshop:

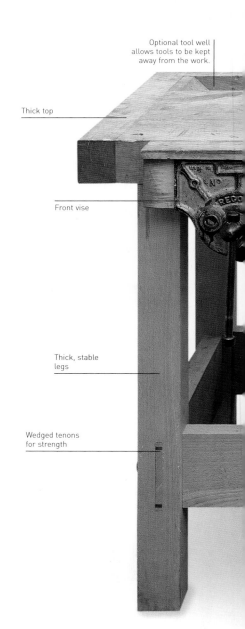

Optional tool well allows tools to be kept away from the work.

Thick top

Front vise

Thick, stable legs

Wedged tenons for strength

Flatness

The top of the bench may be used as a reference surface, so it should be perfectly flat in both directions, with no twisting. It should also stay that way. If it's made of solid wood, it should be laminated from narrow pieces no more than 3 in. (75 mm) wide.

Mass

A good bench will be "chunky," so that it has solidity when you are using it as a base for high-impact work, such as chopping a mortise. Look for a thick top of over 3 in. (75 mm). The legs should also provide a stable, rigid base for the top to sit on, so look for fairly chunky legs with deep rails, especially those running on the long sides.

Portability

You may want to move workshop occasionally, so a large bench that you can't dismantle could be tricky. Look for an undercarriage that can be dismantled, with good, thick bed bolts or something similar that will maintain rigidity.

Height

The optimum height for your bench will depend on your stature and also what kind of work you want to do on it. For detailed work, such as marquetry, you may need a slightly higher bench, while for wood carving you may want something a little lower. A good height can be approximated by measuring from the ground to the crease of your wrist while standing erect.

Work holding

At least one vise is essential, and the bigger the better. This should be on the left front if you are right handed, or the right front if you are left handed. An end vise is also very useful if incorporated with bench dogs (wooden or metal posts that engage in holes in the bench or vise top). A workpiece can be held firmly between dogs in the bench and end vise. A bench for a right hander will have the end vise on the right, and vice versa. Dog holes down the leg of the bench can also support work in the front vise.

It is possible to spend a lot of money on a bench, but this is not necessary. You can make a simple, wall-mounted bench using a 60-minute fire door blank, with a thick, solid lipping around the edge.

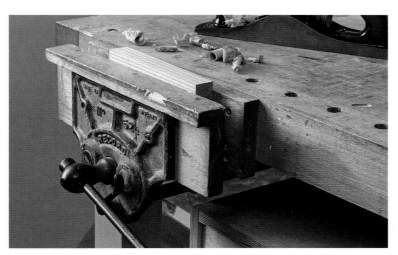

A good-size vise with quick release

Bench dogs are invaluable for wood holding.

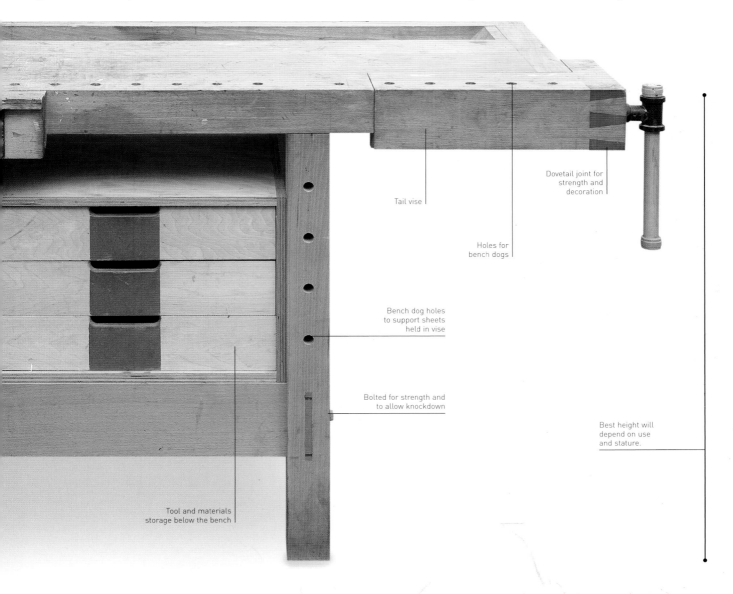

Dovetail joint for
strength and
decoration

Tail vise

Holes for
bench dogs

Bench dog holes
to support sheets
held in vise

Bolted for strength and
to allow knockdown

Best height will
depend on use
and stature.

Tool and materials
storage below the bench

Workshop-made tools

Most of the tools discussed in this chapter can be purchased new or secondhand. However, there are some tools or workshop aids that can easily be made in the workshop, with the materials coming from waste wood.

Bench hook [1]

This useful work-holding device is used to keep the workpiece steady while sawing. It also stops the saw from marking the bench if you saw right through. It consists of a base piece approximately 8 x 6 x ¾ in. (200 x 150 x 20 mm) — this could be plywood or solid wood, with the grain running in the long dimension. Attached at either end on opposite sides are hardwood stocks approximately 5⅜ x 1⅜ x 1⅜ in. (135 x 35 x 35 mm). The stocks are fixed level at one end, with a ⅝ in. (15 mm) margin at the side. If you are right handed, the margin will be on the right, and vice versa for the left hander.

Shooting board [2]

If you don't have a power saw that you can use to cut an accurate clean end, you will probably need a shooting board. It allows the plane to be used on its side to neatly clean up a sawn end. It's also useful for jointing veneer. For stability, good plywood or MDF is best for making one. It can vary in length, but 24 in. (600 mm) is a good size. A simple shooting board may have a base 24 x 10 x ¾ in. (600 x 250 x 18 mm) or thicker. A second piece 22¼ x 7 x ⅜ in. (565 x 180 x 9 mm) fixed to the base creates a wide rabbet for the plane to slide on, with a gap at the end for a stock to be fitted. It is important that the stock end of the second piece is perfectly square with the

rabbet side. The stock piece, 7 x 1⅜ x 1¾ in. (180 x 35 x 44 mm), is fixed at the end at precisely 90° to the rabbet.

If you are right handed, the rabbet should be on the right of the stock, and vice versa. You can vary this design; it's useful to make the stock so that it can be trimmed and slide forward when the end gets damaged. Some people like to stick tough nonslip material such as melamine or Teflon to the rabbet where the plane slides.

It is useful to have a 45° block that can be fitted to the board to convert it into a miter shooting board, the block being located on dowels and butting up to the stock.

Miter block (not shown)

As the name implies, the miter block is used for cutting miters (see page 166). It is difficult to cut a good miter by sawing freehand to a marked line. The miter block helps to hold the saw accurately at the correct angle by running it in previously cut kerfs, assuming it has been made accurately (that is the difficult bit). The block should be made of hardwood, such as beech. The size depends on the work you are doing and the maximum depth of cut of your saw (backsaws give the cleanest cut but have limited depth). But 12 in. (300 mm) long with a 3 x 3 in. (75 x 75 mm) depth and width of cut would be a good standard. Accuracy in making is vital.

Winding sticks (not shown)

A pair is used for testing when a surface is twisted or "in wind" (pronounced to rhyme with bind) — see page 62. One is made in a light-colored wood, such as maple, and the other in a dark wood, such as ebony, or they can be made in any wood and then colored. They must be perfectly straight and of even thickness.

Sawhorses [3]

These are not a substitute for a sound workbench, but they are useful as a temporary support when handsawing or using a track saw, or with a board on top as a gluing table.

Plastic, folding sawhorses are available, or you can make your own. Traditionally, they used to be made with fixed splayed legs that allowed them to be stacked, but they still take up valuable space. You can make folding horses using commercial sawhorse brackets that either hinge or can be dismantled.

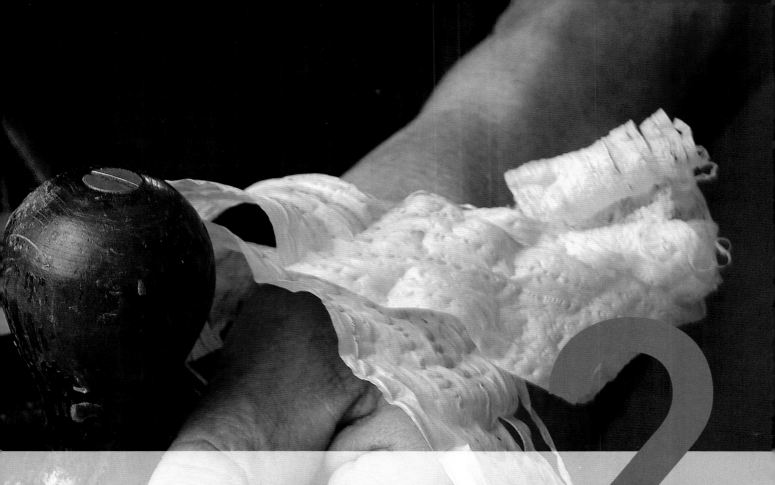

Using Hand Tools

Using hand tools comes naturally to some people, while others struggle with the physicality of manipulating them. Whether you are a "natural" or not, you will achieve much better results if you keep your tools sharp; a really sharp tool (and I mean *really* sharp) is a joy to use, while a blunt tool only leads to frustration. The other vital element for using hand tools is to adopt a rigorous attitude toward accuracy. In general DIY work, you can often get away with being a fraction of an inch out, but for finer work, you should aim to be spot on. With sharp tools and an accurate attitude, it is a matter of method, posture, close observation and practice. In the previous chapter, I talked about the tools you will need, and in this chapter, I show how to use and maintain them.

Sharpening edge tools

Making sure that you have a sharp edge to your tools is really the basis of the craft. This section shows how to sharpen edge tools — those that cut with a single edge, such as a plane or chisel. Sharpening saws (which are not edge tools) will not be covered, because it is beyond the scope of this book. A sharp tool consists of two flat surfaces meeting perfectly with no disruption, rounding or irregularity. In the previous chapter (see pages 25, 28–29), we prepared chisels and plane irons with a flat, polished back. Sharpening consists of creating a similar flat, polished bevel on the other side.

A chisel or plane iron will usually have two bevels. The first of these is the primary (or grinding) bevel, which you will only need to regrind occasionally and which is usually fairly coarsely ground on a wheel at an angle of 25°. The secondary (or honing) bevel is a finely polished bevel, honed at an angle of 30° on a flat sharpening stone or other honing medium. Honing will need to be done frequently, sometimes every 20 minutes or so when an edge is being worked hard.

So, how do you know when an edge needs re-honing? First, are you finding the task hard work? Perhaps it is hard to get the plane to take a shaving, or the cut surface is rough? If so, you should check the edge. A sharp edge cannot be seen. If two surfaces meet perfectly, there is nowhere for the light to reflect off. If you can see a fine bead or little specks of light on the edge, it is not as sharp as it could be. Try feeling the edge carefully. If you lightly pass your finger over the edge (not along its length), you should be able to feel that it might "bite" you. A blunt edge will feel "bland."

How do you know when a bevel needs regrinding? Perhaps you hit a nail and there are large dents or chips on the edge? If so, these chips will probably be too deep to remove by honing, and will need grinding. Or it may be that the honing bevel is too big. Each time you hone, the bevel increases in size, and the wider the honing bevel, the longer it takes to get a good edge. There will come a point (probably when the honing bevel is about the same size as the grinding bevel) at which you decide it is taking too long and that the tool needs regrinding (see bottom left panel).

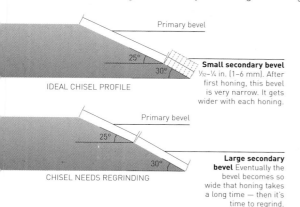

Primary bevel

25°
30°

IDEAL CHISEL PROFILE

Small secondary bevel 1/32–1/4 in. (1–6 mm). After first honing, this bevel is very narrow. It gets wider with each honing.

Primary bevel

25°
30°

CHISEL NEEDS REGRINDING

Large secondary bevel Eventually the bevel becomes so wide that honing takes a long time — then it's time to regrind.

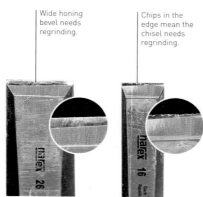

Wide honing bevel needs regrinding.

Chips in the edge mean the chisel needs regrinding.

Checking chisel edge

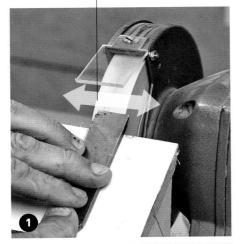

Move chisel from side to side.

1

2

Edge is ground to 90° before regrinding.

Clinic

Many facets

Burn

Most grinding problems arise when using the dry grinding method:

Tool burns You should douse more often! Sometimes this is caused by impurities that are ingrained in the stone, which make it grind hotter. Using a diamond dresser to dress the wheel will also help. Dressing removes a layer of abrasive to reveal a new clean surface. If the edge does get burned, you will need to grind back beyond the burn.

Bevel has many facets This is caused by not keeping the tool flat on the rest.

Ground end is not square This is usually a problem with freehand grinding on the dry grinder. The tool must be held at 90° to the wheel. To help, make some marks at 90° on the support and make sure that the tool is kept parallel to them.

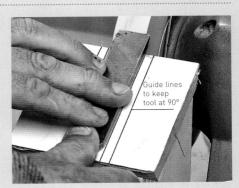

Guide lines to keep tool at 90°

HOW TO GRIND AN EDGE

In the previous chapter, two different grinding tools were described (see page 30), so here is how to grind each.

DRY GRINDING

When dry grinding, it is important to avoid burning the tool edge. Burning is most likely to occur at the tip, and can be avoided by dousing the tool regularly and using a light touch to avoid friction heat.

Most dry grinders come with some form of adjustable tool support or rest. These vary in quality — some are firm and robust, while others are small and flimsy. If you find that the support is inadequate, you could make a support similar to that pictured in the photographs above. In any

case, your support should be adjusted so that the ground bevel is 25°. This can be achieved by offering up a tool that you know is already ground to that bevel and adjusting the support appropriately.

1 Switch on the grinder, place the tool on the rest and move up to engage the stone. Don't worry about sparks — they're not hot. Move the tool from side to side on the wheel.

2 After grinding for a few seconds, douse the end of the tool in water to avoid burning the metal. Repeat this process until grinding is complete.

3 Examine the edge. Burning is indicated when there is little metal to conduct the heat away.

4 If you have to grind away a deep chip in the edge of your tool, it's worth grinding the end flat across at 90° first, then grinding the bevel. This helps to prevent burning, but you should make sure that you then grind the bevel until the entire flat end is removed. Initially, you can grind for longer between dousing, but as the end gets thinner, douse more frequently.

GRINDING GAUGE

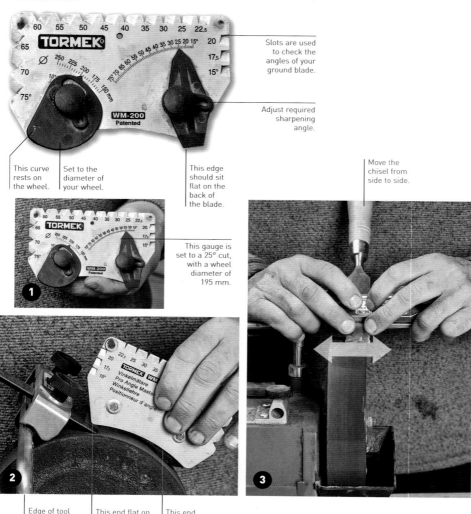

Slots are used to check the angles of your ground blade.

Adjust required sharpening angle.

This curve rests on the wheel.

Set to the diameter of your wheel.

This edge should sit flat on the back of the blade.

This gauge is set to a 25° cut, with a wheel diameter of 195 mm.

Move the chisel from side to side.

Edge of tool butted to stop

This end flat on chisel back

This end on wheel

WET GRINDING

Wet stone grinders usually have some kind of jig arrangement for holding the tool at the correct angle. Most are fairly similar to use.

1 Adjusting the tool in the jig usually involves a setting template or gauge with two adjustments — one for the diameter of the wheel and the other for the angle required.

2 Position the tool in the jig, bevel side down, until the flat of the setting template sits flat on the back of the tool while the end is set on the wheel. Make sure that the side of the tool is butted up to the edge of the jig (this ensures that the end is ground square). If you measure and keep a note of how much the tool protrudes from the jig at this point, you'll find that it's easier in subsequent settings to simply set to this measurement — as long as the wheel is not re-dressed or the jig bar moved.

3 To grind, with the wheel turning, tilt the jig until the edge of the tool is on the wheel. Apply light to moderate pressure and move the tool from side to side. There should always be water on the stone surface — top up the water bath if not. Continue until a new, clean 25° bevel is created.

HOW TO HONE AN EDGE

Grinding produces an edge on the tool, but it's quite coarse. Honing creates the exquisitely sharp edge that we are looking for. It should be a fairly quick process, allowing you to get back to the work as quickly as possible. The basic method described is similar whether you are working freehand or with a guide, and is aimed at getting a sharp edge quickly. Honing media were discussed in the previous chapter (see page 30); whichever medium you use, the honing method will be the same. There are two approaches — freehand honing and using a honing guide.

Rock tool to find the flat of the grinding bevel (25°), then lifted a smidgeon to get the honing bevel of 30°

COARSE

MEDIUM

FINE

3

4

Light pressure applied on the back stroke

6

Rubbing away the burr

Pressure applied to the right of the blade.

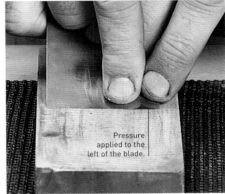

Pressure applied to the left of the blade.

FREEHAND HONING

1 When honing, feeling for a burr on the back edge tells you that the edge is sharp. However, if there is already a burr on the back edge from grinding, you will not be able to feel the honing burr. So first remove the grinding burr by rubbing the back flat on the stone.

2 Apply lubricant to the surfaces, if required — in this case, water stones are being used, so a spritz of water will suffice. Here, I am using three stones — 100, 4,000 and 10,000 grits.

3 Start on the coarse stone and offer the tool to the surface, bevel side down, holding as shown. By slightly rocking the tool, you should be able to feel the grinding bevel sit flat on the surface. Now, lift the tool slightly to add an extra 5° to the angle.

4 Keeping the tool at this angle, and applying fairly light pressure, draw the edge over the honing medium from end to end. On delicate media, such as water stones,

as shown here, or finishing film, only apply pressure on the back stroke.

5 After two or three strokes, feel for a burr on the back of the edge. On newly ground edges there should be a burr, while edges with a wider honing bevel may take more strokes. If there is no burr, continue honing a few strokes at a time, until a burr is found.

6 As soon as you have just a burr, the tool is sharpened and it now needs polishing. Progress to a finer grade stone and apply three or four strokes, and so on. After the final grade, turn the tool over and rub with the back absolutely flat on the honing medium to remove the burr (although often the burr has fallen off by this point).

7 The edge should now be perfectly sharp.

FREEHAND HONING PLANE IRONS

When sharpening plane irons, a slightly cambered edge is often desirable. This can be achieved by applying differential pressure to either side. After honing on each grade as described in Step 6, move the fingers to apply pressure first on one side for three strokes and then on the other for three strokes. This is enough to give a camber of a few thousandths of an inch.

Homemade setting template ensures the correct protrusion of the tool.

Use an engineer's square to check that the tool is at 90°.

Apply pressure on the back stroke.

Pressure applied to the left of the blade

HONING WITH A GUIDE

There are several different honing guides on the market. One of the simplest guides is used in this demonstration — the Stanley.

1 Fit the tool in the guide, bevel side down.

2 Either use the plastic setting tab or a workshop-made setting template to determine the protrusion of the edge for a 30° bevel.

3 If using the setting tab, check that the tool is square in the guide using an engineer's square.

4 Lubricate the honing medium surface, if required. Apply the edge of the tool to the sharpening medium, with the bevel and guide wheel on the surface. Make two or three strokes, pressing only on the back stroke if the medium is soft, and then check for a burr.

5 Proceed through the grades in the same manner as described with freehand honing (see page 55, Step 6).

6 If you want a camber, make differential strokes as described in freehand honing plane irons (see page 55).

Clinic

Can't get a burr when freehand honing
This is probably because you are honing at a low angle. Sometimes this is shown as abrasion on the heel of the bevel. It could be that you are finding the bevel okay, but then allowing the tool to drop down. Try to picture your hands moving parallel to the surface, maintaining the angle.

Can't get a burr when using a guide
Sometimes this happens when using a guide after previously working freehand. Your freehand honing may have been slightly steeper than the guide setting, so the honed bevel does not extend to the very edge of the tool.

Edge still not sharp after honing
If you ground off the end of the blade to remove a chip and then ground the bevel, it is sometimes easy to miss that the bevel has not extended to the very edge, leaving a flat on the end.

The edge digs a chunk out of the water stone or finishing film This is caused by pressing down on the forward stroke. Sometimes this can happen on very fine finishing film, which is more delicate, if a piece of grit gets under the edge. This can be prevented by good hygiene around the sharpening station.

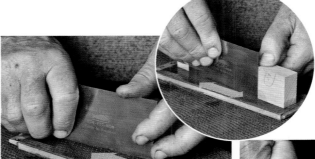

Tip: Holding the scraper against a square-edged piece can help to maintain it at 90° on the stone.

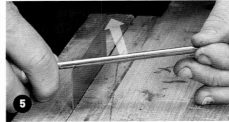

Tip: Use a square-edged piece of wood clamped in the vise next to the scraper to help keep the file square with the edge.

SHARPENING A CABINET SCRAPER

A cabinet scraper needs sharpening when it no longer removes shavings, just dust, or if it is damaged so that it leaves lines in the scraped surface. Usually all four burrs on the scraper will be worked until they are blunt, then all four sharpened together. Sharpening can involve either re-turning the burr or completely renewing the burr. Re-turning the edge can be done two or three times until the whole edge needs renewing.

Dust on the left from a blunt scraper. Shavings on the right from a sharp one.

RENEWING THE BURR

Renewing the burr involves removing any rounding of the edge from previous burr creation, then turning a new burr.

1 Place the scraper in the vise with the edge protruding (you may want to do this in a metalwork vise, if you have one). Use a medium mill file to file a square edge, using strokes along the edge.

2 You should have square edges now, but they will have file marks in them that would show as lines on the scraped surface. Remove the file marks by rubbing the edge at an angle of 90° on a medium-grit sharpening medium. Doing this on a water stone will damage it, but a diamond stone works well, or you could use finishing film, or even wet-and-dry paper on float glass.

3 Feel the edge to check for any remaining file marks. When it feels quite smooth, rub the flat of the scraper on the sharpening medium to completely remove any burr left from the filing process.

4 You should now have smooth, square long edges. Now you need to work harden the new edges. Place the scraper flat on the workbench about 1¼ in. (30 mm) from the edge, and place a burnisher (or screwdriver shaft if you don't have a burnisher) resting on both the scraper edge and the bench edge. Rub backward and forward, applying moderate pressure, three or four times.

5 Now create the cutting edge. Position the scraper in the vise. Place the burnishing tool on the edge at the far end, angled down at about 5°, with the handle close to the scraper. Applying moderate downward pressure, draw the burnisher toward you along the edge, moving the handle away from the scraper as you move it. Imagine you are dragging the corner over into a burr. Repeat this about three times.

6 Turn the scraper around and repeat on the other corner. Then turn the scraper over and repeat Step 5 on the two corners on the other edge.

7 You should be able to feel a pronounced burr on the edges. To re-turn a burr, simply repeat Steps 4–6.

Planing

Of all the hand woodworking tasks, planing is perhaps my favorite. A really sharp plane makes a lovely swishing noise as it cuts, and leaves a beautiful burnished surface. Apart from being fun to use, the plane is also one of the most useful tools in the workshop, because it is able to perform many tasks with great finesse.

PLANING TECHNIQUE

Planing is all about momentum, so it is good to get your body weight behind the plane. For planing an edge, stand facing toward the planing direction, with your left foot forward, and tuck your elbow into your hip. As you start the cut, lean back slightly, then lean forward as the cut progresses — in this way, you are using your body weight to drive the plane.

Start the cut with the plane on the wood surface and the blade slightly back from the front edge. Begin with moderate downward pressure at the front. Once the shaving is started, reduce the downward pressure. It can be beneficial to angle the plane slightly to give a guillotining cut.

For planing an edge, hold the plane with your left-hand thumb in front of the knob and your fingers gripping the underneath. You can then use your fingers as a fence to change the position of the plane on the edge, which is useful when trying to square an edge.

Grip for planing wide surfaces. Note angled presentation gives a smoother, guillotining cut.

For surface planning, the hold is on the front knob, as shown here.

At the start of the cut, rock backward so that your weight is on your back foot.

As the cut progresses, rock forward onto the front foot and extend your arms. In this way, your body weight drives the plane.

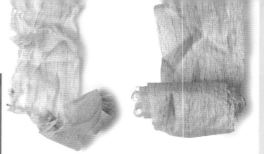

Broken shaving (above)   Unbroken shaving (above)

Always look at the shavings as they come off the blade. They will tell you where the wood is being cut and whether the plane is performing correctly.

Thick shaving (below)

Shaving thicker on the right — plane biased to the right

Thicker on left — plane biased to the left

Clinic

Plane won't cut This could be for a number of reasons:

• Is the blade in the wrong way up? This is easily fixed!

• The adjustment may be incorrect — the blade is not protruding enough to cut, or it's so far out that it just digs into the wood without cutting.

• Is the chip breaker back from the edge? Sometimes the breaker can slide forward so that it covers the blade edge. Aim for 1/32 in. (1 mm) back from the edge.

• Is the mouth too small? If the blade edge is too close to the front of the mouth, it clogs with shavings, preventing the cut. It should be around 1/32 in. (1 mm). Adjust this by removing the blade and adjusting the frog position.

• Very occasionally this may occur if the blade has been sharpened at a steep angle, causing the heel of the bevel to rub instead of the tip cutting.

Surface is rough This could be because you are planing against the grain, causing tear out. Try turning the piece around in order to plane in the other direction. A really sharp blade helps with tear out, but sometimes it's just that the wood will not play ball! If the roughness is at the start of the cut, try angling the plane, and make sure that you start the stroke with the blade slightly back from the wood and apply pressure at the front.

Planing is hard work Your blade may be blunt or you are taking shavings that are too thick.

Plane is sticking Rub the sole of the plane with candle wax so that it slides easily.

ADJUSTING A PLANE

When setting up the plane (which you have to do each time you sharpen or dismantle it), the aim is to set the blade so that it takes a fine shaving of a uniform thickness across its width. To achieve this, you use the blade angle and depth adjusters described in the previous chapter (see page 27).

1 Hold the plane up to the light with the sole uppermost, so that you can sight down the sole. You are looking for the blade to be just showing above the sole — an even hair's breadth all the way across. You can adjust the blade height with the adjusting wheel, then get it level right across with the lever.

2 Try out the cut on a piece of scrap wood. Take a cut with the wood under the middle of the plane, so that the shaving comes out from the middle of the blade. You are aiming for a fine, even shaving across the width that comes away from the wood without too much effort.

3 When you have an even shaving, try using the plane shifted over to one side so that the shaving comes out from the edge of the blade. You should find that the shaving is tapered across its width, being thicker on the side you have biased to, especially if you have honed the blade with a camber. The same should apply for the other side. This feature is an important consideration when you come to use the plane for squaring up (see page 67).

WHY ARE THE FACE SIDE AND FACE EDGE IMPORTANT?

Establishing and marking up your reference surfaces at the start of a job is vital. Reference surfaces are two adjacent faces that are perfectly flat and square to each other, known as face side and face edge. These are your datum surfaces, marked as shown.

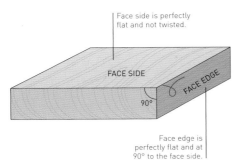

Face side is perfectly flat and not twisted.

FACE SIDE

FACE EDGE

90°

Face edge is perfectly flat and at 90° to the face side.

Why are they so important? First, they aid accuracy in your work. Having created your face side and edge, make sure that jointing occurs on these surfaces. Most jointing takes place on one or two surfaces — table and chair legs and most carcass work, for example. Using established datum surfaces helps to make sure that parts jointed into these surfaces are square and that the complete piece will be true.

Second, they help with orienting the parts. When working on a piece with many parts, it can become confusing as to which piece goes where and which way up. Always keep the faces on the inside and facing up. For example, a table will have the face sides of the rails on the inside with the face edges at the top, and the legs will have face sides and edges facing inward. For drawer sides, the face side is on the inside and the edge is on the top. As long as you are consistent, this convention will aid you in knowing how a particular piece fits into the whole.

And finally, they make notation easier. It is easy to become confused and disheartened if you have to spend a long time figuring out how pieces fit together. Sometimes, although a piece may be numbered, it can be upside down. Using a strict face side and face edge convention removes this problem, thus simplifying your notation.

Planing to this line

Wedge to keep wood from rocking

1

BENCH

2

3

4

PREPARING A FACE SIDE AND FACE EDGE

Always start a project by preparing the wood with face sides and face edges that are straight and square with each other. These surfaces will be used for marking and reference throughout the project. You may have bought the wood from the woodyard as rough boards; if you don't have a machine to prepare them, you will need to use a hand plane.

1 Check the board to be flattened against a straight edge. It's likely to be curved and, if so, secure it to the workbench with the concave side up. It could be secured between bench dogs or butted up to a stop that is fixed to the bench. If it rocks, steady the board with wedges placed underneath.

2 You need a fairly long plane for this — a no. 5½ jack plane or longer would work well. Start by planing diagonally and progressively across the board to remove any cupping. You may find that the cut is better in one direction than the other — in which case, turn the board around so that you are cutting with the grain.

3 Scribble the surface with a pencil — this will help to show where wood is being removed when planing.

4 Check for flatness occasionally with a straight edge.

CONTINUED ▸

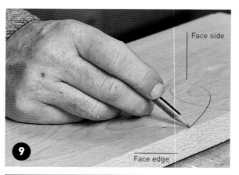

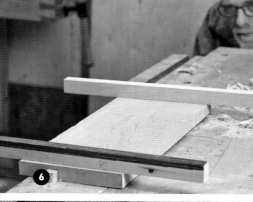

Clinic

The face edge is domed across the width This can be caused by tilting the plane when trying to correct squareness. The correction is achieved entirely by the position of the plane on the edge, not by tilting it.

The edge is curved along the length You may be applying undue pressure on the surface. You should press down at the front of the plane at the start of the cut to get the shaving started and ensure that the plane is flat on the surface. After that, the shaving should help to pull the plane down onto the wood with reduced pressure from you.

Use fingers under plane sole to position plane on the edge.

---

5 When the board is flat across the width, start planing along the length to remove the diagonal planing marks and to flatten, checking occasionally with a straight edge.

6 Use winding sticks to check whether the surface is twisted. Place the sticks at either end of the board and sight down the length. If the sticks are not level, the board is twisted. Alternatively, if you have a surface that you know is flat, you could invert the board on this to check for twisting.

7 You can use the edge of the plane sole as a straight edge to check for flatness.

8 When the board is flat, finish with a sharp, finely set blade to take fine shavings along the full length of the board. This should give a clean, flat surface with no ridges.

9 Decide which edge will be your face edge, and mark the planed face side to point to the face edge. Be bold about this so that the mark can be seen easily!

10 Start planing the face edge to remove saw marks and unevenness. When it is smooth, check for a flat surface along the edge with a straight edge.

11 Check for square at intervals along the edge, using an engineer's square against the face side. Make sure that the stock of the square is pushed firmly against the face side — if not, you will get a false reading. You will also get a better reading if you test against a good back light.

12 If not square, use the plane position to correct the edge. If the edge is high on the right, try moving the plane over so that it is biased to the right. Or, you may find that the edge is out of square differently along the edge — perhaps high on the right at the beginning, and then on the left at the end. You can correct this by moving the plane across, starting with a bias to the right and moving across to a bias on the left. Watch the shaving coming off the blade to check where it is cutting.

13 To correct undulation along the edge, plane locally to remove high spots, but try to finish with a continuous shaving of the length.

14 When the edge is square, mark it boldly as face edge, with the mark pointing to the face side.

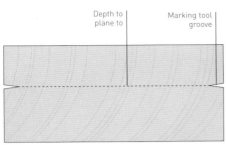

Depth to plane to — Marking tool groove

You can tell when you are very close to the line, because thin slithers start to flake off from the edge of the line. That's the time to back off to a finer shaving.

Note thumb gripping back of the frog.

3

PLANING DOWN TO A LINE

You can use the hand plane to dimension pieces to a required thickness and width. This usually involves planing down to a line created by a marking gauge (see "Marking a piece to be cut to width or thickness," page 67).

1 When dimensioning to width, any waste should be sawn off, leaving just a few fractions of an inch to plane off to reach the gauge line. Imagine the gauge line as a "V" groove — you are aiming to create a surface in line with the bottom of the "V." Be careful not to overshoot when planing to the line — you can start with thick shavings, then back off to thinner as you get closer.

2 When you have finished, check with the gauge to see if you have hit the mark. On wide surfaces, check for flat with a straight edge, because there can be a tendency to plane at the edges but not in the middle.

 Try this!

> It is easy to overshoot and plane below the line. As you approach the line, take only a couple of shavings at a time. Also, it is easier if the planed surface is brought down parallel to the gauge line, so that you don't hit the line at one end but not the other.

PLANING END GRAIN USING A SHOOTING BOARD

Planing end grain can be difficult. The block plane, with its low cutter angle, is good for freehand planing, but there is a danger of breakout. Breakout occurs when you plane end grain and run off the back edge — the cut causes the grain at the end of the cut to split away. This can be overcome by using a shooting board.

The shooting board was introduced in the previous chapter (see pages 48–49). Here's how to use it:

1 Place the workpiece on the board, with the edge butted up to the stock. A plane runs on its side along the rabbet on the board. A jack plane is about right.

2 Grip the workpiece against the stock, with slight pressure against the sole of the plane, but not enough to push the plane away from the rabbet.

3 Push the plane up and down the rabbet so that the end of the workpiece is trimmed. Concentrate on keeping the side of the plane flat on the board. You may find it convenient to hold the plane by the frog rather than the handle. There is a comfortable area for the thumb to rest on the back of the frog.

FOR CLINIC, SEE NEXT PAGE ▶

Clinic

FOR TECHNIQUE, SEE PREVIOUS PAGE

Plane won't cut The blade must be set very fine — too thick and the blade will just jam up against the edge of the piece. You need to keep some pressure on the workpiece so that it engages with the blade, a little like a bacon slicer.

End is not square Make sure that you keep the side of the plane flat on the board. If it tips over, the cut will not be square. You will also trim the end of the shooting board stock, possibly allowing breakout to occur at the back of the cut. Also check that the side is square with the sole of the plane. If it's not, you can "fudge" it a little by adjusting the blade square to the side.

The end of the plane bangs into the workpiece This happens when you bring the plane too far back. The sole of the plane should always be in contact with the end of the workpiece.

Adjust the angle until a good cut is achieved.

Knuckles on the surface help to control the cut.

USING A CABINET SCRAPER

The cabinet scraper is used for woods that are difficult to plane where you are experiencing tear-out. When scraping you only use about 1 in. (25 mm) of the edge in the center — this is achieved by flexing the steel between fingers and thumb. A well performing scraper should give definite shavings rather than dust.

1 Hold the steel on the wood surface with your fingers along the outer edge and both thumbs in the center, toward the bottom. Flex the scraper between your fingers and thumbs. Angle the steel vertically at around 30° and apply moderate pressure as you push the scraper forward. You may have to adjust the angle until you get a good cut.

2 Sometimes you can achieve a better cut by slightly skewing the scraper horizontally. I also find it useful to work with my knuckles rubbing on the surface, as they help to control the depth of cut.

USING THE HAND ROUTER

Nowadays the work of the hand router can easily be done by an electric router. However, if you enjoy using hand tools, you might use the hand router when excavating the waste from dadoes, such as the recesses into which shelves would be fitted in a bookcase. This is done using a combination of the hand router and paring. The hand router is an effective tool for cutting thin layers across the grain. For example, it could be used for grooving a dado joint.

1 Mark one edge of the dado with a knife, then offer up the shelf piece and accurately mark the width of the dado with the knife. Make the knife lines as deep as possible.

2. With a long paring chisel cut a deep chamfer to the knife line, working across the grain.

3. Saw the line of the dado edges with a crosscut backsaw.

4. Pare away most of the waste between the cuts to leave a layer about $^{1}/_{16}$–$^{1}/_{8}$ in. (2–3 mm) deep to be cut away by the router.

Clinic

The wood breaks out at the end of the cut If you cut from the inside outward, the ends of the cut will be delicate because you are cutting across the grain. Always work from the outside inward.

The plane will not cut The angled blade can be difficult to get the hang of, and this is not helped if it's blunt. Unfortunately, the blade is also difficult to sharpen.

Grain running parallel to the cut, making shaving difficult

> Try this!

> It can be difficult to hold the small spoke-shave blade for sharpening. To combat this, you can use a piece of wood with a suitable saw cut in the end. The blade can then be slotted into the cut to hold it in place for sharpening.

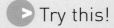

Tool tilted to round corners

5. Set the router depth to remove a fraction of an inch or so of the waste. Holding the handles on either side, work the router across the dado, removing cross-grain shavings.

6. Repeat, progressively resetting the depth of cut; the final depth will be set against the gauge line on the side.

MASTERING THE SPOKE SHAVE

The spoke shave is used for shaping curves. It is a difficult tool to get the hang of, requiring some sensitivity to the wood and its grain direction. However, when you have mastered the technique, it's a very satisfying tool to use, giving a sense of close contact with the material being worked.

The method for adjusting the spoke shave varies — some shaves have thumbscrews for moving the blade, while on others the blade is positioned with finger pressure or by tapping the body on the edge of the bench. As with planing, spoke shaves perform best with finer shavings.

BASIC SPOKE SHAVE TECHNIQUE

1 Hold the shave with your thumbs behind the blade — on some models, there are shaped areas for the thumbs to rest on —

and with your index fingers at the front on the side. Your thumbs and index fingers control the angle of the sole on the work.

2 Take the cut by pushing the shave away from you. You will need to adjust the angle and position of the sole until the blade engages with the wood. Grain direction is very important when spoke shaving, so make sure that you are cutting with the grain. This may mean turning the piece in the vise or changing position.

3 There will be a tricky part where the grain runs parallel to the cut, making it difficult to decide which direction to cut. This bit often needs tidying with a cabinet scraper later.

4 When the main curve has been formed, the shave can also be tilted and used to round the corners of the work.

Marking and measuring

Accuracy is essential in woodworking, and this starts with marking and measuring. Close attention here will save you from having to correct errors later in the project. Whenever you use a marking knife, always make sure that the flat side of the knife faces the measuring tool.

You should have a number of marking and measuring tools in your tool kit that can be used for a number of different tasks.

MARKING UP A PIECE TO BE CUT TO LENGTH

1 If both ends need to be square, start by truing one end on the shooting board (see page 63) or trimming on a chop saw. If possible, use a steel rule to mark the dimensions because this will be more accurate than a tape measure.

2 Working from the trued end, lay the rule on the workpiece with the correct measurement aligned with the end. Mark the dimension off the end of the rule by pricking with a marking knife.

3 Place the knife in the previous mark and then slide a square up to the knife, making sure the stock is held firmly against the face side or face edge. If possible, grip the square as shown to firmly clamp it against the face.

4 Make a knife cut along the edge.

5 Turn the workpiece and place the knife into the previously marked line, where it intersects the corner. Slide the square up to the knife as before and make another cut. You may have to turn the square to make sure the stock is against a face. Marking is easier if the knife is against the outside face so that you can run right through without hitting the stock.

Note thumb and fingers clamping the square in place.

By marking this side, the knife will hit the stock.

6 If you are marking a very wide piece, you may need to place a straight edge, such as a steel rule, against the square to get extra length.

MARKING A PIECE TO BE CUT TO WIDTH OR THICKNESS

Marking for width or thickness is usually done using a marking gauge (see page 20) and always working from the planed references of face side and edge (see page 61).

1 Offer up a rule to the gauge, with the end against the stock, and move the stock until the point of the pin sits on the appropriate measurement. Then tighten the locking screw and recheck.

2 Hold the gauge with your thumb below and index finger above the stock, and the rest of the fingers grasping the shaft.

3 Place the gauge on the workpiece, with the stock against the face and the corner of the shaft on the surface. Rotate the gauge until the pin engages with the surface. This will give you a trailing action as you push the gauge away from you.

4 Mark the two surfaces on either side, and at each end if the piece is quite wide.

Clinic

Lines do not meet.

Squared lines around the piece do not meet up This may occur for a number of reasons:

• Because your wood is not true — check that your face side and face edge are straight and square.

• You didn't do all the marking from the reference faces.

• The square may have moved while cutting the line, due to pressure from the knife. Try to hold the square stock as firmly as possible against the edge.

• You may not have positioned the square precisely on the previous line as you moved around the piece. This is helped by positioning the knife and sliding the square up to it.

Gauge lines are not straight Although a relatively simple tool, the gauge can be difficult to master. Correct grip is important, as well as having the pin angled for a trailing action. Instead of looking at the path of the pin, look at the position of the stock against the face — if a gap appears there, the line will wander. Concentrate on keeping that area gap-free.

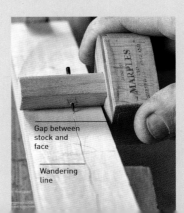

Gap between stock and face

Wandering line

MARKING A PENCIL LINE PARALLEL TO AN EDGE

There are three simple methods for marking a pencil line parallel to an edge:

You can use a pencil gauge (a marking gauge with a pencil instead of a pin) in the same way as a marking gauge (see page 67). The pencil gauge shown here is workshop made.

For a rough-and-ready line close to the edge, simply hold a pencil and use your middle and ring fingers as a fence.

Use a combination square, set to the correct measurement. With the stock of the square against the edge as a fence, and a pencil against the end of the rule, run the stock along the edge.

MARKING FINE MEASUREMENTS FOR FITTING AND THICKNESS

Sometimes you may wish to measure pieces to fit, such as when fitting a dado joint, for example. These are such fine measurements that a rule will not do. In this case, you should use a vernier gauge (see page 20). With this tool, you can measure the internal dimension of the slot and the width of the fitting piece down to fractions of an inch.

A vernier gauge can also be used to precisely check if a planed piece is the same thickness at each edge.

Measuring an external dimension.

Measuring an internal dimension.

MARKING ANGLES

To measure and mark out angles, you should use a sliding bevel.

1 The angle between the stock and plate can be adjusted and set using a protractor.

2 Or it can be offered up to the work to copy a required angle.

3 Once the angle is set, it can be used in the same way as the engineer's square.

 ## Good practice

As mentioned earlier, precision and accuracy are key when marking and measuring your work. While the main tip is to keep practicing, here are a few further pointers for improving accuracy:

Use a sharp pencil When you need to be accurate, use an H or 2H pencil and keep it well sharpened. For less accurate marking, such as face side and edge marking, an HB pencil is often better because it is darker and stands out well.

Use a knife or gauge If you are sawing or chiseling to a line, use a knife or gauge to make the line; then you can feel the tool engage with the line.

When measuring, use a steel rule. Invest in a set of rulers — 6, 12, 24 and 36 in. (150, 300, 600 and 1,000 mm). Always use these for measurements up to a yard or meter. For larger measurements, make sure that your tape is accurate; often the sliding tab at the end of the tape causes a false reading.

Get a vernier gauge Sometimes 0.01 in. (0.25 mm) can be the difference between a good fit and a bad fit, but you can't measure such small increments with a rule. Using a tool that works to this level of accuracy also encourages you to think in those terms.

Be methodical about creating your datum surfaces Make sure that your face side and edge are true and square with each other before you start any marking out or dimensioning from those surfaces.

Check your squares are truly square by marking a line from a straight edge, then turning the square to check that it matches up with the line from the other side.

Pencil line aligns with square

At each stage, check that everything is square (assuming that it is supposed to be) — tenon shoulders, panel edges and also frames on dry clamping and glue-up (measure the diagonals).

Jointing first If you are making something with curves or tapers, try to do all of the jointing first, while all of the datum surfaces are present. Then tackle the shaping, where you may be cutting away the datum.

Try to keep faces straight and clean when paring. This makes it easier to see where you are cutting in relation to the marks.

Work from accurate drawings Either computer generated, such as CAD or Sketchup, or full-size rods (drawn with a sharp pencil — see the glossary on pages 256–57 for more information on rods). If you have to change a dimension while working, make sure that you also change it on the drawing, because not doing so usually leads to confusion and inaccuracy later on.

Finally, remember that accuracy is more crucial in some cases than in others. For example, the length of a tenon is not crucial, because there is usually clearance at the bottom of the mortise, but the distance between the shoulders of a rail with tenons at either end is very important.

Sawing

Sawing accurately is an essential woodworking skill, but it can be difficult to acquire. The secret to it is good technique and practice. Of all the woodworking skills, sawing is possibly the one that requires the most practice to perfect. Sawing operations can be divided between rough sawing to get parts close to a required dimension, and detail sawing for precision dimensioning and jointing. Use handsaws for rough sawing and backsaws for detail sawing. The principle with all sawing is to cut on the waste side of the line. Usually the line will have been measured from an edge or end, so you need to cut on the non-measured side of the line. Always consider safety when sawing — you guide the start of the cut with your thumb or forefinger. Take gentle strokes with the saw while your digit is in the danger zone; once the cut is started, move your finger and saw with more vigor.

USING HANDSAWS

Wood for a project may come into the workshop as large sheets of plywood perhaps, or long rough-sawn boards that need to be reduced. If you don't have a circular saw, you can use a handsaw. You use a ripsaw for cutting solid wood along the grain; crosscut saws are used for crosscutting solid wood and for any cut in man-made board. Crosscut saws can be used to rip, but it is harder work.

RIPPING

Ripping is best done with a 4–6 TPI ripsaw, although a disposable 8 TPI hard-point saw could be used.

1 Mark the line of the cut. If the piece is small enough, it can be placed vertically in the vise. Usually it will have to be placed across two sawhorses (see page 48), with the starting end overhanging.

2 Position yourself with your right knee on the board about 16 in. (400 mm) back from the start of the cut. If possible, get your eye over the top of the cut so that you have a stereoscopic sight of the saw. The line of your arm should be in line with the saw.

3 Hold the end of the wood to the left of the line and use your thumb to guide the saw onto the line. Keep your thumb up from the wood surface in case the saw jumps at the start of the cut. Start the cut with light strokes, holding off some of the weight of the saw. The saw angle should be about 60° from the board.

4 Once the kerf has been established, you can move your thumb away and go at it with more vigor, but not "hammer and tongs"! Use steady, long strokes, keeping your arm in line with the stroke and your eye on the line of the cut to make sure that it's following the marked line.

5 As the cut progresses, you will have to move the board on the horses, ending with the saw outside the second horse or turning

CROSSCUTTING

Crosscutting is best done with a 7–8 TPI crosscut sharpened handsaw or an 8 TPI hard-point saw.

1 Mark the line of the cut and either place the piece on sawhorses (see page 48) or clamp it on the bench. If you are using sawhorses, position yourself over the cut so that your arm is in line with the blade and with your knee on the board to stabilize it. If there is a lot of overhang, use another sawhorse to support it.

2 The start of the cut is the same as for ripping (see previous page), but the saw is held at a shallower angle of around 45°. If the saw is sharp, you shouldn't need to press it into the wood — just let the weight of the saw do the work.

3 When you come to the end of the cut, go gently and reach your left hand over to support the waste; otherwise it may come away, taking a splinter of the non-waste with it.

Chamfer

The saw kerf is on the waste side, just kissing the knifed line.

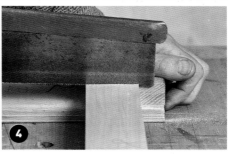

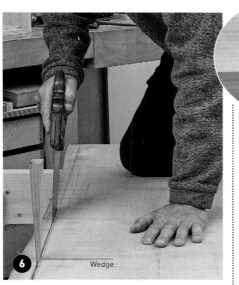

Wedge

the wood around and sawing the final bit from the other end. Always try to keep the cutting area as close to the support as possible.

6 Sometimes sawing will become difficult because the kerf is closing up and pinching the saw. A wedge driven into the kerf will alleviate this problem.

 Try this!

> All sawing operations are easier if you have the support as close to the cut as possible. This reduces vibration and increases workpiece stability.

USING BACKSAWS

The common backsaws are the carcass and the dovetail. The dovetail, as the name implies, is used mainly for dovetailing, and will be dealt with in the joints chapter (see pages 153–65). However, the carcass saw is the workhorse saw for general, detailed bench work. Carcass saws are usually sharpened for crosscutting. This may be to cut a piece to length or may be for a partial cut for a joint shoulder.

1 Mark the line of the cut with a marking knife (see page 66). Then, using a wide, sharp chisel, pare a slight chamfer on the waste side of the line. This provides a slope for the saw to sit into.

2 Place the workpiece on a saw hook. Start the cut at the back corner. Guide the saw into the chamfer with the tip of your index finger, and angle the saw up about 5° from horizontal. The saw should drop onto the cut line easily.

3 Use light strokes to start with, almost holding up the weight of the saw.

4 Once the cut is started, progressively bring the saw down onto the line until you are sawing the whole width of the piece horizontally. Work steadily with long strokes, without pressing down, until you are through or reach the stop line. Let the weight of the saw do the work. If the saw is sharp, you won't need to force it into the wood.

Cut will finish here.

Clinic

The cut is not square:

• The saw may be blunt on one side, which will cause vertical drift. Feel the teeth — are they sharper on one side? The saw may need sharpening if it can be, or replacing if not.

• Check your stance. Is your arm in line with the saw blade or are you looking to one side of the blade? This can make the cut out of square in both dimensions. Practice cutting with different stances.

• If there is some of the knife cut left on the top surface, when crosscutting with a backsaw, you may be bringing the saw down to the knife line too quickly. It should be brought down progressively over a number of strokes after you've established the cut on the corner.

The cut is ragged:

• The saw may be blunt. When using a carcass saw, you can sometimes get a ragged corner on the bottom edge where the last bit breaks between the knife cut and the saw. This usually falls off easily.

• A ragged cut with a handsaw may mean that your saw is too coarse.

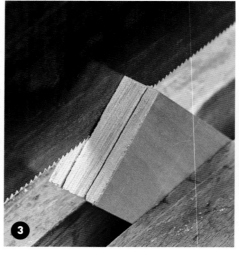

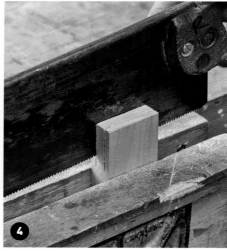

Saw down until you meet the shoulder line on both sides.

RIPPING WITH THE CARCASS OR TENON SAW

The ripping cut goes with the grain and would normally be done to cut the cheek of a tenon or lap joint (see pages 129–43). A tenon saw is best for this, because it is sharpened rip style, but a carcass saw will also work.

1 Mark the line of the cut using a gauge. Place the piece low in the vise at an angle so that a line from corner to corner is roughly horizontal.

2 Start the cut at the top corner on the waste side of the line and saw down so that the cut runs diagonally from corner to corner.

3 Turn the piece around in the vise and repeat Step 2.

4 Finally, with the piece vertical in the vise, saw down to the line to remove the remnant.

 Try this!

> If you are having trouble controlling the cut, try holding the saw with your index finger pointing toward the cut.

Chiseling

Chisels may be the most useful tools in your kit — they can be used for everything from heavy waste removal when cutting joints to very delicate and nuanced paring. For heavy work, the chisel is driven with a mallet, while for paring, hand pressure is usually enough.

In all chisel work, it gives more precision if you work progressively down to a line rather than trying to cut directly on the line. If you try to cut straight to the line, the force of the large area of waste acting on the bevel will push the edge beyond the line.

When chiseling, always make sure that both hands are behind the sharp end of the tool. It is not safe to hold the piece with one hand in front of the chisel. Use a holding device on the workbench instead (such as a "C" clamp). Wear eye protection when chopping down with a chisel and mallet (when chopping a lapped dovetail, for example), because pieces of wood can fly off with force.

Finally, remember to keep your chisels sharp, because a blunt tool is more dangerous than a sharp one. This may seem counterintuitive, but a blunt tool requires more force to work it, so you have less control over it.

Bad practice — blade can slip.

Safe chiseling — both hands behind the sharp end.

PARING

Paring is the progressive removal of waste by a series of very thin cuts with a chisel. It is often used to remove waste up to a saw cut.

I'm using my body weight to drive the chisel down.

PARING END GRAIN

This can be done with the wood vertical in the vise, using a similar method to side-grain paring (see overleaf), or it can be done with the piece flat on the bench, as shown above.

1 Clamp the piece on the bench with a piece of waste underneath.

2 Hold the chisel handle in your right hand with a reverse grip. Use your left hand to position the end of the chisel.

3 Use your body weight to press down on the chisel to make the cut.

Clinic

Pared surfaces are ragged and uneven
This may be because the chisel is not sharp or you are driving it with only your arms — using your body weight gives a cleaner cut.

The cut surface drops below the line
You could have cut to the line too soon. A large mass of waste above the line can push the chisel below the line when you make the cut. You need to be very careful when engaging with the line.

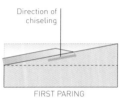
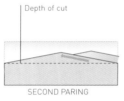

Direction of chiseling

Depth of cut

FIRST PARING

SECOND PARING

FINAL PARING

The flat part of the chisel sits here to provide a reference for the cutting part.

Only this part is cutting.

You can feel the chisel "click" into the gauge line. Note just a sliver above the line.

PARING SIDE GRAIN

It is easier to pare across the grain than with the grain — it gives better control. Often hand paring as shown here would follow removal of waste with mallet and chisel (see page 75, opposite).

1 Clamp the piece in the vise. With the chisel handle in your right hand, use your left hand to guide the end into the wood. Keep your index finger under the blade and pressed against the edge of the workpiece and your thumb on top. Pressing down with your thumb helps to engage the chisel edge with the wood to start the cut.

2 Using your body weight when paring horizontally gives a smoother, more controlled cut. Tuck your elbow into your hip and move your body forward to drive the chisel through the wood. A sharp chisel should slice cleanly.

3 Often you will be paring to a knife or gauge line; work down to the line until there is just a slither left, then drop the chisel into the line. You should feel the tool engage in the line so that you cut precisely to it.

4 Do not pare right through to the back of the workpiece to avoid breakout at the back. If you need to pare right across, turn the piece to come from the other side.

5 Often a wide chisel is used for paring, but only part of it is cutting. The rest is riding on an adjacent, previously pared surface as a reference for the cutting part.

6 It is easier to see what you are doing if you keep the pared surface flat and clean. Using your body weight to drive the cut helps with this.

Annual rings
curved upward.

USING A MALLET AND CHISEL FOR REMOVAL OF WASTE

For heavy removal of waste, the chisel can be driven with a mallet. When removing a lot of waste from a dado, it is useful to chop with chisel and mallet and then finish with hand paring. Use a bevel-edge or firmer chisel for this.

1 Saw the shoulders, then break up the waste first with a few cross-grain saw cuts.

2 With the workpiece in the vise, take a reverse hold on the chisel with your left hand, so that the blade leaves the back of your hand. Rest your elbow on the workpiece to steady your hand, then position the chisel for the cut, angled slightly upward. Each cut should only remove a ¹⁄₁₆ in. (2 mm) layer.

3 Hit the handle of the chisel firmly with the mallet until the waste comes away.

4 Work your way down to the line, then turn the work to come from the other side.

Tip: The cut is usually cleaner when working with the annual rings curving up toward you. Look at the end grain to establish this.

MAKING DEEP CUTS WITH A CHISEL

Chopping with a mallet and chisel is the best method for deep cuts, such as mortises. This is best done with a mortise chisel (see page 24).

1 Mark the area to be cut and clamp the piece on the bench, preferably over the leg.

2 Holding the chisel with a reverse grip in your left hand, guide the chisel into position with your right hand. Start about ⅛ in. (4 mm) in from the edge of the mortise.

3 Hit the chisel firmly with the mallet, then move it forward about ⅛ in. (4 mm) and repeat until you are just short of the other end of the mortise.

4 Turn the chisel over so that the back faces forward and lever out the waste.

5 Repeat this process until you have reached the required depth. Chop out the remaining endpieces using the chisel with the back facing out.

Clamping and holding

It's often said that you can never have too many clamps, but I think the truth is that the number of clamps you own determines their use. Often you can hold work with fewer clamps, as long as you use them creatively. Clamps come in many shapes and sizes — they are used not just for clamping pieces together while gluing, but also for holding and steadying a piece while you work on it.

The aim when clamping is to close up the joint surfaces and apply moderate pressure. Once this is achieved, no more pressure is required, and it is wasted effort to tighten further. Clamp pressure should always be close to the joint, as pressure remote from the joint leads to distortion. Try to match the clamp to the job — sometimes using a large clamp on a small job can distort it, leaving it twisted when you remove the clamps. It can also be very inconvenient to have long bar clamps sticking out unnecessarily in your workspace.

GLUING YOUR WORK

The golden rule of gluing up is, "Always do a dry run first." There are three reasons for this:
• You will find out whether the piece fits together well and can correct any problems. It's very difficult to do this once the joints are covered in glue.
• The dry run means that you will have all of the correct clamps, ready and adjusted, when you start the glue-up process.
• Gluing up is a hectic procedure — it's the culmination of the project, and you have to get everything right before the glue sets. By allowing you to find possible pitfalls in advance, a dry run helps to take the stress away!

How much glue should you use?
It's difficult to quantify this, but most beginners use too much glue. You should aim for just a slight bead of squeeze-out on edge joints when the joint is clamped up, and not large dribbles running onto the bench! This is something that only comes with experience. For most joints that are inserted — mortise and tenon or dowel joints, for example — you need to avoid squeeze-out. Put the glue in the hole rather than the spigot (perhaps, if the joint is loose, add just a smear on the tenon), and this way you reduce the risk of squeeze-out.

> ## ▶ Try this!

> Make sure that the surface you use for gluing up is flat, so that it can be used as a reference to make sure the work is not twisted.

Some woods (oak and walnut, for instance) will stain black if the clamp bar is against the wood with glue squeeze-out present. This can be prevented by applying masking tape to the bar.

Clamping blocks protect the wood.

Angling the clamps will pull your frame back to square.

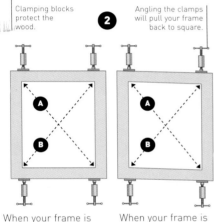

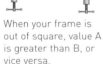

Winding stick

Winding stick

When your frame is square, values A and B are equal.

When your frame is out of square, value A is greater than B, or vice versa.

CLAMPING UP FRAMES

Bar clamps are best for clamping over long distances; you could use "F" and "C" clamps for anything less than 12 in. (300 mm).

1 Position a clamp at each jointing point. Use clamping blocks to prevent the clamps from bruising the work. Magnetic or bar-holding blocks are very useful here (see page 34).

2 When the joints are closed up, check that the frame is square by measuring the diagonals. Using a square to check can give a false reading if the components have distorted under pressure.

3 If the diagonals are not equal, the frame can be corrected by moving the clamp heads so that they are pulling in the direction of the long diagonal.

4 Check that the frame is not twisted — make sure that the clamps are resting evenly on the reference gluing surface and that the frame is resting on the bars all around. If the gluing surface is not true, you check using winding sticks or a level.

5 Sometimes the ends can be lifted by the clamps. Check for this with a straight edge, or check for light showing under the winding sticks.

6 Wipe off any glue squeeze-out with a damp rag, or wait until it has hardened to a pliable consistency and then remove it with a chisel.

CLAMPING UP CARCASSES

Carcasses (meaning case constructions such as cupboards, chests and boxes) can be difficult to assemble, because you need to clamp in a number of different directions. Use a mix of clamps, depending on the distance — "F" and "C" clamps for short distances, and bar clamps for longer. Break the assembly into stages if you think that you will not be able to get it glued and clamped in time (approximately 20 minutes for most PVAs). Make the same square and twist checks and adjustments as you would for frame clamping. Where pressure has to be applied in the middle of a carcass, make upcurved bearers. Clamping at either end will transfer pressure to the center. Sometimes you have to be creative when arranging clamps for a carcass.

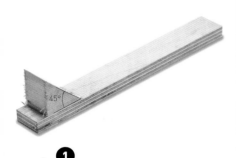

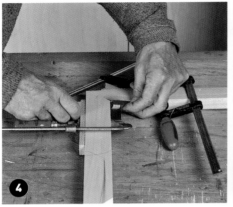

CLAMPING MITERS

There are various methods that you can use to clamp miters, including commercial systems based on ratchet straps and corner blocks. However, a simple workshop-based method uses "C" or "F" clamps to apply angled blocks at the corners. These blocks can be glued on or just clamped in place, depending on how many clamps you have available.

1 For a 90° joint, cut two triangular blocks with 45° corners. If you have clamps available, glue the blocks onto strips of wood (plywood or MDF, perhaps). If not, glue the blocks straight onto the ends of the workpieces. Introducing a layer of newspaper into the joint will aid knocking the blocks off later.

2 If you are using blocks on strips, fix the strips onto the ends of the workpieces using "C" or "F" clamps.

3 You should now be able to exert pressure across the joint at 90°, using a "C" or "F" clamp. Apply glue and clamp up.

4 Use an engineer's square to check alignment.

5 After the joint has set, stuck blocks can be knocked off by tapping them sideways with a hammer.

6 If clamps are scarce, this method works well even if you clamp up pairs of diagonal corners in two parts rather than all corners.

▶ Try this!

> This method of clamping can also be used on mitered carcasses, using wider miter clamping blocks.

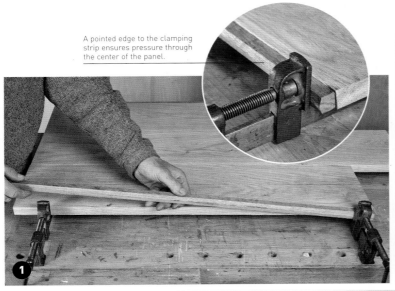

A pointed edge to the clamping strip ensures pressure through the center of the panel.

Masking tape prevents the wood from reacting with the metal of the clamp.

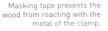

Light showing indicates that the surface is not flat.

> ## Try this!
>
> Adjusting clamp tension can relieve the bow across a board. Tighten the top clamps to push the middle down, and the bottom clamps to push it up. Moving the clamping strips can also help; moving them up slightly can raise the edges, and vice versa.

CLAMPING PANELS

Bar clamps are the tool of choice for gluing up panels. You might need to do this for a tabletop or a wide door panel — any piece that consists of a number of boards to be jointed side by side.

1 Protect the edges of the piece by using clamping strips.

2 You will need a bar clamp approximately every 18 in. (450 mm) along the panel, alternating the positioning above and below. If they were all on one side, the components would spring up in the middle.

3 Before tightening the clamps, check that the components are aligned correctly — tap them into place with a mallet if not.

4 After tightening, check that the joints have closed up well and add more clamps if necessary.

5 Check for flat using a steel rule, and for twist using winding sticks or a level. This can sometimes be adjusted by changing the tension in the clamps or moving the clamping strips up or down to change the pressure point.

6 Any glue squeeze-out can be wiped off with a damp cloth or carefully scraped off with a cabinet scraper after hardening.

Using Power Tools

Power tools can be a mixed blessing — some woodworkers like the quick results that you get with machinery, while those who enjoy the journey as much as the destination find them a distraction. Some power tools are simply not accurate enough for fine woodwork, and others are only suitable for roughing out. The router is the exception — if you have just one power tool, it should be a router. It's so useful that it is covered in detail in Chapter 4.

Power tools should always be used with care, not just because they are dangerous, but also because they work fast and before you know it you have damaged your work. However, with an understanding of the way in which each machine works, you can make sure that they are on your side.

Drilling

Power drills can be defined by their power source — those that plug into a power supply (almost extinct now!) and those that are cordless and driven by a rechargeable battery. The introduction of cordless drills has led to the development of the lightweight drill/driver, which can be used as a powered screwdriver. The creation of these lighter drills has almost replaced the simple hand drill, although there are still tasks for which the latter is invaluable, especially where access is limited.

Marking the position for the drilling with an awl.

Some drills are designed mainly for heavy drilling into masonry and have SDS (special direct system) chucks. These are not suitable for woodwork, but adapter chucks can be fitted. Most cordless drills have keyless chucks.

Often you will want precision drilling for your work, which is difficult to achieve with a handheld drill. A bench-mounted drill press is an option, or the power drill can be fitted in a vertical drill stand. This consists of a vertical column on which runs a sprung bracket to which the drill is fitted. Pulling down a lever lowers the drill, and the spring returns it to the top position. The accuracy of these drill stands depends on the build quality. Look for a solid column and base, and little play in the sliding bracket. Fit a piece of wood to the baseplate to allow drilling through the workpiece. The stand can be clamped to the workbench.

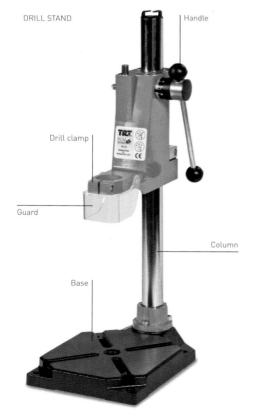

DRILL STAND

Handle

Drill clamp

Guard

Column

Base

Using a square helps to keep the drilled hole vertical, and masking tape shows the drill depth.

FREEHAND DRILLING

To aid accuracy, place a square close to the drill as a guide. It's worth marking the drilling position with an awl. Depth can be controlled by attaching some masking tape to the drill or using a drill stop collar.

A drill stop collar can be used as an alternative to masking tape.

DRILLING FOR SCREWS

In softwood, you can often get away with driving screws straight into the wood without preparation. When working with hardwoods, pilot, clearance and countersunk holes are required to avoid splitting. The diameters of the clearance and pilot holes are determined by the size of the screw used.

CHOOSING PILOT HOLE DIAMETER

The following chart shows the best pilot hole diameter for commonly found screw sizes (you can approximate to some degree). Some screws are sold with the diameter indicated by number, while others are sold by shank measurement.

Pilot holes		
Screw Number	Screw gauge	Pilot hole
4	1/8 in. (3 mm)	5/64 in. (2 mm)
6	9/64 in. (3.5 mm)	7/64 in. (2.8 mm)
8	5/32 in. (4 mm)	1/8 in. (3.2 mm)
10	13/64 in. (5 mm)	9/64 in. (3.6 mm)
12	7/32 in. (5.5 mm)	5/32 in. (4 mm)

Try this!

> Clamp a piece of scrap wood underneath the workpiece when drilling right through. This prevents unsightly splintering or breakout when the drill bit emerges.

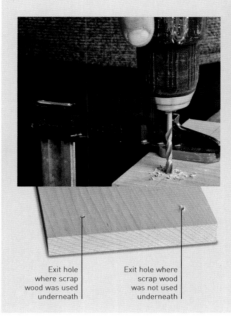

> While drilling deep holes, occasionally lift the drill bit out of the wood to allow the waste to be expelled. This allows for a cleaner and quicker drill.

Exit hole where scrap wood was used underneath

Exit hole where scrap wood was not used underneath

DRILLING TO ATTACH TWO PIECES TOGETHER

To screw two pieces together, you need a clearance hole in the upper piece and a pilot hole in the lower piece. You also need to deal with the screw head — it can be left visible but countersunk level with the surface, or recessed below the surface in a counterbored hole that can later be filled. Counterboring is also useful when joining thick pieces without a screw that is long enough.

COUNTERSINKING

Countersinking involves recessing the screw head in a conical recess at the top of the clearance hole. The top of the head sits level with the surface or just below it.

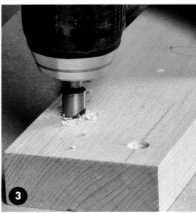

1 Mark the position of the screw with an awl.

2 Using an ordinary twist bit, drill a suitable clearance hole right through the piece.

3 Countersink the clearance hole with a countersink bit. Aim to countersink so that the head sits just below the surface.

CONTINUED ▶

4 Hold the piece in position (clamp, if necessary) and mark the position of the pilot hole through the clearance hole, with either an awl or a screw.

5 Remove the countersunk piece and drill the pilot hole, using masking tape or a drill stop collar to indicate depth.

6 Screw the pieces together.

Mark left by screw or awl

Mark left by screw or awl

Use a screw to mark the drilling position.

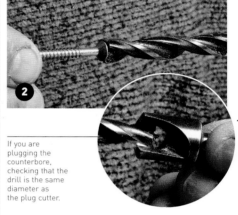

If you are plugging the counterbore, checking that the drill is the same diameter as the plug cutter.

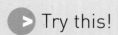

THE FINISHED RESULT

Try this!

> Brass screws are relatively soft, and so the heads can break off at the shank. Drive in a preliminary steel screw of the same gauge, lubricated with wax, to define the thread, then screw in the brass screw.

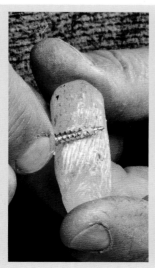

COUNTERBORING

In counterboring, the screw head is sunk entirely below the surface in a hole wider than the diameter of the head. The hole can be plugged later.

1 Mark the screw's position with an awl.

2 Select a drill slightly wider than the screw head for the counterbore hole. A spur point or forstner bit will give a cleaner hole. If you are planning on plugging the hole later, choose a bit the same diameter as the plug cutter (see Step 9).

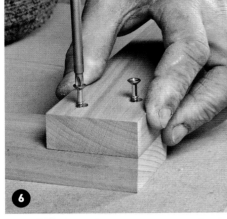

> Good practice

> When you need to use a spur point or forstner bit to drill a wide hole concentric with a narrower one, always drill the wide hole first, because the bits need a solid center to work.

THE FINISHED RESULT

3 Indicate the drilling depth with masking tape or a drill stop collar. A bit of arithmetic may be required to make sure that the drill does not come right through.

4 Drill the counterbore hole.

5 Select a suitable bit and drill the clearance hole through the counterbore hole.

6 Hold the piece in position (clamp, if necessary) and mark the position of the pilot hole through the clearance hole with either an awl or a screw.

7 Remove the counterbored piece and drill the pilot hole, using masking tape or a drill stop collar to indicate depth.

8 Screw the pieces together.

9 The counterbore hole can be filled using a cross-grain plug. These can be made using a plug cutter, rather like a drill with a hollow center, which leaves a circular cut with the plug left in the center. They can be difficult to use with a handheld drill, being difficult to get started in the cut; they work better in a drill press or stand.

10 Drill the plugs.

11 Lever them out.

12 Smear glue in the counterbore holes and tap in the plugs. Make sure that the grain directions are aligned.

13 When the glue is dry, level off with a block plane and abrasive.

Using a circular saw

With the correct blade, the portable circular saw can give a very clean, straight cut. This is enhanced if the saw has a plunge facility and is fitted to a track. The introduction of track saws means that sheet materials can be dimensioned cleanly and accurately without a table saw. Without a track this is more difficult, and the edge may need to be cleaned up a little with a hand plane.

SAFETY

It is very important to consider safety before you use a circular saw. There are a few key rules that you should follow:
- Wear ear and eye protection.
- Have good dust extraction by connecting up to a vacuum. If not, wear a dust mask. Always wear a dust mask when cutting MDF.
- Check that cables are well away from the line of cut.
- Always work with the correct cutting depth — this should be with no more than ⅛ in. (3 mm) of tooth protruding below the cut material.
- Always disconnect the saw when changing blades.
- Make sure that the blade guard is covering the teeth at all times.
  - Before using the machine, check that the blade guard is functioning correctly. Does it return to the closed position when released?
  - Do not lift the guard up other than to allow the saw to start cutting.
  - Don't fix the guard in the open position.
  - Make sure that the guard has dropped back to cover the blade before putting the tool down; otherwise the machine may run away over your foot!

- Don't try to change direction or angle the saw in the groove, or kerf, formed by the teeth. This could result in the saw running out of the kerf in an uncontrolled way.
- When ripping, place a wedge in the kerf to make sure that it does not pinch the blade.
- The saw should have a riving knife just behind the blade — this helps to prevent the wood from pinching the saw blade. Never remove the riving knife.
- Check for nails or other foreign objects in the line of cut before cutting.
- Use the correct blade for the job.
- Think ahead! Make sure the work is well supported so that, when the cut is completed, the two parts can be controlled. If they tilt away from each other as they are cut, there is a danger of pinching the blade. You can also lose control as pieces fall apart at the end of a cut.
- A sharp saw is a safer saw.

BLADE SELECTION

You will need at least two blades for your circular saw — a coarse blade for ripping solid wood (this would have around 14 teeth, depending on its diameter), and a second finer blade for crosscutting and for sheet materials such as plywood and MDF (this would have around 70–80 teeth). For a very fine cut, choose a triple-chip blade — the teeth are sharpened with alternate teeth trapezoidal in shape. This aids removal of the central waste, giving a very clean cut, especially in veneered or laminate boards.

CIRCULAR SAW TECHNIQUES

In some situations, you may only need a piece of wood roughly cut to dimension, and so you can use the kerf indicator on the saw base as a guide. However, sometimes you require a more accurate, cleaner cut. In this case, you should either use the fence provided with the saw, or clamp a straight edge to the workpiece for the saw base to run against. It's worth measuring the distance from the edge of the base to the near side of the blade and writing it on the base for future reference. The straight edge would be clamped at this distance, parallel to the intended line of cut.

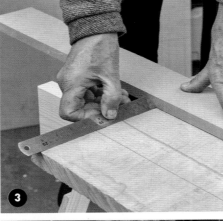

 Try this!

> When using a straight edge to guide the saw, check that it is fitted in the right place by taking just a nip out with the saw. You can then adjust to the line and set the other end to the same measurement.

Tip: The technique for cutting solid wood will vary from that used for man-made boards, but for both you need to ensure good support for both the workpiece and the offcut. Be aware that the sudden imbalance caused when a large, inadequately supported piece is cut in two could be dangerous.

Usually, cutting solid wood is asking more of the machine than cutting sheet materials — cutting a 3 in. (75 mm) oak board is more challenging than ¾ in. (18 mm) MDF. There is also more danger of the saw binding in the kerf with solid wood.

CROSSCUTTING SOLID WOOD

For crosscutting narrow pieces, the chop or miter saw (see page 43) should be the tool of choice if you have one. If not, here's how to go about it.

1 Make sure that the workpiece is adequately supported. If the offcut is quite small, it can be allowed to drop away. If it's heavy, it needs support so that it will not break off at the end of the cut, or drop and pinch the blade. Also check that the blade will not cut through into a precious or damaging surface, such as a bench top or concrete floor.

2 Check that you have a fine tooth crosscut blade fitted and that the depth adjustment is correct (no more than ⅛ in./3 mm greater than board thickness).

3 Mark the line of cut. If you are clean cutting, use the fence or clamp on a straight edge, as described on the previous page. Make sure you are set up for cutting on the waste side of the line.

4 Lay the saw base on the edge of the wood, with the blade away from the wood, and switch on. Check that the front of the blade is aligned with the marked line and push the saw forward. The blade guard should swivel back as you push against the edge; if not, it can be tilted back slightly using the small knob at the back of the blade to start the swivel. Try to keep a two-hand hold on the saw — the handle at the back and the knob at the front.

5 Progress the cut, making sure it is aligned with the fence or clamped straight edge. Listen to the sound of the motor — if it starts to drop, reduce your feed speed.

6 At the end of the cut, lift the saw away, switch off and check that the blade guard has swung back to cover the blade.

RIPPING SOLID WOOD

Ripping is trickier than crosscutting — the cut is harder work for the saw, and there is more likelihood of the blade binding in the kerf. The cut is usually longer, perhaps the whole length of an 8 ft. (250 cm) board.

1 Check that the workpiece is supported and the blade is set up as described in Step 2 on the previous page.

2 Decide on the line of cut. You can follow the line freehand, but will probably have problems with the cut wandering from the line. It's safer and a better cut if you use some guidance, either the fence or a straight edge. The fence will only work for cuts up to about 8 in. (200 mm) from the edge; the edge also needs to be straight. It is best to use a straight edge, fitted as described on page 86, "Circular Saw Techniques."

3 Switch on and start the cut as before. Once the cut has lengthened (say 2 ft./ 600 mm), you could put a wedge in the kerf.

If you have an assistant, they can do it; otherwise, back off from the cut slightly and switch off.

4 Drive a wedge in so that it splays the kerf.

5 Check that the blade is free running by moving the saw backward and forward. It's not a good idea to switch on if the blade is nipped by the kerf or stuck in any way. Switch on and continue the cut.

6 At the end of cut, lift the saw away, switch off and check that the blade guard has swung back to cover the blade.

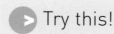

Try this!

Always fix the straight edge to the kept piece, not the offcut side. In this way, if you wander from the line, it will be in the waste section rather than in the piece you need.

CUTTING MAN-MADE BOARDS

Ripping and crosscutting do not apply to man-made boards, even though the surface layer may have a grain direction. The problem here can be that the top surface may be chipped out when cutting across the surface grain direction. This can be overcome by scoring the line of cut with a utility knife—this will sever the fibers and avoid chipping. Cut with the show side (the side that will be most on display) facing down. The main problem with man-made boards is their size. They usually come in 8 x 4 ft. (2440 x 1220 mm) sheets, and it's quite difficult cutting these with a power saw. If possible, get them cut by your supplier, even if it's just in half.

1 When cutting man-made boards into two large pieces, make sure both the kept piece and the offcut are supported. If you are cutting down the middle of the long dimension, for instance, lay the board on a couple of long support boards — say, 16 x 96 in. (400 x 2,400 mm) — on the floor, either side of the line of cut. The board is

⊳ Try this!

> If there's no access for clamps to secure the straight edge, stick it down with double-sided tape. Make sure that the surface is not dusty and press it down firmly.

USING A TRACK SAW

The track saw already incorporates the straight edge that we clamped on previously. The saw clips onto an aluminum extruded straight edge so that it runs true. The saw also plunges, so the blade is driven into the cut from above rather than a blade guard swinging away.

1 Set up the saw for the correct blade and depth of cut as before.

2 Lay the straight track precisely on the line of cut; nonslip strips on the bottom stop it from moving.

3 Drop the saw onto the track so that it locates and slides.

4 Bring the saw back to the start. Switch on, plunge the blade and push forward. Unplunge and switch off at the end of the cut.

lifted enough so that the saw is not cutting into the floor, both pieces are supported and the boards are stable enough for you to walk (or crawl) on.

2 Clamp a straight edge in the appropriate position and check it.

3 Set up the saw with a fine tooth or triple-chip blade and to the correct depth.

4 Start the cut in the usual way. If the blade starts to bind some way into the cut, drive a wedge into the kerf.

5 At the start of the cut, keep the front of the base against the straight edge; at the end, concentrate on the back and follow through right to the end of the cut.

6 At the end of cut 1, lift the saw away, switch off and check that the blade guard has swung back to cover the blade.

CHOP AND SLIDING COMPOUND MITER SAWS

If you are using power tools in your woodwork, it is important that all parts are accurately dimensioned at the start. When working in this way, parts must be uniform — catering for the nonstandard wastes time and almost defeats the object of using machines. You can do this dimensioning using a handsaw and perhaps fine adjusting with a shooting board, or you could use a chop or compound miter saw. Using a good saw of this type to cut parts cleanly to length at the start of the job can save time later on. As the name implies, these saws are also useful for mitering, and they can also be used for cutting simple dadoes and tenons.

Chop saws have a single action, where the blade tilts down to cut the workpiece. Sliding compound miter saws have an additional sliding action, so they can be pushed through the workpiece. The sliding facility means that wider boards can be cut.

The table and fences on these saws are usually quite short; extensions can be bought, but they are usually fairly light weight for site work. It's worth making some that suit your workshop situation, similar to those shown below.

CONTINUED ▶

Simply made fence and support tables aid stability when cutting long boards.

Safety

The ability for the blade on these saws to plunge or slide means that you need to be particularly careful about safety. The manual will provide safety instructions, but here are some important ones.

- Make sure that the saw base is firmly secured to the bench or work surface, so that it cannot tip or shift while in use.
- Check that the safety features, such as the moving blade guard, are functioning correctly before use.
- When cutting a long piece, there is a danger of tipping as the piece is cut through. Make sure that the workpiece is supported along its length; an extension of some sort is useful for this.
- With mitered cuts, it can be difficult to predict the path of the saw, so if possible, rehearse the cut with the blade stationary before actually cutting.
- Where possible, clamp the workpiece rather than holding it manually, especially with longer pieces.
- Never use a cross-handed hold (e.g., holding the right side of the workpiece with your left hand).
- When holding a piece for cutting, try to hold both the piece and the fence. This means there is less danger of your hand being pulled toward the blade.
- When using a sliding saw to cut wide boards, bring the saw toward you beyond the workpiece, switch on and plunge down, then push the saw away

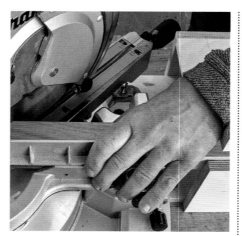

Hold the workpiece by gripping both piece and fence together.

from you. Avoid cutting on the pull stroke, because it is unstable.
- When using a sliding saw for just short plunging cuts, lock it in the back position so that it cannot unexpectedly jump forward.
- After the cut, allow the blade to come to a stop in the workpiece before lifting it, and wait for it to stop before removing any small offcut pieces.
- You may want to use stops for cutting pieces to length. Don't use the stop on the offcut side of the saw, as the offcut could wedge against the stop and be ejected.

STRAIGHT CUTTING OR CHOPPING

1 If squareness is important, check the cut on a piece of scrap wood first and adjust if necessary.

2 Mark the line of cut and offer the piece up to the fence.

3 If your saw has a laser guide, align the guide with the cut mark. Usually, the cut is to the right side of the laser line. If you do not have a laser, press the safety release and drop the stationary saw down to position the workpiece under the blade.

4 When the position is good, clamp the piece to the table. With the saw elevated, switch on, engage the safety release and bring the saw down on the front edge of the piece, making sure that your hand is well away from the blade.

5 Longer offcuts may be unstable, in which case they should be clamped down or supported remotely.

Stop clamped to fence

Cutting multiple parts to length

1 For repeat cuts, some form of fence extension is useful for clamping stops to.

2 Trim one end on each piece.

3 Clamp the stop to the fence.

4 Trim the other end, with the piece butted up to the stop.

When cutting wide boards, plunge down at the front first, and then push the saw forward.

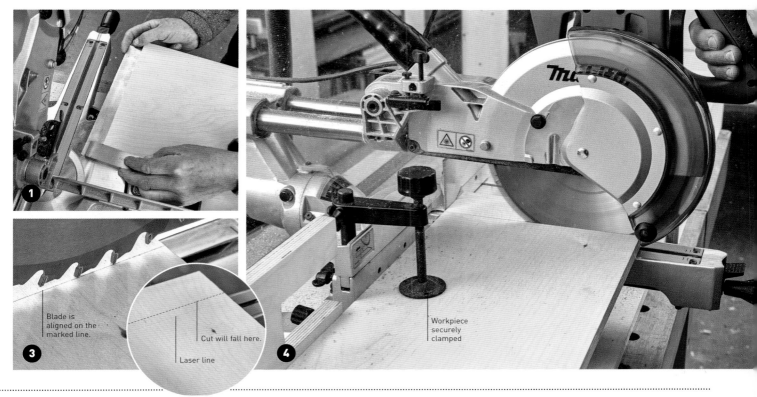

1

3 Blade is aligned on the marked line.

Cut will fall here.

Laser line

4 Workpiece securely clamped

Mitering

Most saws allow the saw to be turned on the table to make frame miter cuts, and also for the blade to be tilted over to make longer box-miter-like cuts. Both functions can be engaged at the same time to obtain a compound miter. When cutting with a tilted blade, adjust the fence to prevent the saw from cutting into it.

The cut is the same as for a square end, although more care should be taken over safety, because the angled cut can make the path of the blade confusing.

MITER

BOX MITER

COMPOUND MITER

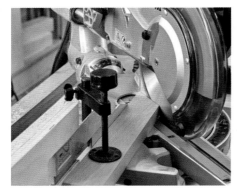

Miter

Box miter

Compound miter

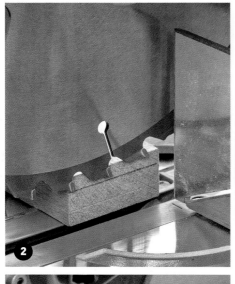

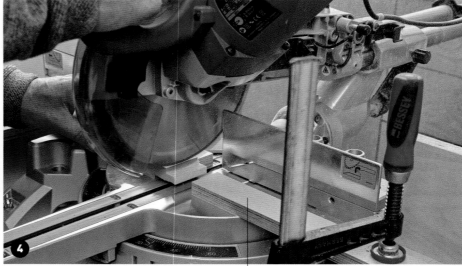

Packing piece ensures cut to back of workpiece.

Stop clamped in position to determine length of tenon.

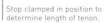

Dadoes and tenons

Sliding compound miter saws should have a facility to limit the height of cut, so that it doesn't cut right though the workpiece. This can be used to make repeated cuts to remove waste to depth for forming dadoes and tenons. This is useful when cutting a batch of joints. Now let's look at using this for tenons.

1 Mark the tenon thickness with a mortise gauge on an offcut of the same thickness as the workpiece.

2 Set the height stop so that the blade is level with the top gauge line.

3 Make repeated cuts in the test piece, moving it forward after each cut until you have removed about ¾ in. (20 mm) of waste. Flip the piece over and repeat on the other side, then check the fit in your mortise. Adjust the stop until you have a snug fit.

4 If the cut does not extend to the back of the workpiece, place a packing piece between fence and workpiece.

5 Clamp a stop to the fence so that the blade is aligned with the marked tenon shoulder.

6 Now cut the tenon, using repeated cuts up to the stop — first on one face, then flip over to the other face.

7 You should now have an accurate tenon, central in the workpiece.

Using a jigsaw

The jigsaw is of limited use in furniture making, because the cut is rough and erratic. However, it does have uses for roughing out, especially if you don't have a circular saw or band saw. It is useful for cutting out a section in the center of a panel, although this could be done more neatly, if a little more dustily, by a router. It can also be used to rough cut curves.

1

2

BLADE SELECTION

Most manufacturers have a coding system with related icons to aid with blade selection. Look for a blade that is classed for fine cutting in wood — this is likely to be a bimetal (BIM) taper ground blade with a high TPI (teeth per inch). For cutting curves, a narrow blade will allow for a tighter curve.

CUTTING ACTION

Standard blades cut on the upstroke (there are down-cutting blades, mainly used for cutting worktop material without chipping the surface laminate). The action of the blade should be to pull the saw down onto the surface.

Straight lines can be cut freehand, or a straight edge can be clamped to the surface for the edge of the saw base to run against, but this depends on the saw running true with the base.

Measure the distance from the blade to the edge of the plate.

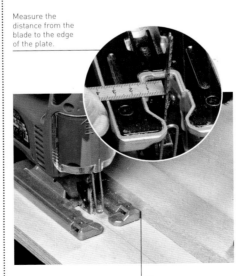

Plate runs against the clamped guide.

1 For cutting a section out of the center of a panel, drill holes wide enough to insert the blade at each corner.

2 The cut can be started with the blade in one of the holes and then rotated in the hole at each corner. Any cut with the jigsaw is likely to need cleaning up later using a router or hand tools.

Refer to your saw instructions for guidance on how to change the blade.

Try this!

> When using an extractor with the sander, the extractor hose often rubs up and down the edge of the workpiece, possibly damaging it. You can avoid this by suspending the hose above the work, perhaps attached by a wire to the ceiling.

Using sanders

There are two types of sanders that you will find useful for most work — a belt sander for rough surface preparation on large surfaces, and a random orbital sander (ROS) for the finer finishing.

Tracking control knob

The belt sander is not a finish sander. For furniture work, a good sanding regime would be to belt sand with 120 grit (80/100 on very uneven surfaces), then progress to 150 and 180 grit on the ROS. The ROS is distinct from an orbital sander. The orbital sander has a single orbiting motion of less than ¼ in. (5 mm) diameter. This tends to leave small circular scratches in the surface. On the ROS, the orbit is complemented by the disk also rotating. This tends to prevent the circular scratches.

The dust bags that come with sanders are usually inadequate, so if possible, plug in a vacuum extractor. Otherwise, wear a dust mask.

THE BELT SANDER

The belt sander is a useful tool for sanding large surfaces, such as panels and tabletops, and can almost replace hand planing for leveling these surfaces. On small or narrow surfaces, the belt sander should be used with some care, because it is capable of removing a lot of wood in a short time — especially off a corner, if you drop off the edge. However, if you follow these belt sanding rules, it can save a lot of hand-sanding time and elbow grease.

To change a belt, most sanders have a lever on the side for moving the forward roller so that the belt is loosened, and

the new belt can then be slid into place. When fitting a new belt to the sander, check that the arrows on the inside of the belt are pointing in the direction of rotation. After fitting, run the sander and check the tracking of the belt to make sure it is running fully on the wheels. If the belt runs off the machine side of the wheel, it can get shredded. Most sanders have a turn knob at the front that controls tracking.

Tip: If you haven't used a belt sander before, set the speed to slow for your first outing as its get up and go on full speed can be a surprise.

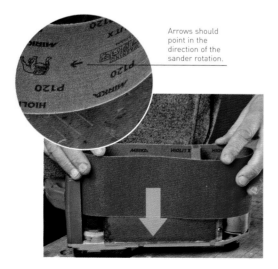

Arrows should point in the direction of the sander rotation.

Clinic

Narrow blemishes about 3–4 in. (75–100 mm) long show up when a finish is applied These are scratch marks left by "nose diving" the sander onto the surface after switching on. Often, they are not evident until the finish is applied. Make sure you have the sander on the surface before you switch on (see Step 2, right).

Marks left by sander nose diving.

Keep the sander parallel with the grain of the wood and moving around all the time.

Aligning holes in Velcro-backed sanding disk

Abrasive mesh disk

Clinic

Small whorls in the surface are caused by the oscillating action of the sander
This is usually a problem on cheaper sanders or when the disk has become clogged. They are often difficult to spot, not showing until you put the first coat of finish on. Change clogged disks.

USING A BELT SANDER

The sander is a little like a miniature tank, and it's your job to stop it from charging off! If you hold it back, it will want to throw the surface it is sitting on backward.

1 Make sure the workpiece is secured to the bench in a vise, between bench dogs or with clamps.

2 Always have the sander on the surface before switching on. If you switch on and then place it on the surface, there is a risk of nose diving — the front of the sander pad hits the surface first and leaves a slight depression.

3 Work with the front-to-back axis of the sander aligned with the grain. The action of the sander leaves slight scratches in the surface, but they are not so evident if they run with the grain. You can move it around in any direction as long as you keep the alignment correct. Don't press down on the machine. Belt sanders are quite heavy, so let the weight do the work.

4 Keep the machine moving. As mentioned before, the sander can remove a lot of wood quickly; if you work it in one spot, a depression will be formed. If you want to sand away a blemish, you should work around the area in circular motions as well as concentrating on the one place. In this way, the depth of cut is distributed over a larger area.

1

THE RANDOM ORBITAL SANDER (ROS)

While the belt sander can do the rough work of surface preparation, the ROS does the final sanding before finish application and also the light sanding between coats. It's a less aggressive tool than the belt sander, so it cannot remove deep blemishes so quickly, but it is also less likely to damage the surface.

To set up the sander for use, locate the sanding disk so that the holes in the disk align with those in the base. These holes will vary from sander to sander, so make sure you get the correct pattern when ordering disks. Most sanders use Velcro-backed disks. Abrasive mesh disks (Abranet) are very good, having very good dust-extraction properties.

USING A ROS

The surface should be fairly smooth at this point, having already been planed, scraped or beltsanded. For final surface preparation, you could use aluminum oxide 180-grit disks — perhaps 150, then 180 for surfaces with slight blemishes remaining.

1 In use, the weight of your hand and the sander should be sufficient for you not to need to press down hard. Keep the sander moving over the whole surface in a random motion.

2 Avoid tilting the base to try to work with the edge on a difficult spot, because this can lead to an uneven surface.

3 For light sanding between coats of finish (de-nibbing), use 400- or 500-grit aluminum oxide. Be careful at corners, where it is easy to sand through the finish.

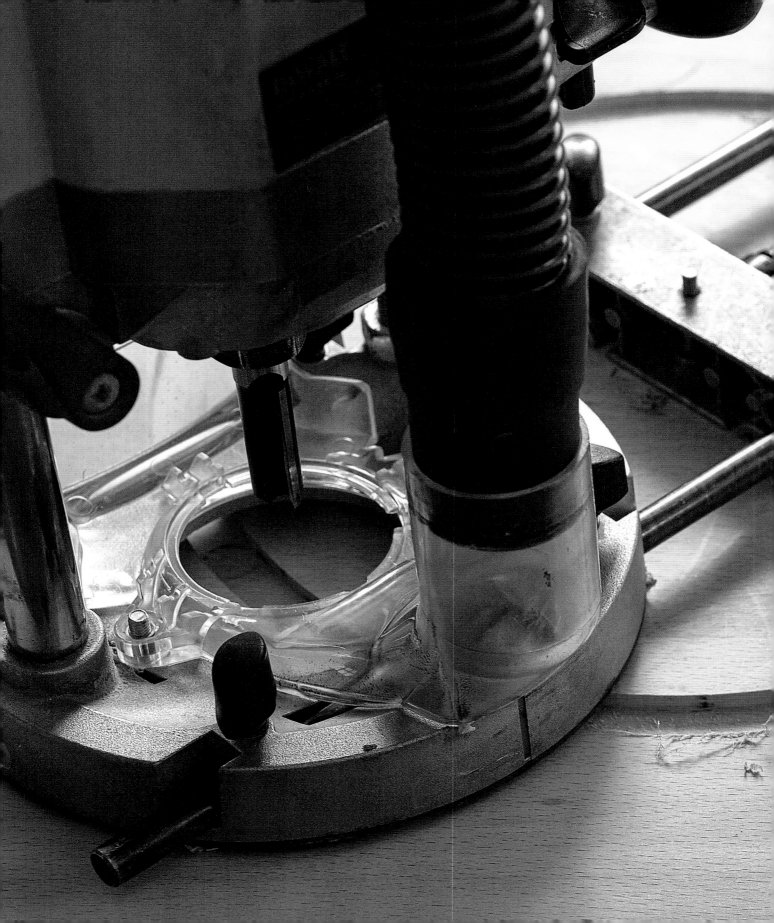

Routing

4

The router is an extremely versatile tool that can allow you to work effectively and accurately. However, many people find it intimidating — it's noisy, with a fast-rotating cutter that can cause damage to you or the workpiece. There are five essentials that can help you make friends with your router, so that it becomes a valuable tool in your workshop. These are: common sense; an understanding and respect for health and safety considerations; understanding feed direction; looking for and anticipating issues that may affect the quality of cut; and using jigs and fixtures to aid safety and accuracy.

This chapter will introduce some of the many functions that make the router so versatile, and address these five essentials along the way.

Getting started with the router

The router can be a real workhorse in the workshop. Here, I introduce some basic tasks it can perform. As you become familiar with it, I am sure you will discover others.

SAFETY WITH HANDHELD ROUTING

With handheld routing, both hands should be holding the router handles so that they do not come into contact with the cutter. The important safety considerations for handheld routing are:

- Disconnect the power before changing the cutter or otherwise handling the "business end" of the router. This avoids mishaps should the machine be switched on accidentally.
- Be aware that the cutter can continue turning for a time after switching off, so don't allow your fingers near it until it has finished turning. When finishing a cut, return the router to the unplunged position so that the cutter is shielded by the base.
- Wear ear defenders and eye protection.

- Connect the router to a vacuum extractor, because it can produce a lot of dust. In some situations, it can be dusty even with extraction — when edge molding, for instance — and so you'll need to wear a dust mask. Wear a mask at all times when routing MDF.
- If you have long hair, make sure it is securely tied back.
- Secure the workpiece firmly, either in the vise or clamped in some way. Never hold the workpiece in one hand and rout with the router in the other.

Dust extractor

Use good dust extraction when routing.

Make sure the workpiece is held securely, and hold the router with both hands.

Always return the cutter to the up position before switching off.

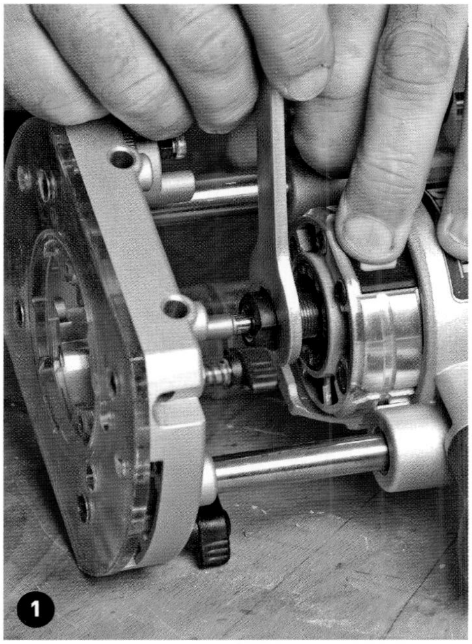

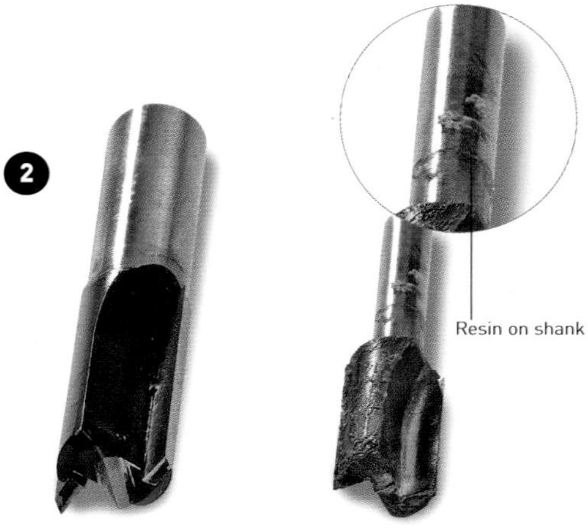

①

②

Resin on shank

CLEAN CUTTER　　　DIRTY CUTTER

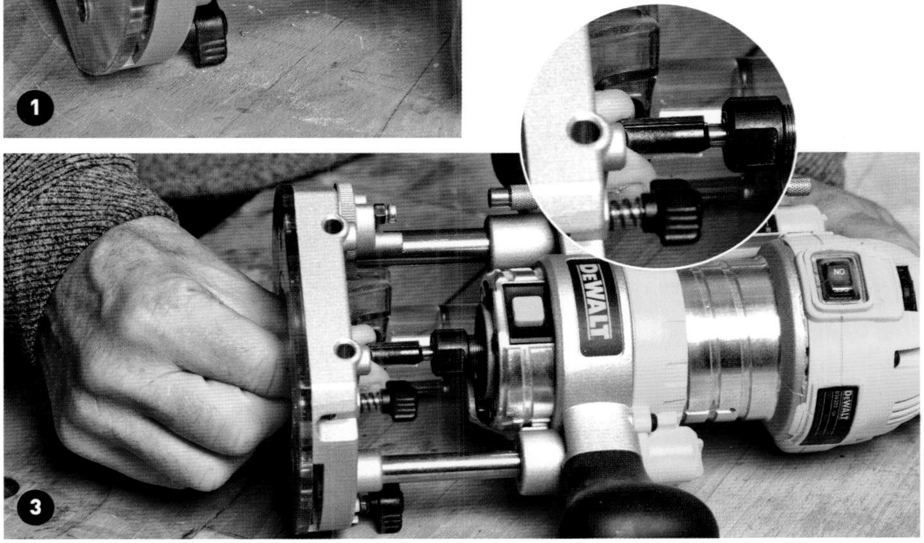

③

SETTING UP THE ROUTER

There are a number of steps that you need to go through to set up the router prior to switching it on.

CHANGING CUTTERS

1 Remove the previous cutter by slackening off the nut. The shaft will have some form of locking device to aid this — either a locking nut and additional spanner, or a press lock above the collet. Most routers have a safety measure in which the nut slackens off, but the collet will not release the cutter. The nut requires further turns to actually release the cutter.

2 Check the new cutter — is it sharp; is the shank clean and undamaged; are there resin deposits on the cutters? Damage or residues can cause imbalance leading to vibration, which affects the finish quality.

3 If it is blunt, you can sharpen the cutter with a small sharpening stone (see "Maintaining Cutters" on the next page). If all is well, insert the cutter shank at least three-quarters of the way into the collet (some cutters have a depth indicator on the shank) and tighten up the nut. It should be tight but not over-tight.

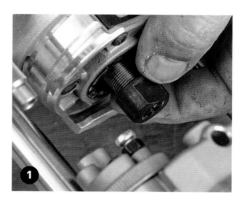

MAINTAINING CUTTERS

Blunt or damaged router cutters will affect the quality of your work. Blunt cutters will slow down the cutter speed, leading to burn marks and a ragged cut. Dull cutters can be re-sharpened, but damaged ones with chipped edges are best replaced.

Chipped edge

Burn marks

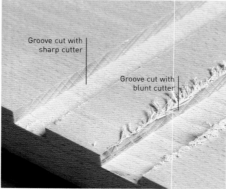

Groove cut with sharp cutter

Groove cut with blunt cutter

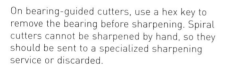

On bearing-guided cutters, use a hex key to remove the bearing before sharpening. Spiral cutters cannot be sharpened by hand, so they should be sent to a specialized sharpening service or discarded.

High-speed steel cutters can be sharpened on an oil or water stone. Tungsten carbide will require a small diamond stone; some are known as credit-card stones. The sharpening should only be done on the flat faces of the cutters — working on the outside face will change the dimension and profile. Try to sharpen the cutters evenly, because the slightest imbalance between the two will lead to vibration and a low-quality cut. Cutters can only be sharpened in this way a few times. Eventually, the cut quality deteriorates and they should be discarded or sent away for sharpening.

CHANGING COLLETS

If you have a half-inch router, you will have occasion to change the collet — down to ¼ in. or 8 mm, perhaps.

1 Remove the collet nut from the shaft — the collet should come away with the nut.

2 Pull the collet away from the nut and spring in the replacement.

> ## ⊳ Try this!

> It can be difficult to remove the collet from the nut when you want to change size. Try drilling a hole slightly narrower than the collet in a piece of wood that is a little thicker than the length of the collet. By pressing the collet into the hole, it should be reduced enough for you to be able to pull the nut off. You can store the collet in this hole. Pressing the other collet into the hole from the other side pops out the stored collet and also releases the other from the nut.

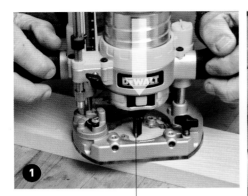

Cutter on
wood surface

Depth stop

Bottomed out

Bring the stop down
and lock it.

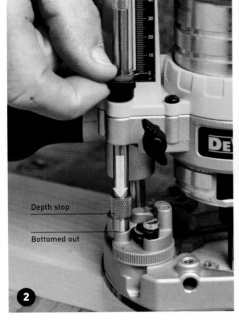

Molding cutter
set as required.

Some routers have a micro-adjuster on
the depth stop — this is useful for making
fine adjustments after a test cut.

SETTING THE DEPTH STOP

On your router there will be some form of adjustable depth stop.

1 To set the depth for grooving or rabbeting, bring the cutter down to the wood surface and lock it.

2 Bring the depth stop right down until it is bottomed out. On some routers, you will have a movable cursor. Bring this to zero, or a convenient number if zero is not available.

3 Raise the depth stop the required depth, reading the dimension from the cursor, and lock the stop. If you don't have a cursor, you will need to raise the stop relative to the bottomed-out position.

4 If you are using a molding cutter, the depth setting will depend on the profile required. The curve of the cutter may be set to blend with the top surface, or set below the surface to give a step to the molding. Test the cut on scrap wood to get the correct position. Then, with the cutter at the depth required, bring the stop down and lock it.

5 The depth stop usually drops onto a stepped capstan. This can be turned so that you can plunge down to the final depth in stages.

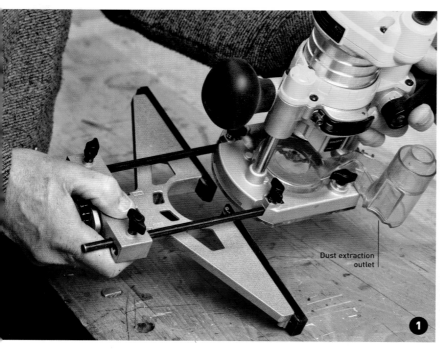

Dust extraction outlet

Cutter tips at 90° to fence.

SETTING THE FENCE

If the cutter is not bearing guided (see page 109), you are likely to need the fence.

1 Insert the fence rods into the base and thread the fence onto the rods. This is usually done so that the dust extraction is to the front, with the fence rods sticking out to the right.

2 Use a piece of scrap wood to aid setting the fence position — mark the position of the cut on the scrap, using a marking gauge perhaps. Then, bring the stationary cutter down to the surface, with the cutter tips at 90° to the fence.

3 Adjust the fence until the cutter tips are aligned with the marked line. Some routers have a fence micro-adjustment feature, which makes fine adjustment easier.

4 When cutting a rabbet, the cutter will be set in the line of the fence. Some routers have a permanent gap in the fence to allow for this, while others have movable faces on the fence that can be positioned on either side of the cutter.

5 When you think that the fence is set correctly, check that all the various retaining turn screws are well tightened.

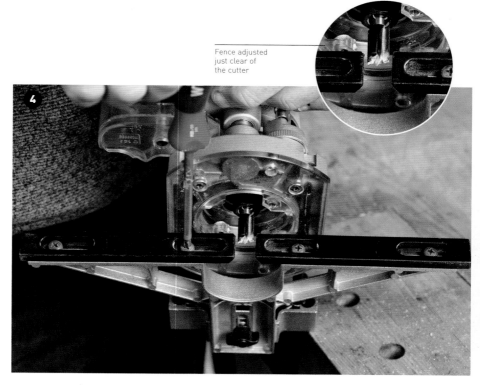

Fence adjusted just clear of the cutter

▶ Try this

> If your router does not have movable faces on the fence, there is a danger of the fence tilting as the edge of the workpiece moves into the gap in the fence. To avoid this, stick on your own temporary facing, approximately ¼ in. (6 mm) thick and ¾ in. (20 mm) wide, so that support is provided right up to the cutter. Double-sided tape is good for attaching temporary facings.

If necessary, cut a recess in the temporary facing for the cutter position.

DEPTH OF CUT, CUTTER DIAMETER, FEED SPEED AND RPM

The cutting efficiency of the router depends on balancing the width of the cutter, the depth of cut, the speed setting and the feed speed. There is an optimum speed for any cutter; if the speed drops below this, the quality of cut will be impaired.

Most routers now have a speed control that changes the RPM of the motor (see chart, right). The chart shows the recommended maximum speed for a given cutter diameter. However, cutter speed is mostly a matter of trial and error, with many cutters working better below maximum speed; this is particularly true of longer cutters, where vibration may be greater. You will need to develop a sensitivity to the way the cutter sounds and is performing and set the speed accordingly.

Having set the RPM, the efficiency of cut is dependent on the router maintaining the set speed. If the cut is too deep or fed too fast, the motor will slow down, leading to a ragged cut. Maintaining the motor speed is a trade-off between the size of cut and feed speed. It could be suggested that you should never take a cut deeper than the half width of the cutter. However, rather than following rules, it is better to listen to the sound of the motor as you're working. If the sound drops, the motor is slowing down, so you need to reduce either the feed speed or the depth of cut. Reducing feed speed can lead to burning of the wood as friction heat builds up, so reducing depth of cut may be the best option.

Cutter diameter	Speed
Less than 1 in. (24 mm)	24,000 RPM
1–1⁹/₁₆ in. (25–40 mm)	18,000 RPM
1⁹/₁₆– 2⁹/₁₆ in. (41–65 mm)	15,000 RPM
More than 2⁹/₁₆ in. (65 mm)	10,000 RPM

Tip: In all machine woodworking, always listen to the sound of the motor and cutter. If it doesn't "sound right," there is usually a problem that needs addressing, either with the machine or the operator.

Making the cut

Having done the setup, you can now go ahead with the cut. The first element to consider is the feed direction, which is critical to the quality of the cut.

Depending on feed direction, the rotation of the cutter pulls the router either into or away from the work. When using the router hand held, the cutters have a clockwise rotation. Feeding the router with the workpiece on the left of the direction of travel pulls the router against the wood, making for a clean, controlled cut. Feeding the other way around (with the workpiece on the right) means that the action of the cutter will force it away from the work, giving an uneven cut and less control. This may be the most important lesson to learn in routing! Now, let's look at the various cuts that can be taken.

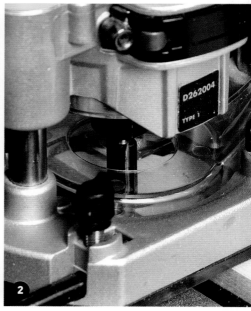

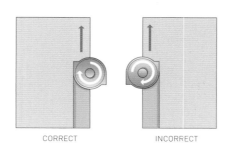

Incorrect feed direction
The uneven cuts shown here are because of incorrect feed direction.

CORRECT   INCORRECT

GROOVING AND RABBETING

When grooving or rabbeting, make sure that the cutter is never reversed or switched off in the cut — both these actions can spoil the quality of the cut.

MAKING A CUT

Using the following steps is good practice when working with the router:

1 Place the router on the work, with the fence on the right, and switch on.

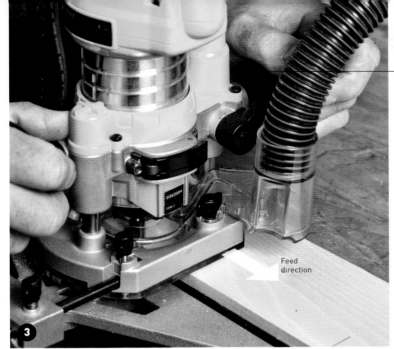

Locking lever

Feed direction

 Try this!

> For stopped rabbets, grooves or moldings, stops clamped to the workpiece can help to make sure that you start and stop in the correct position. Place the router at the start position, mark its back edge and clamp a stop there. Then move the router to the stop position, mark the front edge and clamp another stop there. This helps to prevent burning, because you don't need to slow down to check whether you are nearing the stop position. It also helps with accuracy at the start of the cut.

Marking the stop position

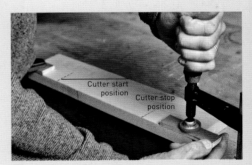

Cutter start position
Cutter stop position

Clamping the stop position

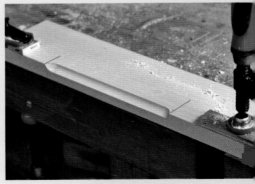

The finished cut

2 Position the cutter over your start position and plunge down to the optimum cutting depth (see page 103).

3 Use the locking lever to fix the depth of cut. Push the router forward to make the cut, listening to the motor speed. Try to avoid pausing, especially at the start and end of the cut, because this will lead to burn marks.

4 Stop at the required position, unlock the plunge and let the cutter withdraw from the work.

5 If you need to make another cut, return to the start and repeat. If not, switch off the router and wait for the cutter to stop.

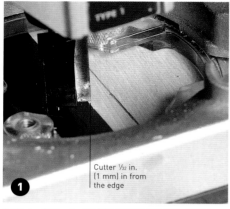

Cutter 1/32 in. (1 mm) in from the edge

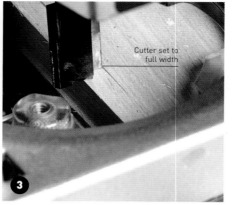

Cutter set to full width

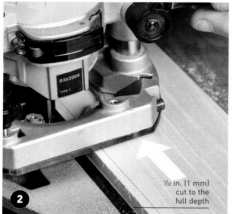

1/32 in. (1 mm) cut to the full depth

Note clean edge of rabbet.

Initial cut on a piece of scrap wood

GETTING A CLEAN EDGE AT THE BOTTOM OF A RABBET

When rabbeting, the cut can be rough, with splintering or breakout where the bottom of the rabbet meets the side face. This occurs because the bottom of the cutter does not cut as efficiently as the side. This can be overcome by back feeding — the only time that the feed direction will be the same as the cutter force.

Prevent this kind of splintering by back feeding.

1 To back feed, set the fence so that the width of cut is 1/32 in. (1 mm) or less and set for a full-depth cut.

2 Feed the router in reverse to a normal cut. This will give a shallow, clean-bottomed cut at the edge.

3 The router can then be reset for a full-width cut.

4 Continue to use in the normal way. Note that back feeding only works if a very narrow cut is made, because the forces involved are much reduced.

Tip: For rabbets, it is better to use a large bit, cutting the rabbet with just the outer part of the bit. Using a bit just a little bigger than the rabbet can lead to splintering and an uneven cut.

WORKING A WIDER GROOVE

On occasions, you will need a groove that is wider than the available cutter, such as when fitting a panel in a groove. In this case, you will need to take a cut, then move the fence for subsequent cuts. It's best to test these cuts on a piece of scrap wood until the width is correct.

1 Set the fence so that the first cut is to the fence side of the final groove. Make a long test cut in the scrap wood. When the position is correct, groove the workpiece (see pages 104–105).

2 To reset the fence for the full width, offer the panel piece up to the test groove and mark the width. Or you may be grooving between gauge lines. Adjust the fence until the cutter is on the marked width and take

Routing circles and arcs

To cut circles and arcs with a router, you will need a trammel. There are many applications for this — for instance, forming the circumference of a round table, cutting for curved inlay or creating templates that can be used with a bearing-guided cutter.

A trammel is simply a device for retaining the router at a central point around which the cutter can be rotated. Special trammel bars can be purchased, but a trammel can easily be rigged up using MDF or Plexiglas.

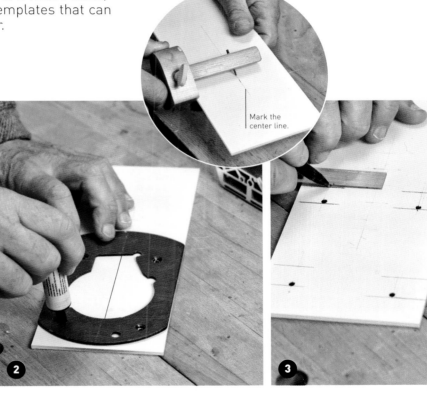

Mark the center line.

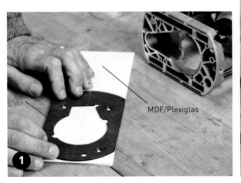

MDF/Plexiglas

①

②

③

....

MARKING A TRAMMEL TO ROUT SMALL CIRCLES

For very small radii, the center point may be under the router base. In this case, you could drill a hole in the base for a center pin, but that's a bit cavalier! Instead, you can make up an adjustable false base.

1 Using ¼ in. (6 mm) MDF or Plexiglas, cut out a rectangular false base that is slightly longer than the router base.

2 Most routers have a removable plastic or Bakelite base. Remove this and use it as a template to mark out the position of at least two of the retaining screws and the cutter center.

3 Mark center lines for the retaining screws and also for the plate center — this will be drilled for the pivot pin.

CONTINUED ▶

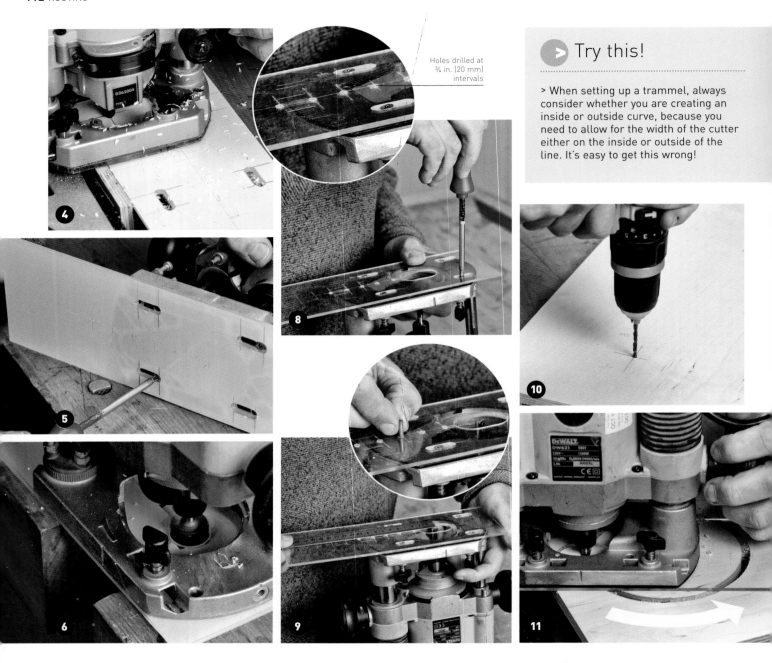

Holes drilled at ¾ in. (20 mm) intervals

4 Use the router to create countersunk slots for the retaining screws.

5 Attach the trammel to the router base, leaving the screws loose so that the base slides freely.

6 Fit a large cutter of approximately ¾ in. (20 mm) diameter in the router. Working over a suitable gap, plunge the cutter and slide the trammel so that a slot is created.

7 Remove the trammel and drill for the center pin adjacent to the cutter slot, at approximately ¾ in. (20 mm) intervals. If you are using Plexiglas, you could remove the protective plastic now.

8 Fit the trammel to the router base and adjust the position until the desired radius is found, the pin locating in a hole in the drilled piece.

9 Fit the center pin, protruding by about ¼ in. (6 mm).

10 Drill a hole in the workpiece to take the trammel pin.

11 The feed direction when using the trammel should be counterclockwise, and the cut may have to be done in a number of passes.

12 If you want the outside of the hole to be clean, it can be useful to leave a couple of small "tags" when doing the final pass — this stops the centerpiece from moving and

Leave a small part of the wood attached.

12

MDF square stuck on with double-sided tape

14

13

Apply packing when using a raised trammel center.

15

> Try this!

> For larger radii, a longer false base can be made. You may want arcs up to or greater than 78 in. (2 m). In this situation, the false base could become a long strip of MDF. There would be no need to slot screw holes in the base—make adjustments simply by re-drilling the pin hole.

possibly damaging the outer edge when it is cut through.

13 The thin tags can be cut by hand and cleaned up with a chisel.

14 If the center pin hole will spoil the finished piece, drill into a piece of plywood or MDF instead and position the plywood/ MDF square with double-sided tape.

15 You may need to apply the same thickness of packing under the router base to level it out.

Tip: Make sure that the work is raised off the bench before making the cut. Otherwise, you may find some attractive curved grooves in your bench top!

Work aids for routing

Using various workshop-made jigs and accessories can make the router capable of very fine, accurate work. The number of jigs is only limited by your imagination, because these are often made as required for a specific job. Here, I describe two useful accessories for cutting square to an edge.

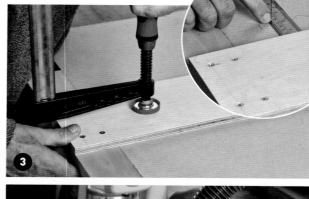

Positioning the straight edge

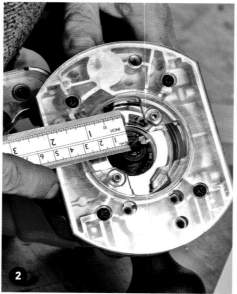

MAKING AND USING A SQUARE GUIDE

1 The square consists of a piece of plywood about 8 in. (200 mm) wide and a suitable length for the cuts that you will be taking. Glue and screw a piece of hardwood, approximately 12 x ¾ x ¾ in. (300 x 20 x 20 mm) to the end, making sure that it is absolutely square to the long edges.

2 Measure the distance between the edge of the router base and the cutter.

3 Position and clamp a straight edge at that distance from the edge of the required groove (inset). Make sure you are working on the correct side of the line.

4 Make the cut with the edge of the base against the straight edge. The feed should be with the straight edge on the left of the forward direction. The cut may be done in a number of passes.

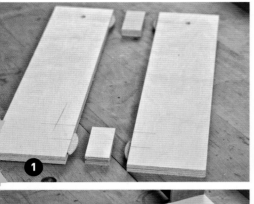

USING A GUIDE BUSH

A guide bush is a collar fitted around the cutter under the router base. The bush is used to guide the cutter against a template or jig. This is useful when you want precision or repeatability when routing grooves and recesses. As an example, we will make a jig to rout a groove 1 in. (25 mm) wide and $11^{13}/_{16}$ in. (300 mm) long, using a bush with a $^7/_8$ in. (22 mm) diameter and a $^5/_8$ in. (15 mm) cutter. Jigs like this can be used in many situations, especially when accuracy is needed. It's often worth spending time making a jig rather than trying to achieve precision by eye.

Establish the width of the template space required so that a 1 in. (25 mm) wide groove is formed. (See calculation, far right.)

1 Cut two pieces of $^5/_8$ in. (15 mm) plywood or MDF, approximately 18 x 4 in. (450 x 100 mm), for the sides of the jig. Cut two pieces precisely $1^1/_4$ x $2^3/_4$ in. (32 x 70 mm) as spacers to form the groove. Reinforce the joints with biscuits (see pages 180–84).

2 Glue the jig together, positioning the spacers so that the groove formed is $12^1/_4$ x $1^1/_4$ in. (307 x 32 mm).

3 If the groove was to be at 90° to an edge, a crosspiece could be fitted as before.

4 Test the template on a piece of scrap wood before using it on the real thing.

5 To use the jig, clamp it in position and locate the router in position, with the collar in the jig groove. Make the cut by feeding up the left side, then down the right, in as many passes as required.

Calculation

Width of template groove =
Width of final groove – width of cutter + width of guide bush.

Width of template groove =
$1 - ^5/_8 + ^7/_8 = 1^1/_4$ in. (25 – 15 + 22 = 32 mm)

A similar calculation can be done for the length of the groove:

Length of template groove =
$12 - ^5/_8 + ^7/_8 = 12^1/_4$ in. (300 – 15 + 22 = 307 mm)

When fitting the bush, make sure that it is concentric to the cutter. Many routers have devices to help achieve this.

Clinic

Cut is uneven when using the simple guide
Check that you are feeding in the correct direction.

Groove too big when using guide bush jig
Some adjustment can be made by sticking masking tape to the inside of the jig or sticking insulating tape to the bush.

The router table

You will get a lot more out of your router if you have the option of putting it in a router table. The router table allows you to make cuts that would otherwise be very unstable with the handheld option.

A router table is simply a table with a hole in the center. The router is attached underneath, so that the cutter can protrude through the hole. The workpiece is usually fed against an adjustable fence. This fence is in two parts — the infeed fence on the right, and the outfeed on the left — that can be slid apart so that the cutter can be positioned in the line of the fence. The larger ½ in. (12 mm) collet machines are better suited to tables than smaller ones. Some routers have a very useful facility to adjust cutter depth though the base — this allows easier adjustment from above when fitted to a table.

Some router tables are rather flimsy. When purchasing, look for those with robust fences and fittings and check that the table surface is flat and strong. Alternatively, you can make a table using a piece of kitchen worktop and a purchased insert plate. You will also need to make an adjustable fence and other accessories.

ROUTER TABLE SAFETY

With the handheld router, your hands are holding the handles, which ensures that they are away from the cutter, but on the table your fingers can easily come into contact with the cutter, so awareness of health and safety is key.

Feed direction

In this situation, feed direction is a health and safety issue; using machines with rotating cutters is all about balancing forces. The rotating cutters are imparting a force in one direction, so you need to make sure that, in feeding the work onto the cutters, you are pushing in the opposite direction. If you and the machine are both trying to force the work in the same direction, it may be pulled out of your hands and thrown across the workshop. Or worse still, if you don't have adequate guarding, your fingers may be pulled onto the cutters. Note that in many of the illustrations the guard may have been removed for clarity.

In a router table, the cutters will be rotating counterclockwise. Therefore, if you feed with the fence on the left of the direction of travel, the force imparted by the cutters will be in the same direction as you are pushing. This means that the forces will not be balanced and the workpiece will be grabbed by the cutters. If you feed with the fence on your right, the cutter force and the feed force will be balanced.

Safety devices

Many safety devices for the router table can be made in the workshop.

Balancing forces

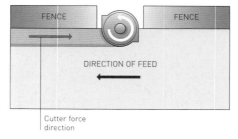

CORRECT: BALANCED FORCES IN THE OPPOSITE DIRECTION

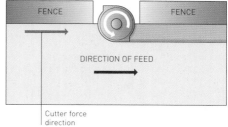

INCORRECT: UNBALANCED FORCES IN THE SAME DIRECTION

Guards

Guards are usually fitted to the fence. If you have made your own table, you will need to make a guard. Always guard the cutter in some way. This could be with a Plexiglas shield or feather boards.

Feather boards

Feather boards are used to apply even pressure as the work is fed over the cutter; they also prevent the work from being thrown back by the cutters. Most commercial router tables will be supplied with plastic feather boards that attach to the table or fence. You can also purchase them separately or make your own in the workshop.

Dust extraction

There are two points for dust extraction on the router table — either through the fence when rabbeting or molding, or through the cutter hole when the cut is remote from the fence opening.

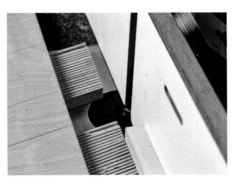

Dust extraction through the fence

Dust extraction through the cutter hole

Push board

A push board is approximately ¼ in. (6 mm) thick, with a notch cut out at the front and a handle attached on top. It's useful for pushing narrow pieces when a guard or feather board restricts access.

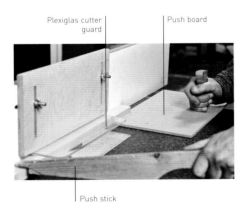

Plexiglas cutter guard

Push board

Push stick

Push sticks

Have an armory of push sticks and other aids for feeding the work over the cutters and under the guards or feather boards. The basic push stick is simply a wooden stick with a bird's mouth cut at the end.

Workshop-made router table and fence. The table hinges up to aid cutter changing. A car jack is used for cutter height adjustment.

Sprung work hold-downs for securing work in progress

BASIC CUTS ON THE ROUTER TABLE

The majority of work on the router table involves grooving, rabbeting or molding with the feed against the fence. The set-up for grooving and rabbeting is similar, a rabbet simply being a groove at the side of the piece!

A digital depth gauge is a useful device for setting up the table for a rabbet or groove — it gives precise measurements of cut depth or distance from the fence.

Cut depth measurement

Distance from fence measurement

An alternative is to mark the cut position on the workpiece and offer it up to set the cutter against the mark. When setting fence position, make sure that the cutter is rotated to maximum width of cut, i.e., cutters at 90° to the fence.

Cut depth setting

Cut distance from fence

The considerations mentioned in the section on feed speed and RPM (see page 103) need to be kept in mind. Often the cut will have to be taken in a number of passes, and you will need to be sensitive to the sound of the router when feeding — either slow the feed rate or reduce the depth or width of cut if the machine is struggling.

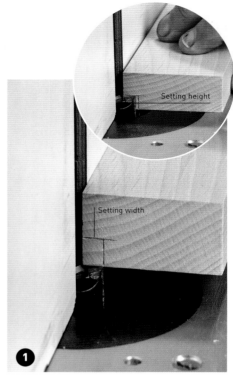

Setting height

Setting width

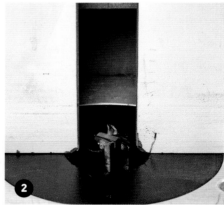

RABBETING

1 Set up the depth and fence position for the first cut using either a depth gauge or a marked piece. For small rabbets, this may be the only cut. For multiple-cut rabbets, set the cutter to full depth, increasing the width on further cuts by adjusting the fence. When rabbeting, the cutter will usually sit in the line of the fence.

2 The fence is in two parts, forming a gap for the cutter. Adjust the fence positions so that the gap is as small as possible.

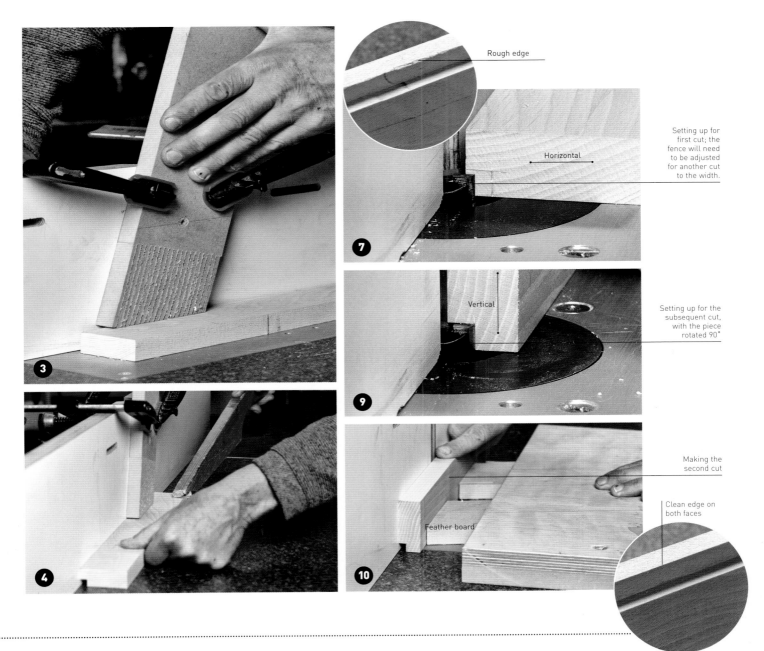

Rough edge

Setting up for first cut; the fence will need to be adjusted for another cut to the width.

Horizontal

Vertical

Setting up for the subsequent cut, with the piece rotated 90°

Making the second cut

Clean edge on both faces

Feather board

3 Fit the feather board by placing the workpiece against the fence. Then fix the board on the fence so that the fingers are slightly compressed and pointing in the feed direction.

4 Make a cut on a scrap piece to check the setting.

5 When the setting is correct, make the cut. Use a push stick or board to push the piece below the feather board.

6 You may find that the cut is irregular at the top of the rabbet. This is because the cut at the end of the cutter is not as efficient as that at the side. With handheld routing this problem can be overcome by back feeding, but this is not a safe practice on the table. Instead, avoid it by taking the cut in two passes and turning the piece between cuts.

7 Set up so that the cutter takes a cut just below the required line but full width if possible. Wider rabbets may need multiple cuts; adjust the fence to achieve the desired width.

8 Make a cut in the usual way.

9 Turn the workpiece around so that the cut is now at 90° to the first. Set the cutter so that the top just brushes the previous cut, and so that the side cuts to the line that was left on the previous cut.

10 Taking a cut now should mean that both of the final cuts are taken with the efficient side faces of the cutter, leaving good clean edges on both faces.

GROOVING

Setting up for grooving is similar to rabbeting.

1 Set up for the cut in a similar manner to rabbeting (see previous page). If you do not have a cutter exactly the right width, the groove will be formed in two or more cuts, moving the fence between cuts. If the subsequent cuts are made on the fence side of the groove, the cutter rotation will tend to grab the piece and cause an uneven cut. Arrange for subsequent cuts to be on the face opposite the fence.

2 If you are grooving to receive a panel or shelf, for example, make a test cut on a piece of scrap wood to check the fit.

3 For wide, deep grooves, adjust the first cuts until full depth is reached, then adjust the fence to give the final width.

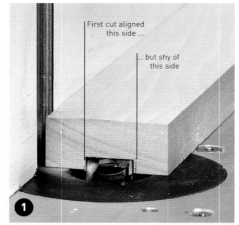

Order of cuts for deep and wide grooves

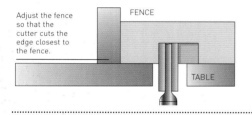

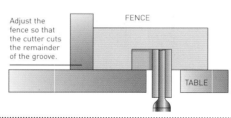

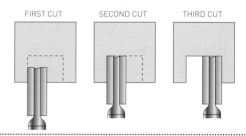

MOLDING

Molding is the shaping of an edge. This may be on a large panel or on a narrow piece that will later be attached, as an edging strip, perhaps. A molding could be seen as a shaped rabbet, so the setup is similar. The molding cutter sits in the line of the fence, with the fence pieces moved up as close as possible. The cut can be taken in one or multiple passes, depending on size.

There are additional considerations. Molding the end of a narrow piece can be difficult, because the piece wants to drop into the gap in the fence.

1 You can overcome this by moving the fence back from the cutter and fixing a board — say, ¼ in. (6 mm) — to the fence, then carefully moving it forward, so that the cutter cuts through it, leaving a Tom-and-Jerry-style shape of the cutter in the board.

2 The piece can then move over the cutter without the danger of it tilting into the gap in the fence.

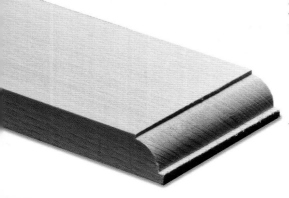

THE FINISHED PIECE

Clinic

Unevenness at the end of the cut
Sometimes the molding may change the line of the board edge so that there is a gap between the edge and the fence beyond the cutter (outfeed fence). This will lead to unevenness at the end of the cut. On some commercial router tables, the fences can be adjusted so that the outfeed fence is offset to take up the gap.

If your outfeed fence cannot be adjusted, you can stick a packing piece of suitable thickness to the outfeed fence. Sometimes this may be so thin that a strip or two of masking tape will suffice.

Selecting a suitable cutter

Inserting starting post

When cut is established, move away from post

Start with piece against the post

USING BEARING-GUIDED CUTTERS ON THE ROUTER TABLE

Handheld routing with a bearing-guided cutter always seems a bit tense! It's a lot easier with a table. The workpiece rests on the whole table surface, so everything is more stable than balancing a router base on the edge of the work.

When using bearing-guided cutters, the work needs to be steadied as it is fed onto the cutter — there is a moment of instability when the cutter engages before the bearing is touching the edge. To provide stability, most tables have a small starting post that can be fitted to the top near the cutter position.

There are additional safety considerations with this function — as there is no fence, dust extraction and guarding have to be catered for. This is usually inadequate on many tables, and it may require some improvisation.

MOLDING

1 Select and fit the cutter and starting post.

2 Turn on the router and offer the piece onto the post and then against the cutter (with the cutter on the right of the workpiece) and start moving it forward. Once the cut is started, you can move away from the post.

3 Continue the cut steadily, with the cutter on the right of the feed direction. Feeding in the other direction can be unstable and dangerous.

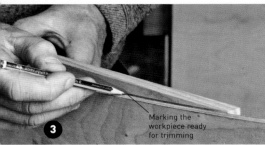
2

3 Marking the workpiece ready for trimming

Bearing on template at start of cut

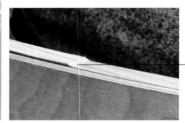
5

6

Cut progressing

4 Make sure the bearing runs along the template.

Cut stopped in progress to show ¹⁄₁₆ in. (2 mm) trimming margin

Clinic

The piece grabs as it engages with the cutter Have you started with the bearing on the template or the piece against the post before engaging? Another cause may be that you have too much to cut. The margin being trimmed should be as thin as possible — certainly no more than ⅛ in. (4 mm) at the most. Routing against the grain can also cause grabbing — try to arrange it so that the cut starts with the grain.

Areas of tear-out or breakout at the end of the cut This is another grain-direction problem. Cutting against the grain will give a rougher finish than other areas, especially if the cutter is blunt. For molding, this can be overcome by making a fine, final cut. For template trimming, if the shape is symmetrical, the piece can be flipped over on the template so that the cut is with the grain. You need to make sure that the second cut blends with the first. When cutting a concave curve, there can be an area of delicate grain that could break off at the end of the cut; flipping the workpiece on the template may also help here.

Second cut being taken

TEMPLATE TRIMMING
Trimming to a template was introduced in the handrouting section, but actually it's a task more easily done on the router table.

1 Create the template in ⅝ in. (15 mm) MDF or plywood, using the router and trammel (see page 111–113) or freehand. Make it overlength, if possible, so there is an area of template beyond the workpiece.

2 The workpiece can be fixed to the template using double-sided tape or screws, but an efficient and elegant way is to use toggle clamps. Fit two toggle clamps to the template so that they hold the piece firmly. They may need to be lifted on blocks to give height above the workpiece. Stick abrasive paper to the template at the clamp positions to increase the clamp hold.

3 Mark and cut the workpiece to the template shape, with a margin of approximately ¹⁄₁₆ in. (2 mm) for trimming, and fix it to the template.

4 Fit a bottom-mounted bearing-guided straight flute cutter (about ¾ in./20 mm diameter is good) and adjust so that the bearing works against the template edge and the cutter against the workpiece. (The cutter illustrated has replaceable blades.)

5 If the template is longer than the workpiece, you can engage the template with the bearing before the cutter hits the work; otherwise you will need to use the starting post.

6 Make the cut with the template going forward on the left side of the cutter.

Tip: Birch plywood creates better templates than MDF. If you do use MDF, it doesn't take screws very well, so if you have to put toggle clamps on blocks, screw the blocks on from below (through the MDF into the block) with the screw holes countersunk.

Measure to proposed end of cut.

Move piece onto cutter and forward in one motion.

Start cut with workpiece against the stop.

Clinic

Uneven cut Because you are dropping or angling the work onto the cutter, it is not possible to use a feather board, so you rely on manual feed. In this situation, it's worth reducing the depth of cut and going to full depth in a number of cuts.

Burning This is more important with stopped moldings, like a chamfer, and is likely to occur at the start and end of the cut when the work is stationary on the cutter. It's worth practicing the start and end on some scrap pieces. The piece should be moved forward as soon as it meets the fence, and angled away as soon as the end stop is reached. Dropping the cutter speed a little can also help.

STOPPED CUTS

Stopped cuts may sometimes be required on the router table. In a stopped cut, the length of the cut does not run out of the end of the work but is stopped short. There are three issues with doing this on the table:
- The workpiece is upside down, so you can't see where the cut is happening.
- It is difficult to control the workpiece when starting and ending the cut, resulting in uneven cuts.
- There are safety issues with attempting stopped cuts freehand. At the start of the cut, the wood can be thrown as it engages with the cutter.

Fortunately, these problems can be addressed using simple precautions. Controlling the work at the start and end of the cut is achieved by clamping stops to the table fence. Correct positioning of the stops is critical.

MAKING A STOPPED CUT

1 For the back stop (the one that the workpiece will be against at the start of the cut), measure from the planned start of cut to the opposite end of the workpiece.

2 Clamp a stop on the infeed fence at this distance from the outfeed side of the cutter.

3 For the front stop, take a measurement from the proposed end of cut to the front of the workpiece.

4 Clamp a stop on the outfeed fence at this distance from the infeed side of the cutter.

5 Set up for the cut in the usual way and make a test cut on a scrap piece the same length as the workpiece.

6 For rabbets and molding (see pages 119–20), offer the workpiece up to the infeed stop and angle it onto the fence, moving forward in one motion to avoid burning. At the end of the cut, angle the piece away as soon as it touches the stop. Use a push stick.

Infeed stop

Angle up vertically

7 Grooving is more tricky — the piece has to be dropped onto the cutter. This can be a little fiddly with a guard in place, but don't be tempted to remove it. With the motor running, hold the piece by the infeed end and position it against the infeed stop, slightly angled up from the cutter. With the piece against the fence, lower it down to the cutter and feed forward. At the other end, lift it vertically away from the cutter, preferably with a push stick.

Jointing

5

Woodwork is all about jointing, but this is about more than strength of construction — well-fitting joints are an indicator of quality and can have a decorative element, showing that a piece has been made with great care. Being able to cut clean, true joints efficiently is an important skill.

In this chapter, you'll find some of the most commonly used joints. In woodwork there is often more than one way of doing things, and so it is with jointing. You can choose to cut the joint entirely by hand or to use some power-tool assistance. Machines take some time to set up, so they are more efficient when you have to cut a batch of joints. They also require that the parts are accurately dimensioned, because any discrepancy will be

Halving joint

A halving joint is used to cross-joint pieces on edge, usually at 90°, and is commonly used in sets for making partitions in boxes or trays. It is not a very strong joint, as there are no shoulders to stabilize the wide cut edge.

1

Tools needed

Marking knife

Light clamp, such as peg or quick clamp

Engineer's square

Marking gauge

Vise

Carcass saw

Narrow bevel-edged chisel

Mallet (optional)

Coping saw (optional)

THE FINISHED JOINT

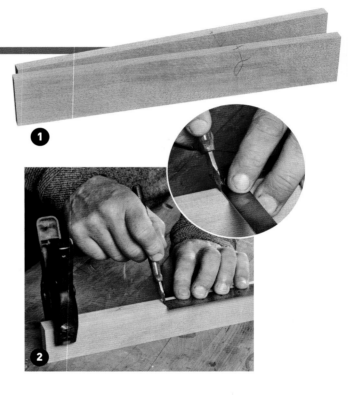

2

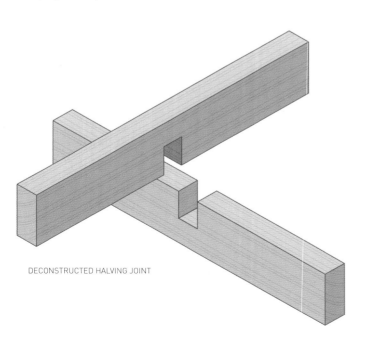

DECONSTRUCTED HALVING JOINT

MARKING UP AND CUTTING A HALVING JOINT BY HAND

Accurate marking out is crucial in cutting a halving joint. In this demonstration, a single joint is cut in the center of two pieces 12 x 2 x ⅜ in. (300 x 50 x 10 mm).

1 Start by marking out the joints. Prepare the parts to dimension with face side and face edge and squared ends. Clamp these together with one face edge uppermost and the other face edge down (this is so that the joint ends up with both face edges uppermost) and the ends aligned.

2 Measure 5¹³⁄₁₆ in. (145 mm) from the end and mark across with a knife and engineer's square (inset).

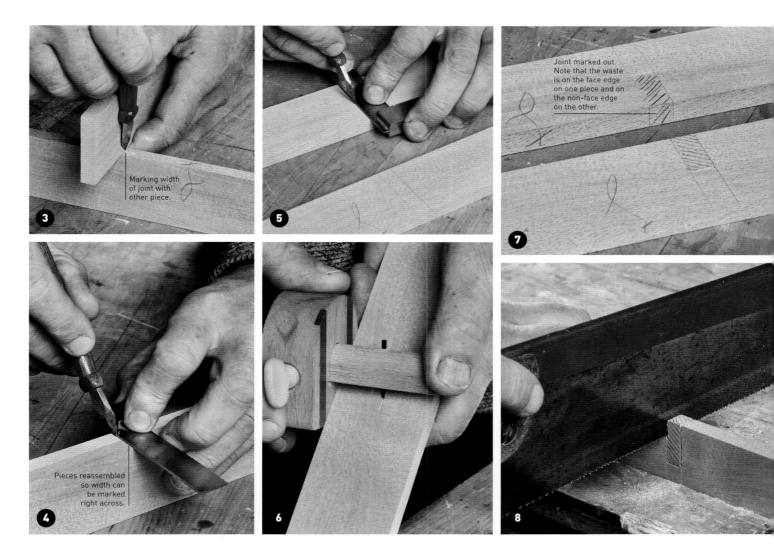

Marking width of joint with other piece.

3

5

Joint marked out. Note that the waste is on the face edge on one piece and on the non-face edge on the other.

7

Pieces reassembled so width can be marked right across.

4

6

8

3 Remove the two pieces from the clamps and use one to mark the width of the joint on the other. (If you have an offcut of the correct thickness, you could use this instead of disassembling the pieces.) Be careful to align the piece on the correct side of the previously marked line and make a knife mark.

4 Reassemble the pieces precisely, clamp and square the mark across.

5 Remove from the clamp and mark the joint lines down the sides using a marking knife and engineer's square.

6 Set a marking gauge to exactly half the width of the pieces and mark between the knifed lines, working from the face edge.

7 Mark the waste from the knifed edge to the center — on one piece this should be a face edge, and on the other the non-face edge.

8 Place each piece in a vise and crosscut with a carcass saw (as described on page 71) down to the gauge line on the waste side of the lines. You may be able to speed things up by taping the pieces together, with the waste parts uppermost and the divider lines aligned, and sawing them in one — but this only works if your sawing is spot on.

> ## ▶ Try this!

> If the dividers are thin, flexing and vibration may be a problem. Clamping a support piece in the vise behind the workpiece can help.

CONTINUED ▶

> Try this!

> For thicker dividers, you may need to cut across the waste with a coping saw or take additional vertical cuts in the waste to break it up, then tidy up with a chisel.

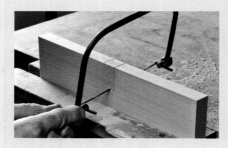

Working back to gauge line

9

10

9 The dividers here are thin enough to chop out the waste with a chisel. Start a few fractions of an inch back from the gauge line and work back to it. Hold the chisel with a reverse grip and press down or use a mallet.

10 Try assembling the dividers — they should slide together neatly.

Clinic

The dividers won't slot together The slots are too thin. Look closely — are there knife lines left? If so, you'll need to pare back to the line. If there are no knife lines, you may not have marked the slots wide enough. You could offer a divider up to the slot, mark a new width with a knife and pare back to it. If they are all tight, another option may be to lightly plane the dividers to thin them down.

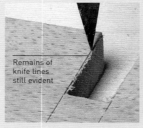

Remains of knife lines still evident

Paring back to knife line

Joint will not push down.

The dividers slot together but are not level on top This is usually because the slots are not deep enough. Pare a little more away from the bottom of the slot — it doesn't matter which one of a pair.

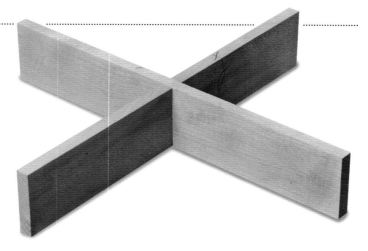

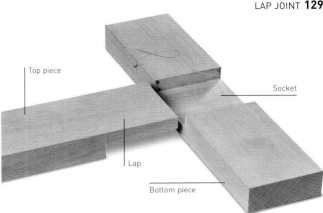

Top piece

Socket

Lap

Bottom piece

Lap joint

The lap joint is used mainly in cabinetwork for frame construction. There are various configurations of this joint. The sequence shows how to make a "T" lap joint. It can be cut by hand or using a router, and both methods are demonstrated here. The lap joint is an excellent hand-cut joint for practicing your paring technique.

Tools needed

Marking knife

Steel rule

Engineer's square

Pencil

Marking guage

Carcass saw and/or tenon saw

Paring or bevel-edged chisel

Mallet

Hand router (optional)

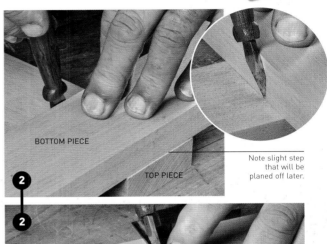

BOTTOM PIECE

2

TOP PIECE

Note slight step that will be planed off later.

2

TOP PIECE

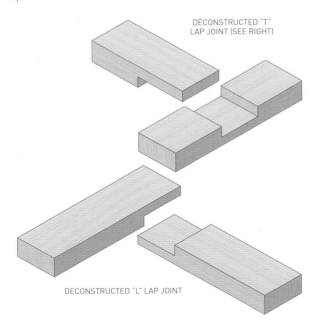

DECONSTRUCTED "T" LAP JOINT (SEE RIGHT)

DECONSTRUCTED "L" LAP JOINT

CUTTING A LAP JOINT BY HAND

For this exercise, a "T" or middle lap is cut with members being 2⁹⁄₁₆ x ¹³⁄₁₆ in. (65 x 24 mm).

1 Prepare the parts with face side and face edge. In this demonstration, the two parts of the joint will be named the top piece and the bottom piece.

2 On the top piece, use the bottom piece to mark the lap shoulder position with a marking knife on the non-face side. Square this across and down the edges (do not mark the face side, because this will show when the joint is assembled).

CONTINUED ▶

> Try this!

> It can be useful to make the lap slightly overlength, perhaps by 1/16 in. (1 mm), so that the end of the lap protrudes slightly when assembled; the overlap can then be trimmed off after the gluing up process. Usually this joint will be part of a frame, so the critical dimension when marking out is actually the distance between the shoulders at either end.

5

3

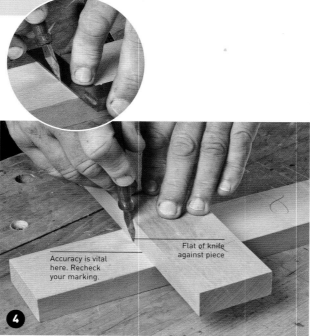

Accuracy is vital here. Recheck your marking.

Flat of knife against piece

4

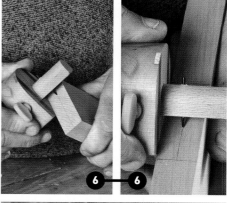

6 — **6**

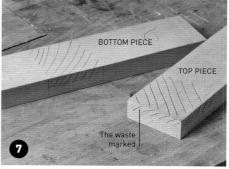

BOTTOM PIECE

TOP PIECE

The waste marked

7

---

3 On the face side of the bottom piece, mark with a knife and square the position of one of the socket shoulders.

4 Now lay the top piece on the marked position. Carefully mark the width with a knife and square it across. Check the accuracy of the marking against the piece (this marking is vital to the quality of the joint).

5 Using a pencil, square the markings on the face down the edges of the bottom piece.

6 Set a marking gauge to half the thickness of the pieces. Mark the thickness of the lap from the face side on both pieces. On the top piece, mark all around the end.

7 Mark the waste areas on both pieces with a pencil.

8 Start by cutting the socket in the bottom piece. It may be worth rereading the sections on crosscutting with a carcass saw, paring, and chisel and mallet before starting (see pages 71, 73, 75). On the waste side of the shoulder lines, chamfer to the knife line using a wide chisel, and then saw down to the gauge line with a crosscut saw.

9 Make additional cuts about 3/8 in. (10 mm) apart in the waste area to aid chiseling away the waste.

10 You can either remove the waste solely with a chisel, or begin with a chisel and then cut to final depth with a hand router. Begin with a chisel and mallet and, with an upward-sloping cut, work your way down to the gauge line until there is just a slither left above the line.

11 Switch to more delicate hand paring to pare to the line (feel the chisel drop into the line for the final cut). Turn the piece around and repeat on the other side.

Mortise and tenon joint

The mortise and tenon joint has a long history and was probably one of the earliest known woodworking joints. Uses range from large pegged joints in wood-framed buildings to short stub tenons in a chest of drawers.

Tools needed

Marking knife

Steel rule

Suitable-sized chisel, either mortise or bevel-edged

Mortise gauge

Engineer's square

Marking gauge

"C" or "F" clamp

Combination square

Carcass or tenon saw

Vise

Sharp chisel for paring

This joint consists of a spigot (tenon) worked in the end of the rail piece, and a slot (mortise) in the upright or stile. The configuration of the joint can vary, depending on its use — strength can be increased by locking the joint with pegs, or by extending it right through the stile and splaying it using wedges driven in from outside. Normally, the finished joint is hidden within the construction, but if the tenon extends right through, contrasting wedges or decorative shaping of the end of the tenon can provide visual interest.

Mortise and tenons usually come in sets — for instance, eight jointing the rails to the four legs of a table. Cutting a set of joints requires accurate marking and cutting. This is especially true if the joint has a decorative element — you don't want to highlight a badly cut joint!

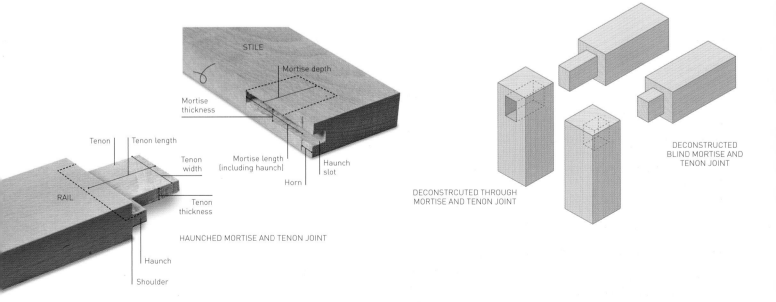

STILE

Mortise depth

Mortise thickness

Tenon | Tenon length

Tenon width

Mortise length (including haunch)

Haunch slot

Horn

RAIL

Tenon thickness

Haunch

Shoulder

HAUNCHED MORTISE AND TENON JOINT

DECONSTRCUTED THROUGH MORTISE AND TENON JOINT

DECONSTRUCTED BLIND MORTISE AND TENON JOINT

5/8 in.
(15 mm)
haunch
slot

3/8 in. (10 mm)
horn

1⁹/₁₆ in.
(40 mm)
mortise

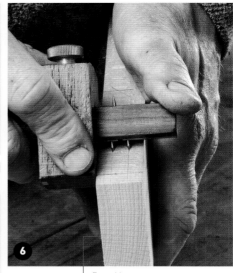

Face side

> ## Try this!

> It is easy to overrun when using marking and mortise gauges. To prevent this, make dimples with the gauge pins where you want to stop, before you begin. The cut will stop when the pins drop into the premade marks.

CUTTING A HAUNCHED MORTISE AND TENON BY HAND

A haunched mortise and tenon has a normal mortise set in from the end of the stile, with an additional shallow slot that extends to the end of the piece. The tenon has an additional step (the haunch) in the bottom corner, which engages with the slot. This joint is commonly used in frame and panel construction — the haunch strengthens the joint and also fills the groove formed in the frame for the panel.

Although mortise and tenons are usually cut in sets, this demonstration shows a single joint being cut. For information on how to mark out a set, see the Oak Side Table project, pages 236–41. In this exercise, the parts are 1 in. (24 mm) thick and 2⁹/₁₆ in. (65 mm) wide.

1 Start by preparing all parts to dimension, with the face side and face edges marked clearly. The mortise should be on a face edge, and the face sides should both be on the same side of the joint.

2 The mortise is marked out on the face edge of the stile. Start by lightly marking the position of the rail outside edge. In normal construction, the stiles are made a little overlength, so that the rails are positioned about 3/8 in. (10 mm) in from the ends. The 3/8 in. (10 mm) horns, as they are known, are trimmed off after assembly.

3 There will be a 9/16 in. (15 mm) haunch on the outside and a 3/8 in. (10 mm) shoulder

on the inside, leaving the width of the mortise at 1⁹/₁₆ in. (40 mm). Mark the width of the mortise with a marking knife, 9/16 in. (15 mm) and 2³/₁₆ in. (55 mm) from the lightly marked rail outside edge position.

4 Normally, the thickness of the mortise and tenon should be around one third of the total thickness. Here, the thickness is set to the width of the nearest matching chisel — 5/16 in. (8 mm). Set the points of the pins of a mortise gauge to the corners of the end of the chisel.

5 Find the center of the piece. This can be done by setting the gauge centrally and

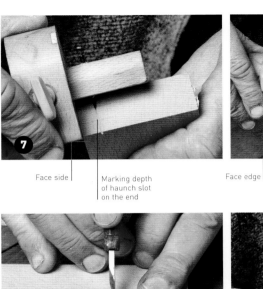

Face side

Marking depth
of haunch slot
on the end

Face edge

Marking inner
shoulder
⅜ in. (10 mm)

Marking outer
shoulder
⅝ in. (15 mm)

Face edge

Cut ¹⁄₁₆ in.
(4 mm) short
of lines

1

Face
side

Marking length
of haunch
⅜ in. (10 mm)

10

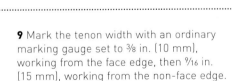

11

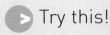

> ## Try this!

> When chopping the mortise, place an engineer's square against the piece to check that both it and the chisel are vertical.

Cutting the joint

You are now ready to cut the joint. Review the relevant sections on the use of chisels and backsaws before proceeding (see Chapter 2, pages 71 and 75).

making a mark on the face before marking from the other side. If the marks line up, they are central; if not, adjust the gauge until they are.

6 Mark the mortise position, working with the gauge stock against the face side.

7 Mark the depth of the haunch slot on the end with a mortise gauge set to ⅜ in. (10 mm).

8 Now mark the length of the tenon. If it is not a full through tenon, it will usually be about two-thirds of the stile width — say, 1¾ in. (44 mm). Measure this from the end and mark around with a marking knife and engineer's square.

9 Mark the tenon width with an ordinary marking gauge set to ⅜ in. (10 mm), working from the face edge, then ⁹⁄₁₆ in. (15 mm), working from the non-face edge.

10 Mark the tenon thickness with the mortise gauge, which should be unchanged from marking the mortises. Work with the stock against the face side.

11 Finally, mark the length of the haunch with a marking knife (inset), in this case at ⅜ in. (10 mm).

1 Cut the mortise first. Using a "C" or "F" clamp, secure the stile to the bench top, preferably over a leg. Position yourself facing the end of the rail, so that you can judge whether the chisel is vertical. Use the chisel that you used to set the mortise gauge, and position it between the gauge lines about ³⁄₁₆ in. (4 mm) from the end (the ends of the mortise will be trimmed accurately once the full depth has been reached). Using a wooden mallet, chop down repeatedly, moving the chisel along about ³⁄₁₆ in. (4 mm) each time (see "Try this!"). Stop approximately ³⁄₁₆ in. (4 mm) from the end. Hold the chisel with the bevel facing the direction of travel, occasionally checking that it is vertical.

CONTINUED ▶

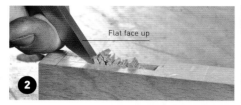

Flat face up

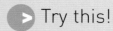

Final cut to line

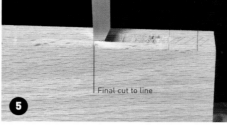

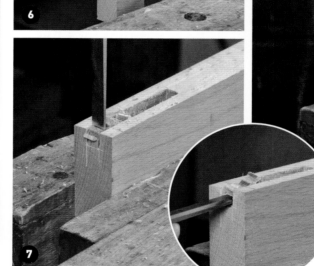

2 The first chop line should be ³⁄₁₆–¼ in. (4–6 mm) deep. Lever out the waste with the flat face of the chisel uppermost. You may need to chop vertically at the end to remove sloping waste left by the chisel bevel.

3 Repeat this process until you reach full depth. I like to use a small combination square to check depth (for other options, see "Try this!", above). This can also be used for checking that the ends are vertical. Full depth is actually the length of the tenon plus approximately ¹⁄₁₆ in. (2 mm). The extra is an allowance for glue squeezed to the bottom of the joint on assembly.

4 Resist the temptation to pare the sides of the mortise, because this would widen it, and both mortise and tenon need to remain the width of the chisel.

5 After reaching full depth, move around to face the side of the rail and chop away the remaining ³⁄₁₆ in. (4 mm) at either end. You will find it easier to judge vertical from this side. Do not chop directly to the line; work back to it.

6 Finally, cut the haunch slot. Carefully saw the sides down to the marked depth.

7 Then chop and pare away the waste to the line.

8 Use the combination square to check the haunch depth.

9 Cut the tenon to fit the mortise (it is worth doing a few practice cuts in some scrap wood before working on the real thing). Follow the method for cutting the tenon cheeks as described in "Ripping with the carcass or tenon saw" in Chapter 2 (see page 72) — saw the diagonals, then saw horizontally.

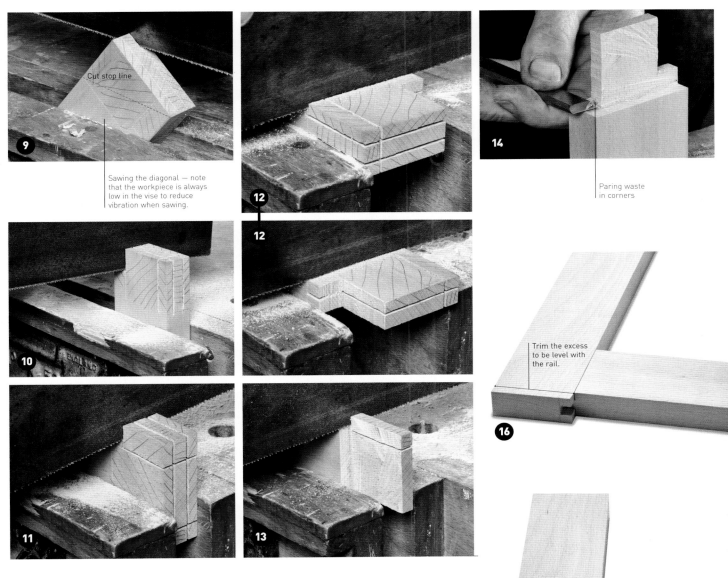

Sawing the diagonal — note that the workpiece is always low in the vise to reduce vibration when sawing.

Paring waste in corners

Trim the excess to be level with the rail.

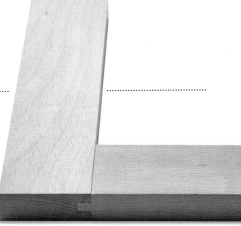

THE FINISHED JOINT

10 Now cut the tenon to width. With the rail vertical in the vise, saw down the gauge lines at either end of the tenon. You don't need to angle the piece as before, because the width of the cut is quite short. Remember that the cut will be shorter on the haunch side!

11 Cut the end of the haunch. Use a sharp chisel to cut a chamfer on the waste side of the previously knife-marked lines, then use a crosscut carcass saw to make the cuts.

12 Repeat Step 11 to cut first one shoulder, then the other.

13 Repeat Step 11 to cut the end shoulder.

14 You will probably have some uncut waste in the corners of the shoulders. Using a sharp chisel, pare this off, working across the grain.

15 Try the fit, making sure that the face sides are adjacent. Your joint may not fit together well initially — it might be loose or tight, or it may not fit together all the way through. The joint should slide together with moderate pressure or light tapping from a mallet. (See "Clinic" on next page.)

16 After gluing up, trim off the horn, level with the rail.

Clinic

If the tenon is tight, try fitting it diagonally. If it goes in diagonally, the problem will be in the width; if not, address the thickness problem first.

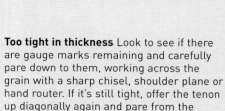

CHECKING FOR WIDTH AND THICKNESS

Too tight in width Check the edges of the tenon — you may see bruising on the faces. If the bruising is only at the end, it may be that the mortise is wedge-shaped — you can check this with a combination square. If it is, pare the mortise just at the bottom at the appropriate end.

Bruising shows that the joint is tight widthwise.

The tenon is square against the side at the bottom, but there is a gap at the top, showing that the end is not square.

Too tight in thickness Look to see if there are gauge marks remaining and carefully pare down to them, working across the grain with a sharp chisel, shoulder plane or hand router. If it's still tight, offer the tenon up diagonally again and pare from the tighter of the two ends.

Remaining gauge marks

Pare across, not from the end.

A little too loose Use a gap-filling glue such as Cascamite and try to be more precise next time!

Very loose Stick a piece of veneer on one face. Check the alignment of the joint to decide which face to apply it to. It may be better to discard and cut a new rail.

TENON WON'T GO IN FULLY

Mortise is not deep enough Check the depth with a ruler or combination square — sometimes there is one area, usually at one end, where the waste has not been fully removed.

Waste around the shoulder Check closely around the shoulder for any steps of waste left from cutting. Check to see whether the shoulder might be sloping up to the tenon, causing a gap. If so, remove the slope with a sharp chisel or shoulder plane, being careful not to disturb the line of the outer part of the shoulder.

Waste remains in the corner

Paring waste in corners

Check that the haunch is not preventing full engagement.

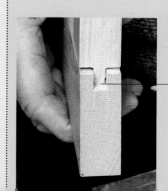

Haunch too long

ALIGNMENT PROBLEMS

Faces not level Check that you have assembled it the right way around! It's possible that you gauged the joint from different faces on the tenon and mortise pieces. It's difficult to correct this without making the joint loose. You could pare across the tenon on the appropriate side, if the discrepancy is not too great.

Rail leans over Check by offering up a straight edge to the side faces. If the faces are not aligned, you can pare from the bottom of the tenon on the side to which it is leaning. Sometimes a slight misalignment can be corrected when clamping up.

Shoulders don't sit well onto the rail face This should be checked after any lean is corrected. Sometimes one shoulder will fit well, but the other has gaps. Correct this by re-knifing the shoulder from the area with the largest gap, and cutting back to the knife line with a wide chisel or shoulder plane. This can only be done sparingly, because it will affect the squareness of the whole assembly.

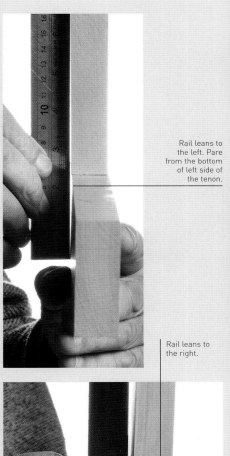

Rail leans to the left. Pare from the bottom of left side of the tenon.

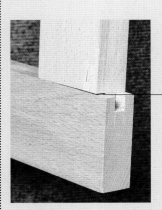

Gap showing at shoulder

Not square Check with a square into the corner. If it's out, then it could be that the mortise is not square. Check with a combination square and correct by paring the bottom of the mortise at the appropriate end.

Rail leans to the right.

Widest gap was here. Align square with this end.

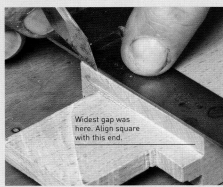

Tools needed

Router and router table

Plunge-cutting, straight flute cutter — the width of the mortise or less

Depth gauge (optional)

Vise

Bevel-edged chisel — slightly narrower than the mortise

Wide, straight flute cutter for tenoning, preferably a tenoning cutter

Carcass or tenon saw

Marking gauge

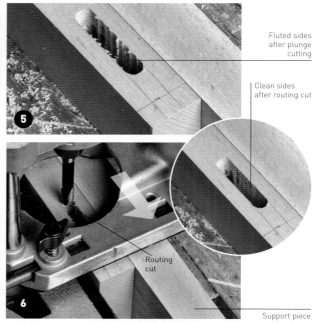

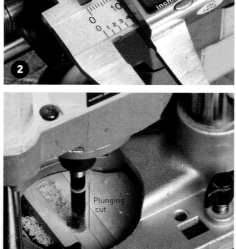

Align with non-fence side of mortise.

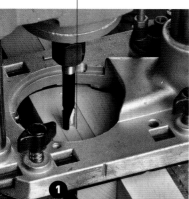

Plunging cut

Fluted sides after plunge cutting

Clean sides after routing cut

Routing cut

Support piece

Haunch routed

CUTTING A MORTISE AND TENON WITH A ROUTER AND TABLE

Mark up the parts as shown in "Cutting a haunched mortise and tenon by hand," page 136.

In frames where both pieces are the same thickness, it is useful if the mortise can be exactly central; this can be achieved by routing the mortise in two cuts, one from either side of the workpiece. In this case, the width of the cutter is not critical (as long as it's narrower than the mortise). In other situations, the mortise gauge should be set to the width of the available cutter. Here, you need to cut a central mortise 5/16 in. (8 mm) wide, so set the gauge to 5/16 in. (8 mm) and centralized on the width to mark the mortise thickness.

Routing the mortises

1 Set up the router with a cutter the width of the mortise or narrower, and make sure that the cutter can plunge cut. In this example, it's 1/4 in. (6 mm) diameter. Adjust the fence (see page 102) so that the non-fence side of the cutter is aligned with the mortise gauge line. Set the capstan (see page 101) to 1/16 in. (2 mm) longer than the tenon — i.e., 1 13/16 in. (46 mm). Have the capstan set to its lowest setting for this.

2 Change the capstan to its highest setting to adjust the depth for the haunch. With the cutter still down to the workpiece surface, adjust the screw on the capstan until the gap between screw and stop is the length of the haunch (3/8 in./10 mm).

3 Place the mortise piece in the vise. Stability can be a problem, so consider having a support piece fixed in the vise behind it. Set the capstan to mortise position.

4 Cut the mortise using a series of plunging cuts, followed by a routing cut that will clean up the edges — position the router on the work, switch on and drill down at the front of the mortise. You may not be able to plunge to full depth, because the waste in the cut will clog the cutter, so only plunge one-third of the depth. Move the cutter forward to take a second cut overlapping the first — you should be able to go deeper this time, possibly full depth.

5 Repeat, going full depth, until you reach the haunch line. Return to go full depth on the starting cuts that weren't cut full depth.

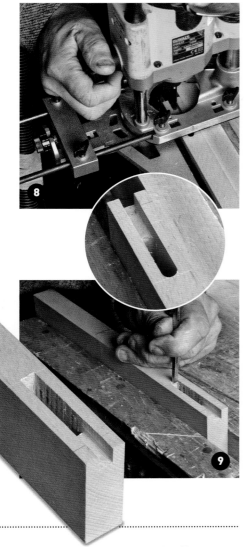

Set the cutter to the gauged tenon line.

Set the cutter to the tenon shoulder or use the digital depth gauge.

Set the cutter to the depth of the haunch.

Majority of the waste is sawn away.

Move the cutter up in ³⁄₁₆ in. (5 mm) increments and take a couple of cuts, moving the workpiece toward the fence between cuts.

Set the cutter to the gauged line or use a depth gauge.

The final cut will be with the cutter set to the tenon edge gauge line.

6 The slot will have fluted sides. To rout these off, plunge down the depth of the router cutters (about ³⁄₁₆ in./20 mm) at the front of the mortise and move forward to the end of the mortise, raising the cutter at the end. Return and repeat until you have routed full depth.

7 Turn the capstan to the haunch depth position and use two routing cuts to cut the haunch slot to full depth.

8 Now turn the workpiece around and repeat Steps 4–7, cutting from the other side. This should leave you with a clean, full-depth mortise and perfectly centralized haunch slot.

9 The mortise will have round ends; square these off with a bevel-edge chisel.

Cutting the tenon

1 You can cut the tenon cheeks on the router table. Set up the table in the same way as when cutting a lap joint (see page 134). Cutting the tenon is the same as the lap, except you also flip the piece over and cut from the other side. It is important to test the setup using an offcut piece of exactly the same thickness. Adjustment is very sensitive because you are cutting from both sides.

2 Having cut the cheeks, adjust the height of the cutter to cut the ³⁄₈ in. (10 mm) shoulder on the face edge side of the tenon. The setting can be done either with a depth gauge or by setting the cutter to the gauge line on the end of the tenon.

3 With the workpiece on the face edge, cut the shoulder. You should use progressive cuts, moving the workpiece toward the fence after each cut.

4 Finally, adjust the fence and the cutter height to cut the haunch. Use a marking gauge set to ⁵⁄₈ in. (15 mm) to mark the edge of the tenon. Also mark the length of the haunch to ³⁄₈ in. (10 mm). Progressively adjust the workpiece position and cutter height until the cut is on these marks.

Dado joint

The dado joint (also known as a housing joint) is used for jointing in shelving, dividers or drawer runners. It consists of a groove — usually running across the grain — that receives the thickness of the shelf or runner. The dado can extend right through and be evident at the edge, or stop short of the edge so that the joint does not show, the front of the shelf being notched out to cover the dado. The joint can take considerable downward pressure on the shelf, but is not resistant to sideways pressure. The introduction of biscuit and domino joints means that the dado joint is not as commonly used as it once was.

1

Tools needed

Square, preferably a long one

Marking knife

Pencil

Marking gauge

Paring or bevel-edged chisel, a little narrower than the board piece — a long paring chisel is best

Crosscut backsaw

Wide bevel-edged chisel

Mallet

Hand router

Dado

DECONSTRUCTED
THROUGH DADO JOINT

Dado piece

Board piece

2

CUTTING A THROUGH DADO JOINT BY HAND

1 Prepare all parts with face side and face edge and to dimension; in this case, each piece is 12 x 6¾ x ⅞ in. (300 x 170 x 22 mm). You will make the joint with the face side facing up on the board and inward on the dado — the face edges should be adjacent. Make sure that the end of the board piece is flat and square.

2 Mark one side of the dado position with a square and marking knife.

Align this edge carefully on the knife line.

Tidying the bottom corner

3 Offer the board piece up on the appropriate side of the line and mark the width with a marking knife.

4 Then square it across with a square and knife. These knife lines should be as deep as possible.

5 With pencil and square, mark the lines down the front and back edges.

6 Set the marking gauge to the required dado depth — this is usually fairly shallow, say ¼ in. (6 mm) — and mark the depth between the pencil lines.

7 Secure the dado piece firmly to the bench.

8 Pare away a chamfer on the waste side of the knife lines, deepening the lines if you like.

9 Saw along the knife lines down to the gauge lines. Keep the cut as horizontal as possible — turn the piece around to attack it from both sides if it is wide.

10 Using a chisel and mallet, make a series of chopping cuts across the width of the dado (just a little narrower than the dado).

11 Pare away the chopped-up waste down to the required depth — you will find a long paring chisel best for this. The sawn sides may require tidying at the bottom corner.

CONTINUED ▶

12

13

12 As you approach the full depth, you can use a hand router to accurately cut down to final depth. Set the cutter depth to the gauged dado depth. You could refer to the method described in Steps 13–14 on page 131 as well. If the cut is too deep to get a good shaving (the tool judders as you take the cut), raise the cutter so that you take only fine shavings and then progressively reset it to the final cut.

13 Put the joint together to check the fit. Take care when checking fit — if the joint is tight, there is a danger of splintering the edge of the dado when you pull out the board piece.

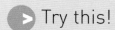 Try this!

> If you don't have a hand router, there are other methods for checking that the bottom is flat:

Checking bottom is level with ruler; you could use the side of the chisel.

Pare down to the gauge lines at either end, and use a straight edge such as a steel rule to check for a flat surface between them.

Checking depth with wheel marking gauge

The modern wheel marking gauge is useful, because it is flat ended and can be used as a depth gauge.

The combination square can also be used to check depth.

Clinic

Board will not fit in the dado Check along the edge of the dado and pare back any areas where the edge is not vertical or the original knife line is still evident. If the fit is very tight, you may see areas of compression on the board piece — these will correspond with irregularities on the dado edge.

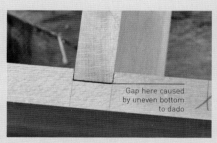

Gap here caused by uneven bottom to dado

The board fits but with gaps at the end This is caused by an uneven bottom on the dado. Check that the bottom is level, using one of the methods described in the "Try this!" box, left.

Board fits but is not square Check for squareness against the joint. If it's not square, the dado may be skewed vertically. Pare the dado edge toward the bottom to correct this.

Tools needed

Square, preferably a long one

Marking knife

Marking gauge

Pencil

Paring or bevel-edged chisel, a little narrower than the board piece — a long paring chisel is best

Wide bevel-edged chisel

Drill and forstner bit

Crosscut backsaw

Mallet

Marking end of board piece

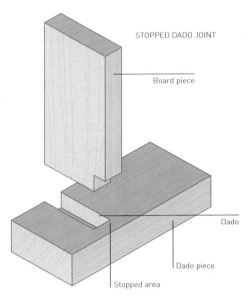

STOPPED DADO JOINT

Board piece

Dado

Dado piece

Stopped area

CUTTING A STOPPED DADO JOINT BY HAND

This is very similar to the through dado joint, except that the dado does not extend to the edge. This can make cutting difficult, because it is hard to saw up to the stopped end.

1 Mark out the width of the dado as in Steps 2–5 of the through dado joint (see pages 144–46), but don't knife too deeply at the front where the stop will be.

2 Set the marking gauge to the required dado depth and mark the depth of the dado at the non-stopped end.

3 Use the gauge setting for the depth of the dado to mark the depth of the notch on the front of the board piece.

4 Set the marking gauge to the length of the stopped area, about ⅜ in. (10 mm) here, and mark a line between the two width lines on the dado piece and on the end of the board piece.

5 Using a pencil, extend the gauged lines on the board piece around the faces to meet each other. This is the notch to be cut out — mark it as waste.

Tip: You may want the front of the board to stop short of the front of the dado piece — i.e., the board piece will be narrower than the dado piece. In this case, be careful to stop the knife lines for the board width short of the face edge; otherwise they will show when the pieces are assembled.

CONTINUED ▸

6

8

7

9

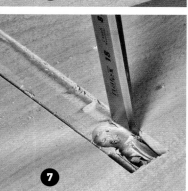

7

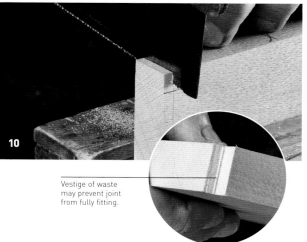

10

Vestige of waste
may prevent joint
from fully fitting.

Clinic

All of the possible issues for through
dadoes also apply here.

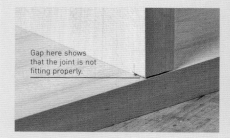

Gap here shows
that the joint is not
fitting properly.

**The shoulder of the notch does not sit
down onto the surface** Check that the
shoulder is square and there is no waste
preventing it from sitting down properly.
If the problem persists, you can either
deepen the dado or plane a little from
the end of the board piece.

Paring away
waste from
corner

6 Chisel a chamfer to the knife lines that
define the width in the same way as you
would for a through dado.

7 It's difficult to saw up to the stopped area.
To assist with this, drill the waste to about
2 in. (50 mm) back from the stopped end,
then chop out and clean up to the knife
lines. A forstner bit that is slightly narrower
than the dado is good for this.

8 Saw along the knife lines — the chopped-
out waste area makes this easier.

9 Proceed as shown in Steps 10–12 of the
through dado joint (see pages 144–46).

10 Cut the notch at the front of the board
piece. Start by crosscutting from the edge.
Chamfer on the waste side of the line and
saw down to the other notch line. Then
turn the wood in the vise and saw down to
remove the notch. Check it for square and
correct if necessary.

THE FINISHED
STOPPED DADO
JOINT

ROUTING DADOES

Both through and stopped dadoes can be cut using a router, and this would be my preferred method. There are a number of ways the cut can be made. If the dado is close to the end of the piece, the fence can be used to guide the cut. If it's more remote, the cut can be guided using a simple square guide as described on page 114, or a guide bush and template as shown on page 115. Here, we will look at the fence and guide bush methods.

Cutting close to an edge

1

> Try this!

> When designing a piece, it can be worth planning for your board parts to be the same width as the cutter you have available. This saves having to make two cuts for a dado.

> If you do have to make two cuts, you could make test cuts in a piece of scrap wood to make sure that your second cut is positioned correctly for the board width.

3

Using two passes to create a wider dado

3

A fence can be used if the cut is close to the edge.

USING THE FENCE FOR CUTS CLOSE TO THE EDGE

1 Mark the joint position with a sharp pencil.

2 Fit a cutter of the same width as the board to be fitted, or slightly smaller.

3 Set the fence so that the cutter is aligned with the marked dado. If the cutter is narrower than the dado, align with the non-fence side of the joint.

4 Set the depth stop.

5 Make the cut, feeding so that the fence is on the right of the feed direction.

6 If the cutter is narrow, move the fence to align the cutter with the other side of the cut, and make the cut feeding in the other direction.

7 There can be a danger of breakout as the cutter exits at the end of the cut. To prevent this, secure a support piece to the back of the workpiece.

7

Support piece prevents breakout

USING A GUIDE BUSH AND TEMPLATE

It's worth reading the section on "Using a guide bush" on page 115 for full details on this.

1 Decide on the size of cutter to be used and calculate the size of template required, as shown on page 115.

2 Make the template in ½–⅝ in. (12–15 mm) birch plywood or MDF.

3 Mark the position of the dado and align the template to cut in that position. Aid alignment by making a cut in the crosspiece of the template with the router set up.

4 Set the depth stop.

5 Make the cut, feeding up the left-hand side and then down the right.

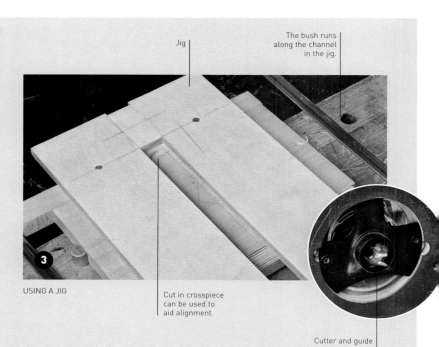

Jig

The bush runs along the channel in the jig.

3 USING A JIG

Cut in crosspiece can be used to aid alignment.

Cutter and guide bush set up

5 Making the cut

THE FINISHED CUT

> Try this!

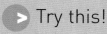

> For through dadoes, breakout can be an issue. To avoid this, clamp sacrifice pieces to the outside of the board to support the grain.

Edge joint

When making tables or wide panels, you are likely to have to joint a number of boards edge to edge. Jointing a wide panel from narrow boards makes it more stable, because warps in wider boards are more pronounced than in narrow ones. When forming these large surfaces, you are looking for an invisible joint with no glue line showing. Some proficiency with the plane is needed for this joint. Review basic planing techniques in Chapter 2 (see pages 58–63) before you start.

Tools needed

Steel rule

Pencil

Vise

Clamp

Jack or longer plane

Hinging boards before putting in vise

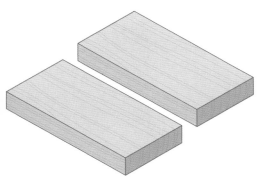

BOARDS READY FOR JOINTING EDGE TO EDGE

PLANING AN EDGE JOINT

When planing an edge joint, you are aiming for two clean edges that will butt together to give a flat surface, with just a paper-width gap between them in the middle. This gap is closed up when the boards are glued and clamped. You can achieve this by planing both boards together. This technique means that you don't have to plane precisely square — when the boards are rotated to fit, any imprecision will be canceled out. However, you do need to have good technique for planing straight along the length.

1 Prepare your boards to a uniform thickness, perfectly flat (see "Preparing a face side and face edge," pages 61–62). Decide on which edges will be jointed and mark them — a cabinetmaker's triangle is good for this, because it is easier and clearer than numbering the edges. Simply draw a triangle across the boards; when they are reassembled, it is clear when the triangle does not come together.

2 For each joint, place the pieces in the vise with the edges level. The boards should be oriented by hinging them together, rather like closing a book. You will plane the "hinged" edges.

CONTINUED ▶

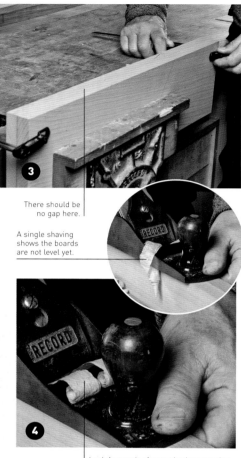

There should be no gap here.

A single shaving shows the boards are not level yet.

Look for a pair of even shavings running the full length of the boards.

3 Look closely at the meeting of the boards in the vise. If there is any warp, there may be a gap between them. Try swapping them side to side so that the gap is lost. If it's still there, lightly clamp them to close the gap. The two boards need to be as flat together as possible.

4 You can use a no. 5 or 5½ jack plane for this, but for longer boards a no. 7 or 8 would work better. Plane the boards together until you get an even shaving across both boards. The plane must be sharp and, for the final cut, finely set.

5 Put the joint together and check the fit (see "Clinic," right).

6 Once the fit is good, the joint can also be biscuited or dominoed to aid alignment or for reinforcement (see "Biscuit jointing" and "Domino jointing," pages 180–87).

Clinic

Is the joint flat vertically? Check by offering up a steel rule to the face at a number of points along the boards. If you can see light, either in the middle or at the top, it's not flat. Put the boards back in the vise as before and re-plane. Be careful when checking this — if the top board was tilted toward the rule and you press it too hard against the surface, the top board will be moved back and you may get a false reading.

Are the edges meeting? Check by lightly holding either end of the top piece and trying to rotate it. You should be able to feel friction as the edges engage at either end. If not, the board will pivot on a high spot somewhere in the middle. If you can feel the friction, grip both boards at either end of the joint and try flexing them back and forth. You want a slight gap in the middle — if the boards flex with no rubbing in the middle, this indicates that gap. Another method of spotting this is to shine a light behind and see if you can see it through the gap. However, the gap should be very fine — only paper width.

Trying to rotate the top board

If there is no clearance in the middle, you should create some using stopped shavings. On just one of the boards, start with a short, fine shaving in the middle of the board, lifting the plane away to end the cut. Then extend to a longer shaving until you are starting and stopping about 6 in. (150 mm) from either end.

Flexing both boards to check for contact in the middle

If you have a high spot, you could try taking stopped shavings locally at the pivot point, then offer the boards up to check the fit again. The shavings between tests should be fine and few. If the high spot is pronounced, it's probably best to put both boards back in the vise and plane them again, paying particular attention to technique.

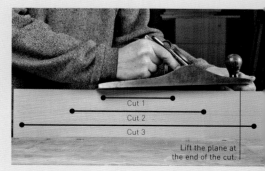

Cut 1

Cut 2

Cut 3

Lift the plane at the end of the cut.

Stopped shavings to remove high point or create slight gap in center of joint

FINISHED THROUGH
DOVETAIL JOINT

Dovetail joint

The dovetail is the iconic woodworking joint. Often when looking at a piece of furniture, people will judge its quality by the look of the dovetails. This is partly because dovetail joints are often on display, whereas other joints are usually hidden within, and partly because the pattern of the tails and pins is naturally appealing. Creating good dovetail joints is simply a matter of method, attention to detail and practice.

Tools needed

Marking knife or scalpel

Shooting board

Cutting gauge

Steel rule

Pin-marking jig (optional)

Dividers

Sliding bevel or dovetail template

Dovetail saw

Vise

Small engineer's square

Coping or fretsaw

Wide chisel and narrow chisel

The dovetail joint is constructed with a series of tails fitting into an opposite series of sockets. There are many different configurations of dovetails, including through, lap, half-lap and secret mitered. In this demonstration, two common dovetail corner joints will be cut — the through and the lapped dovetail.

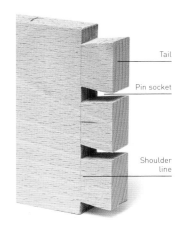

Tail

Pin socket

Shoulder line

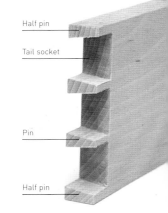

Half pin

Tail socket

Pin

Half pin

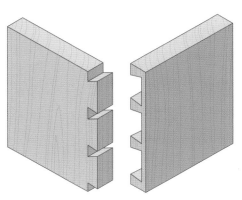

LAPPED DOVETAIL

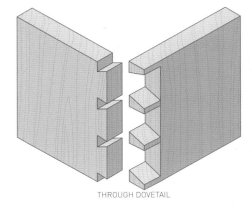

THROUGH DOVETAIL

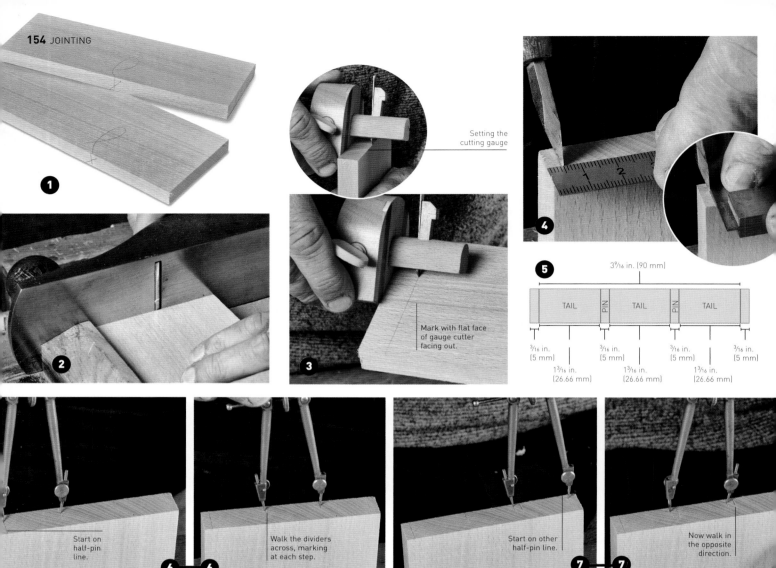

Setting the cutting gauge

Mark with flat face of gauge cutter facing out.

$3^9/_{16}$ in. (90 mm)

| TAIL | PIN | TAIL | PIN | TAIL |

$3/_{16}$ in. (5 mm) $3/_{16}$ in. (5 mm) $3/_{16}$ in. (5 mm) $3/_{16}$ in. (5 mm)

$1^3/_{16}$ in. (26.66 mm) $1^3/_{16}$ in. (26.66 mm) $1^3/_{16}$ in. (26.66 mm)

Start on half-pin line.

Walk the dividers across, marking at each step.

Start on other half-pin line.

Now walk in the opposite direction.

◀ SEE PREVIOUS PAGE FOR TOOLS

CUTTING A THROUGH DOVETAIL BY HAND

Through dovetails are often used in box construction and the backs of drawers. The standard configuration has half pins at each end — so named because they are sloping only on one side — then a series of dovetails with pins in between. The procedure for cutting a set of dovetails is to mark out and cut the tails, then use these as a template to mark the pins.

Normally, the whole set for a box or drawers will be marked together. Here, we will cut a single corner with half pins at either edge and three equal tails in between.

Cutting the tails

1 Prepare the pieces with face side and face edge. In this demonstration, the pieces are $5/_8$ in. (16 mm) thick and $3^{15}/_{16}$ in. (100 mm) wide — length can be arbitrary. Here, a corner is jointed with the face side inward and the face edge on top.

2 Shoot the ends on a shooting board until they are square. The end is shot because marking is done using the end as a datum.

3 Set the cutting gauge to the thickness of the pieces and mark the shoulders with the stock against the shot end. The flat face of the gauge cutter should be facing outward.

4 Mark the position of the tails on the end of the piece. In our example, there will be a $1/_{16}$ in. (5 mm) half pin at either end. Measure this from either edge, then square across.

TAIL LAYOUT CALCULATION

Width of tail $\dfrac{\text{distance between half pins} - (\text{width of pins} \times \text{number of pins})}{\text{Number of tails}}$

Width of tail Metric $\dfrac{90 - (5 \times 2)}{3} = 26.66$ mm   Imperial $\dfrac{3^9/_{16} - (3/_{16} \times 2)}{3} = 1^1/_{16}$ in.

Use index finger to position saw precisely.

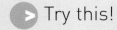

Try this!

> If you don't have a dovetail template, you can use a sliding bevel. To set the bevel, mark the slope on a piece of board. For example, to mark a 1:8 slope on a piece of scrap wood, square a line from the edge, then measure ⅜ in. (10 mm) along the edge and 3 in. (80 mm) along the line and join the two points. Set the bevel to this angle.

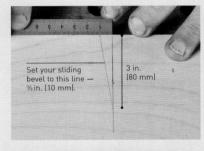

Set your sliding bevel to this line — ⅜ in. (10 mm).

3 in. (80 mm)

---

5 Measure the distance between the half pins. Here, it's 3½ in. (90 mm) — this is the space left for the tails and pins. There will be two 1/16 in. (5 mm) wide pins. Now figure out the width of the tails (see "Tail layout calculation," opposite).

6 Mark the tails using dividers — set the dividers to the width of the tail plus a pin, 1¼ in. (31.66 mm). Start with a divider point on the half-pin line and walk it across to the other end, marking the points.

7 Then set the divider on the other half pin and walk it across the other way.

8 This gives you the marked positions for all the tails, which you can square across. Using the dividers will give more regular tail spacings than if you did it by measurement alone.

9 Mark the slope of the dovetails on the faces. Dovetails in softwood usually have a slope with a gradient of 1:5 or 1:6, while in hardwood it's 1:7 or 1:8. Using a dovetail template, mark the dovetails with a knife (you can also use a sliding bevel set to the angle — see "Try this!" panel, above right) and mark the waste (i.e., the pins).

10 Saw the dovetails with a dovetail saw. Saw to the line as described in the using hand tools chapter (see pages 71–72). (Sawing shy of the line, then paring to it often leads to a worse fit and is time consuming; it may be worth doing a few practice cuts to get your eye in.)

11 Put the tailpiece low in the vise, slightly angled so that the line of cut is about vertical. You could check this with a square.

12 Working on the waste (pin) side of the line, guide the saw into the cut with the tip of your index finger and start with very light strokes. Saw down to the gauge line.

13 Saw all the cuts at that angle, then reposition the piece to take the cuts at the other angle.

CONTINUED ▶

Cut shy of line

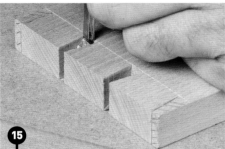

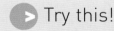

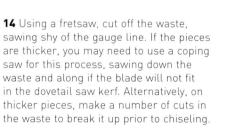

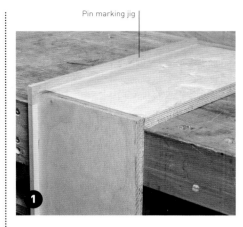

Pin marking jig

Store-bought marking knife

Workshop-made thin knife

Place jig in vise, with end of pin piece level with top surface, and slide tail piece forward until shoulders are in line with back of pins. Both pieces' face edges must be butted up to the raised edge, and face sides should be facing the jig.

Try this!

> Half-pin shoulders sitting below the other shoulders is one of the most common problems with dovetails. Cutting the half-pin shoulders is one of the few times that I would recommend sawing shy of the line and carefully paring to the knife line.

14 Using a fretsaw, cut off the waste, sawing shy of the gauge line. If the pieces are thicker, you may need to use a coping saw for this process, sawing down the waste and along if the blade will not fit in the dovetail saw kerf. Alternatively, on thicker pieces, make a number of cuts in the waste to break it up prior to chiseling.

15 The shoulders between the pin sockets can now be defined with a chisel. If there is a lot of waste to remove, initially use a vertical end-grain paring technique (see page 73). If there is only a small amount to remove, pare horizontally, working back to the gauge line until you can "click" the

chisel into the line for a final cut. Work from both sides, angling the chisel so that there is no danger of undercutting. You should now have a shoulder that slopes up from either side to a peak in the middle. Pare this away progressively until the shoulder is flat or even slightly scooped. Avoid paring right through to the back, because there is danger of breakout. Make sure that the corners are nice and clean, with no remaining waste.

16 Cut the shoulders for the half pins with a normal crosscut. Knife across, then chisel a chamfer to the line and saw to the knife line.

Cutting the pins
You are now ready to mark out and cut the pins. This is the critical part of the job — there is some room for error in cutting the tails, but the pins must be cut precisely for a good fit.

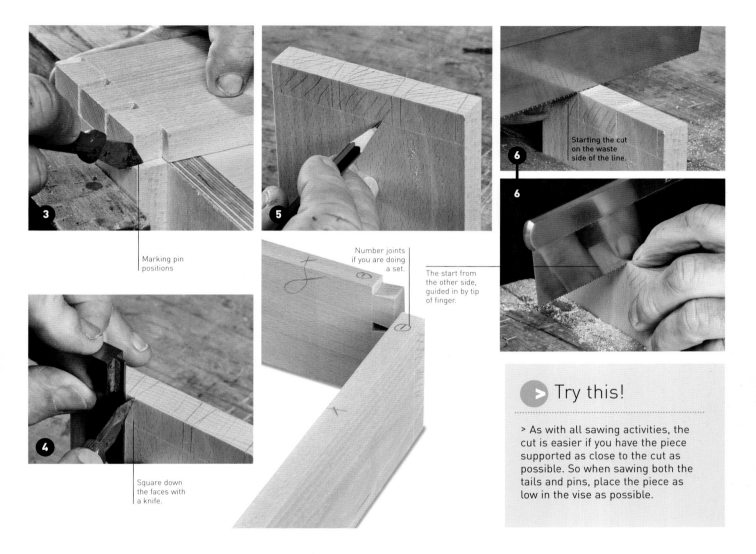

3 Marking pin positions

4 Square down the faces with a knife.

5 Number joints if you are doing a set.

6 Starting the cut on the waste side of the line.

The start from the other side, guided in by tip of finger.

> ## ▶ Try this!

> As with all sawing activities, the cut is easier if you have the piece supported as close to the cut as possible. So when sawing both the tails and pins, place the piece as low in the vise as possible.

1 Traditionally, the pin piece is placed in the vise level with a plane on its side. The plane is moved back and the tailpiece placed on top, with the face sides on the inside of the corner, the face edges adjacent and the socket shoulders in line with the back of the pin piece. The pin position is marked through the sockets with a knife. However, there is a danger of the pieces slipping as you mark, so I would advise making a jig for holding the parts. This is simply two pieces of MDF or plywood precisely jointed at 90°, with raised edging applied to one side.

2 In use, the pin piece is placed in the jig with the face side facing the jig, the face edge against the edge strip and the end level with the top surface. The tailpiece is then placed on the jig in the same orientation, with the shoulders aligned with the back of the pin piece.

3 Mark the pin positions on the pin piece with a knife. Sometimes a normal marking knife is too thick to fit between the tails, in which case you could make a thin knife using a hacksaw blade.

4 Square the pin positions down the faces to the gauge line with a marking knife.

5 Indicate the areas of waste. If you are doing a set, number the joints to aid correct assembly.

6 Place the pin piece vertically in the vise and saw on the waste side of the line down to the gauge line. It's easiest to saw all cuts on one side of the pins, then change position to cut the other side. Aim to saw to the line rather than shy of it. You may find a few practice cuts on some scrap wood useful.

CONTINUED ▶

7 Saw out the waste between the pins, then clean up to the shoulder in the same way as you did between the tails (see page 156).

8 Use as wide a chisel as possible, because it will give a cleaner, straighter shoulder.

9 The joint is almost complete. It's useful to ease the corners of the tails a little back from the ends. This will ease the location of the tails and allow the joints to press home, even if the bottom corners of the pins are not quite clean. Lightly pare away the corner on the face side, starting a few fractions of an inch in from the end.

10 You can now test fit the joint. You are aiming for a joint that slides together snugly, with perhaps a few final taps from a mallet. Any adjusting cuts should be pared across the grain, and only a thin slither at a time; there are only a couple of shavings' difference between a tight and a loose joint.

Saw shy of the line. The fretsaw is not an accurate tool.

Trimming the shaving in the corner

Start the cut a little in from the end and cut on the inside.

Initial chopping cuts to be followed by horizontal paring

Clinic

Here are a few diagnostic tips if your joint does not fit snugly.

Pins are too tight Press the joint lightly together and rock the tailpiece on the pins; you may be able to detect the tight pins, because the tails will engage with the looser ones but not the tight ones. Check whether the edges are aligned — if not, adjusting the pins can help to correct this. Pare thin shavings off the appropriate side of the pins to adjust the edge alignment. If the edges are okay, pare both sides lightly. Looking for the vestiges of the knife markings can also help to decide where to pare.

Joint is too tight/ checking for tight half pins You can see whether the half pins are likely to split by laying a straight edge on the edge to check if they are splaying out. If they are splaying, lightly pare the inside of the half pin to avoid splitting.

Faces of the pins look burnished or compressed This indicates that the pin is too tight. The corners of the pins should stay crisp. If they become rounded, this shows that the corner of the pin socket has not been cleaned out enough.

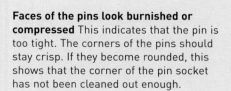

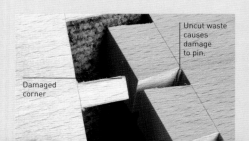

Uncut waste causes damage to pin.

Damaged corner

Joint is loose This is difficult to deal with. If it's loose right across, there is not much you can do, and it's probably best to discard the pin piece and start again. Before you do so, examine the tails to make sure that the faces are square at the sockets.

Gaps between tails and shoulder

Joint will not push home fully — gaps between tails and shoulder First, check that the joint is square. Then see if the shoulders are rounded or out of square. (This is often a problem with pin shoulders — you could make them very slightly scooped.) Look for any little tags or step in the corners between pin and shoulder, because these may prevent full engagement. Pare them away.

Tools needed

Marking knife or scalpel

Shooting board

Cutting gauge

Steel rule

Screwdriver

Crosscut backsaw

Jack plane

Drill

Pin-marking jig (optional)

Dividers (optional)

Sliding bevel or dovetail template

Dovetail saw

Router, with small- to medium-size straight flute cutter (¼–⅜ in./6–10 mm) (optional)

Workshop-made waste-routing jig

Wide chisel and narrow chisel

Coping or fretsaw

CUTTING A THROUGH DOVETAIL WITH ROUTER ASSISTANCE

You can use a commercial dovetailing jig for routing dovetails, but the dovetails from most jigs appear rather bland. Often the pins and tails are the same width, and it is impossible to achieve the very fine pins that can look so elegant in a set of tails. An alternative is to use a router to remove the waste between the pins. The gap between the tails is usually too small for a router bit, but using a router to clear the waste between the pins can save a lot of time, especially if you are dovetailing a set of drawers. In this way, the quality of the joint is still dependent on your skill in cutting, but a lot of the groundwork has been removed. To hold the work while routing, use a workshop-made jig.

Making the jig

The base of the jig can be made in ¾ in. (18 mm) MDF or plywood. A jig about 18 in. (450 mm) wide should be adequate for most work.

1 Accurately dimension two pieces to 18 x 12 in. (450 x 300 mm).

2 Joint them at 90° along the long edge, by biscuiting or dominoing and gluing, or just glue and screw. The corner must be precisely 90° and the surfaces level.

3 Screw and glue a 10 x 18 in. (250 x 450 mm) backpiece of ¾ in. (18 mm) plywood or MDF to the back edge of the base pieces. Countersink the screws below the surface.

4 The 2 in. (50 mm) gap between the backpiece and the front of the jig is for a sacrifice piece that will get damaged in use. Dimension an 18 x 2 in. (450 x 50 mm) piece (hardwood or softwood) to fit neatly into the gap. Screw it in place with countersunk screws in a line 1³⁄₁₆ in. (30 mm) back from the front edge, making sure that it is level on both faces, top and front.

5 Glue a 16½ x 1¾ x 1¾ in. (450 x 45 x 45 mm) strengthening piece centrally into the 90° corner. Be careful to keep everything square.

CONTINUED ▶

6 Make a hardwood crossbar about 18 x 2 x 2 in. (450 x 50 x 50 mm). Plane a very slight convex curve (about ¹⁄₃₂ in./1 mm) along its length on one face.

7 Drill ⅜ in. (9 mm) holes 1 in. (25 mm) from either end.

8 Offer the crossbar up to the jig about 1⁷⁄₁₆ in. (36 mm) below the top edge and mark the position of the holes on the face.

9 Drill into the jig for M8 coach bolts at the marked positions.

10 Fit 100 mm M8 coach bolts in the holes, with the heads at the back. Tap the heads home so the bolts are secured.

11 Thread the clamping bar over the protruding bolts, with the curved face inward, and secure with washer and wing nuts (for a more professional look and a better grip, use M8 female locking levers).

12 Screw a holding piece about 15¾ x 1¾ x 2 in. (400 x 45 x 50 mm) toward the back of the baseplate.

13 The holding piece is used to clamp the jig in the vise.

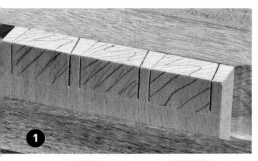

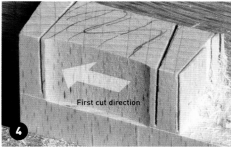
First cut direction

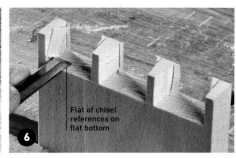
Flat of chisel references on flat bottom

Test cut

Uncut areas to be pared away.

Clinic

Notches in the pins You've come a bit too close to the pin — sometimes the router can jump. This problem can be lessened by working counterclockwise around the waste in the center of the socket, and taking thin cuts with each pass.

When is handmade not handmade?

The term "handmade" is terribly misused today — so much furniture advertised as handmade is evidently not so. As you become more familiar with woodworking methods, you will easily spot the difference. But where should you draw the line between machine and handmade?

I would suggest that it is the critical cuts that make something handmade — the marking and cutting of those faces that are key to the appearance and structure of the piece. For instance, in a dovetail joint, it's your hand-to-eye coordination when marking and sawing the tails and pins that defines their appearance and integrity. The removal of waste with the router is irrelevant. If the router and jig were used to actually define the lines of the tails and pin, then the joint is not handmade.

Routing the waste between pins

1 Cut the dovetails, mark the pins and saw them as before (see pages 154–57).

2 Place the piece in the jig, with the ends of the pins level with the top, and tighten the pressure bar.

3 Fit a small, straight flute cutter (¼–⅜ in./ 6–10 mm) in the router. With the router on the top of the jig, set the depth stop so that the cut will be level with the gauge line. You could use a test piece to check the depth setting before doing the real thing, or take a small cut to test depth.

4 Remove the waste with the router. Routing end grain is easier than side grain, so the cut can normally be done at full depth. Start by taking a very light reverse cut in the socket area. This helps to avoid breakout at the bottom.

5 Then work freehand to remove the socket waste — nibble rather than chomp! Work shy of the saw cut, being careful not to cut into the pin. You will cut into the front of the jig — this doesn't matter, because that's what the sacrifice piece is there for.

6 You should be left with the sockets clear, except for pieces of waste at the edges. Remove the piece from the jig and pare these away, using the flat from the routing as a reference for the chisel.

7 The fitting of the joint is the same as before (see page 158).

CUTTING A LAPPED DOVETAIL BY HAND

Lapped dovetails are commonly used on drawer fronts or any piece where you don't want the ends of the pins exposed. The method for cutting the tails is the same as for through dovetails, but it's more tricky cutting the pins because you cannot cut right through to the back.

Tools needed

Marking knife or scalpel

Shooting board

Cutting gauge

Pin-marking jig (optional)

Dividers

Sliding bevel or dovetail template

Dovetail saw

Crosscut backsaw

Clamp

Wide chisel and narrow chisel

Mallet

6 mm right- and left-skewed chisels (optional)

Selection of chisels

Small combination square

Coping or fretsaw

Waste-routing jig (optional)

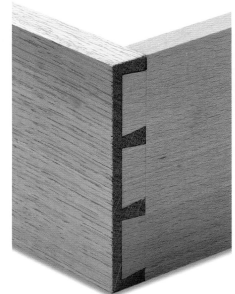

FINISHED LAPPED DOVETAIL JOINT

Shooting the end

1

With a cutting gauge, mark the length of the tails on both sides of the tail piece

Mark the end of the pin piece.

2

TAILPIECE

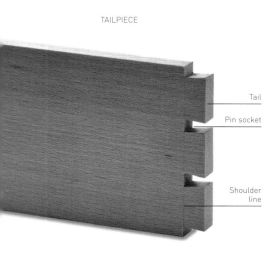

Tail

Pin socket

Shoulder line

PIN PIECE

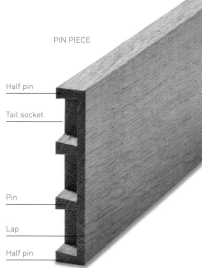

Half pin

Tail socket

Pin

Lap

Half pin

MAKING THE JOINT

1 Prepare the parts with face side and face edge, and square the ends on a shooting board. In this demonstration, the pin piece is ⅝ in. (16 mm) thick and 4 in. (100 mm) wide, with a tailpiece ⅜ in. (10 mm) thick and 4 in. (100 mm) wide. You will cut the joint with the face sides inward and the face edges aligned.

2 Start by marking the length of the tails. This is usually about three-quarters of the pin piece thickness, so the tail length will be ½ in. (12 mm). Set the cutting gauge,

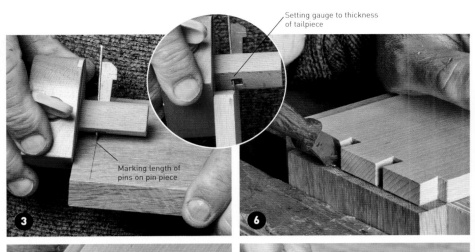

Setting gauge to thickness of tailpiece

Marking length of pins on pin piece

3

Shoulder aligns with back of pin piece.

5

End aligns with gauge line on pin piece.

6

Mark the waste.

7

End cut at the corners on top and bottom gauge lines

8

Taking relieving cuts to aid waste removal

Tip: Very fine pins are an indicator of a quality drawer. However, be careful not to make them so narrow that your thinnest chisel will not fit in the bottom of the pin socket.

Tip: With the saw cuts in the waste, it can be easy to lose track of what is waste and what isn't. Before chopping the waste, mark the pins clearly so that you don't accidentally chop them away.

then mark the end of the pin piece (stock on face side) and also both faces of the end of the tailpiece.

3 Reset the gauge to the thickness of the tailpiece and mark this on the face side of the pin piece.

4 Mark out and cut the tails (see Steps 4–16 of "Cutting a through dovetail," pages 154–56).

5 To mark the pins, fit the pin piece in the pin-marking jig, with the face side against

the jig, and lay the tailpiece in position face-edge side down, with the end of the piece aligned with the gauge line. This should leave the shoulders lined up with the inner edge of the pin piece.

6 Mark the pin positions with a knife.

7 Square the pin positions down the face side and mark the waste area.

8 Place the pin piece low in the vise, but with enough clearance for the angled saw.

Starting the cut on the front corner, cut down on the waste side of the line, with the saw angled so that the cut ends on the top-back and bottom-front corners. Repeat for all the pins. If you are chiseling out the waste, make some additional cuts to break up the waste a little to aid later chiseling.

CONTINUED ▶

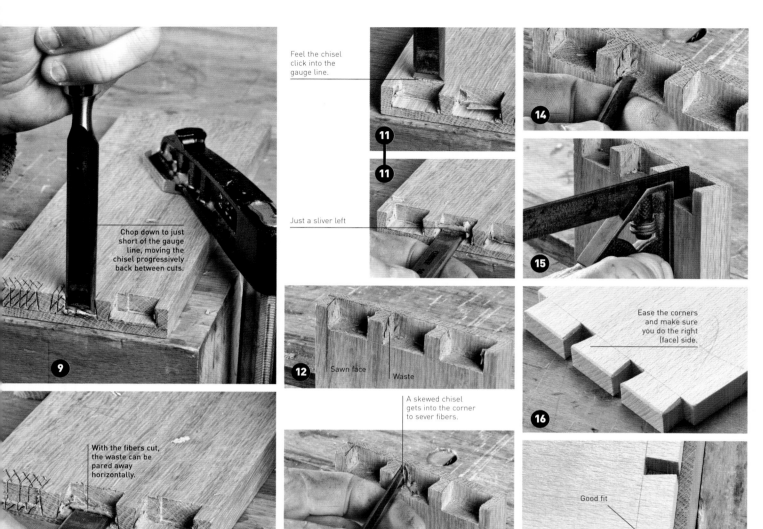

Feel the chisel click into the gauge line.

Chop down to just short of the gauge line, moving the chisel progressively back between cuts.

9

11

11

Just a sliver left

14

15

With the fibers cut, the waste can be pared away horizontally.

10

Sawn face Waste

12

A skewed chisel gets into the corner to sever fibers.

13

Ease the corners and make sure you do the right (face) side.

16

Good fit

17

9 Clamp the piece on the bench and start chopping out the waste with a chisel and mallet. Start about ¹⁄₁₆ in. (2 mm) back from the edge and chop down to just short of the gauge line. Repeat, moving back ¹⁄₁₆ in. (2 mm) or so each time. You may have to do it in stages for greater depths.

10 After a few chops, change to pare out the waste horizontally. By alternating between the two, you should be able to remove most of the waste. The idea is to sever the fibers by chopping down, then lever away the severed waste with the horizontal paring.

11 Work back to the gauged lines until you have just a sliver to remove, then click the chisel into the line and chop or pare away.

12 Clamp the piece low in the vise for final cleaning up. There will be some waste in the corners — you should be able to see the saw cuts, then some waste standing proud.

13 Level the waste to the saw cuts.

14 Use the skewed chisels to pare the bottom of the sockets into the corner. For the hand dovetailing enthusiast, special fishtail chisels are available for this job; otherwise, you can grind chisels to a skewed angle.

15 Use the combination square to check that the shoulder is square with the face, and also that the back of the socket is square to the socket shoulder.

16 The inside corners of the tails and also the inside top corner can be eased a little, as before (see Step 9, page 158). As the inside end of the tails will not be seen, the easing can go around the end of the tails.

17 Try the fit.

Clinic

Lapped dovetail problems and cures are similar to through dovetails, but there may be an additional problem:

The back of the socket is not square with the shoulder In this case, a gap appears at the back of the joint as it is pushed home. This is because the tails are pushed away by the slope of the back. Check the back using the combination square to make sure it's square and pare it if not.

Note how gaps appear at the ends of tails as they are lightly tapped home.

Very slight cutter marks show alignment.

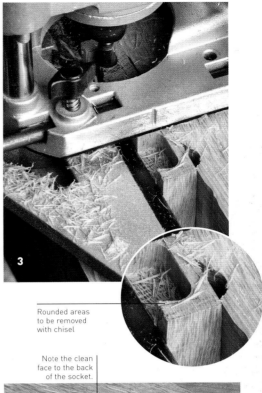

Rounded areas to be removed with chisel

Note the clean face to the back of the socket.

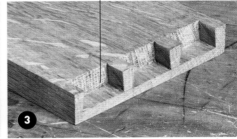

Try this!

> On dark wood, such as walnut, it can be difficult to see markings, either knife or pencil. Sticking white tape on the face overcomes this. Veneer tape is especially good for this.

Tools needed

See "Cutting a through dovetail with router assistance," page 159.

CUTTING LAPPED DOVETAILS WITH ROUTER ASSISTANCE

The procedure is much the same as for through dovetails with router assistance (see page 159).

1 Fit a fence to the router and set it so that the cutter aligns with the gauge line for the back of the socket.

2 Check the setting of the fence on a test piece of the same thickness or by taking a very slight cut to check alignment. Using the fence allows the router to cut a straight back line.

3 Take the cut as before with chisels. The corners of the sockets will need cleaning up with skewed chisels, etc.

Miter joint

The miter joint is commonly found on frames of various types and also on edging, molding and lipping. Here, the miter is sawn across the width of the pieces — I call this a frame miter. A miter is also used for making boxes, where the miter is across the thickness of the pieces — I'll call this a box miter. A miter consists of two pieces meeting at a corner, cut at an angle that bisects the angle of the corner. A wide miter joint has little strength in itself — unless you use a mitered half lap — and so needs additional reinforcement with joints such as a spline, biscuit or domino.

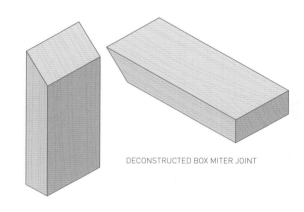

DECONSTRUCTED BOX MITER JOINT

Tools needed

Miter square or
  combination square

Marking knife

Engineer's square

Tenon or carcass saw

Miter shooting board

Jack plane

Block plane

Straight plunge cutter

Router and router table,
  if only using loose splines

It is almost impossible to cut an adequate miter joint freehand. A saw cut is not accurate or clean enough, and planing the cut is difficult as you are balancing a plane on a narrow surface. Miter trimmers are available for precise miter cutting. These use a guillotining action to trim the angle, being either hand- or foot-operated. If you have an accurate chop or compound miter saw, you could use this. Without a miter trimmer or chop saw, the solution is to use specialized shooting boards. The following demonstrations show cutting a frame miter and then a box miter. In these examples, I've used a workshop-made miter shooting board.

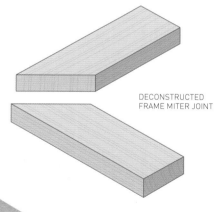

DECONSTRUCTED
FRAME MITER JOINT

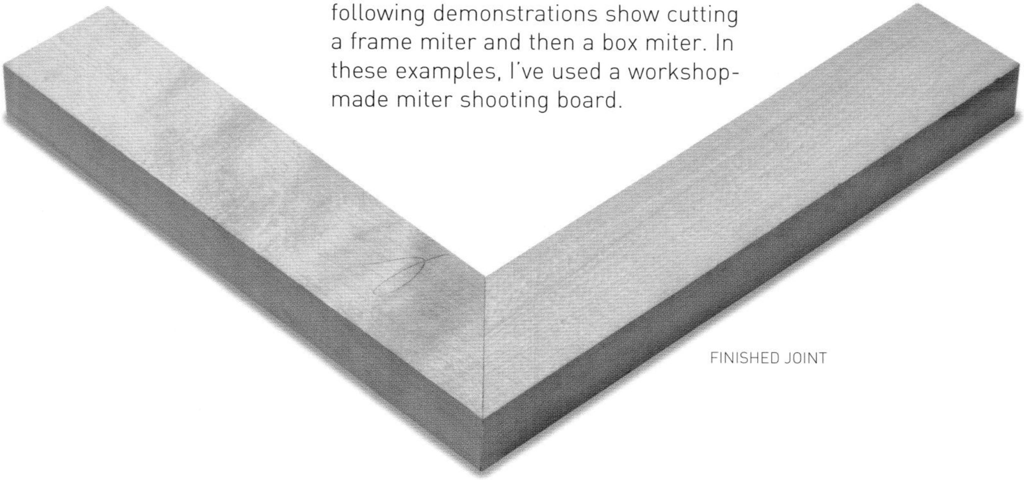

FINISHED JOINT

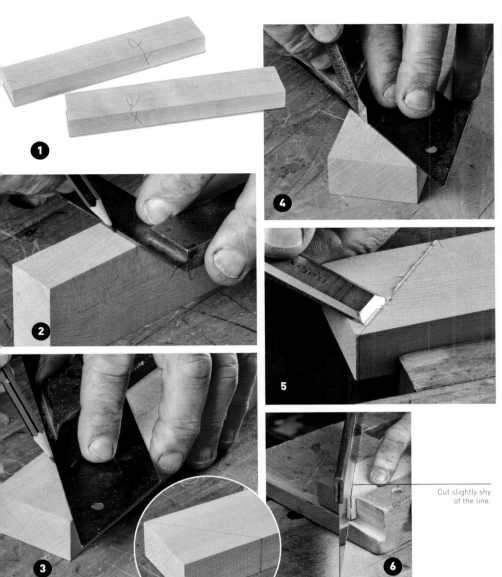

> ## Try this!

> The miters can be cut in a miter sawing box. Miter sawing boxes can be purchased or made in the workshop.

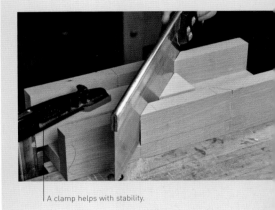

A clamp helps with stability.

Cut slightly shy of the line.

CUTTING A FRAME MITER BY HAND

1 Prepare the pieces with face side and face edge. The face edges should normally be on the inside, and the face sides all oriented the same way. In this example, the pieces are 3 x $^{15}/_{16}$ in. (75 x 23 mm).

2 Mark up the position of the miters on the inside edges.

3 Use the miter or combination square to mark the miter across the face. Then square down the sides to mark the miter on the other face — your lines should meet. Mark the waste side of the line.

4 If you are freehand sawing, mark the line of the miter with a marking knife and suitable square.

5 Chamfer to the line, as with a normal saw cut.

6 Be sure to cut on the waste side of the line, possibly a little shy of the line. You are not aiming for a perfect joint yet — this will come from the shooting board.

7 The miter shooting board is used to plane the mitered ends true. The board can either be made specially dedicated to miter shooting or can be adapted from your normal shooting board (see "Making a miter shooting board," page 169). Place the piece on the board with the edge butted to the miter block, and run the plane along the board in a similar manner to using an ordinary shooting board.

CONTINUED ▶

8 If you are using a shooting board with a central block, and if that block is square, you will get a more accurate miter if you shoot one face in one direction and one in the other.

9 The easiest way to check if the miter is correct is to place the two pieces together and check for 90°, rather than checking individually for 45°.

10 It's also worth checking that the faces are square across the miter.

11 Miters are usually cut as a set — in a frame, for instance. The real test is whether the whole frame assembly fits together with no gaps in the miters — discrepancies can multiply over four corners.

12 Slight errors may be corrected freehand, using a block plane. Otherwise, re-plane selected miters on the miter board, paying special attention to technique.

13 In most situations, the miter will need strengthening in some way. The simplest method is to biscuit the joint (see pages 180–84). Test the size of the biscuit slot in a piece of scrap wood first to check that the miter is long enough for it.

Shooting the second face in the other direction

Marking the two miters together

Check that the miter face is level with the packing piece.

Routing for a loose spline to strengthen the miter joint

If you don't biscuit the joint, an alternative way of strengthening a miter joint is to add a loose spline. A groove is routed in the miter faces to receive the spline.

1 Mark up the miter surfaces for the length of the spline groove; a ¼ in. (6 mm) deep groove must stop at least ½ in. (13 mm) short of the outside end to avoid cutting though the edge. The inside end is not so critical — mark this at about ³⁄₁₆ in. (5 mm).

2 Choose a straight plunge cutter about one-third of the thickness of the pieces. It can be useful to use a cutter to match the thickness of the plywood or MDF you have available — this will be used for the splines.

3 Place the miter piece face side out in the vise, with a level, long packing piece to the front. Make sure that there is no gap between the workpiece and the packing. Set the router fence so that the cutter is central to the workpiece. Set the depth stop to ¼ in. (6 mm).

4 Rout the groove in the end, being careful

not to overshoot on the outside; otherwise you may cut through the edge.

5 Repeat this for both pieces. Make sure that you orient the pieces so that the face side is always facing the fence; otherwise you may have misaligned joints.

6 Make some splines ⁷⁄₁₆ in. (11 mm) wide and a suitable length and thickness. If they are solid wood, the grain should run across the width.

7 Assemble the joints with the splines in place and recheck the fit.

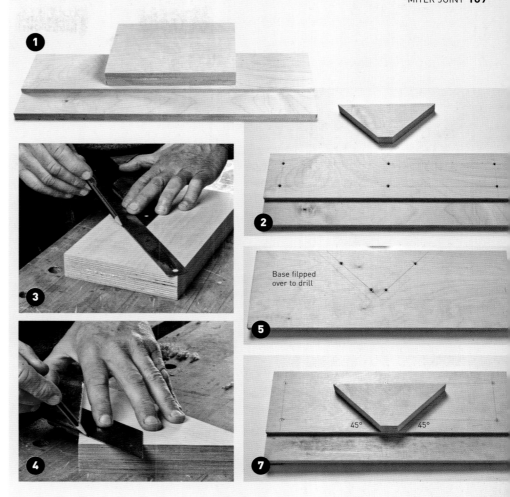

Base filpped over to drill

45°   45°

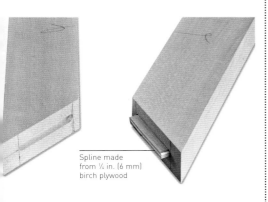

Spline made from ¼ in. (6 mm) birch plywood

> Try this!

> Gluing up can be a problem with miters, because the glue tends to lubricate the joints so that they slide around. See "Clamping miters," page 78, for advice on how to resolve this.

MAKING A MITER SHOOTING BOARD

A miter shooting board is similar to an ordinary shooting board, except that it doesn't have an end stock. There is a triangular stock in the center instead.

1 Prepare the base approximately 25⁹⁄₁₆ x 8⁷⁄₁₆ x ¾ in. (650 x 215 x 18 mm) in plywood or MDF (birch plywood is preferable). Fit a second piece about 26 x 5½ x ⅜ in. (650 x 140 x 9 mm) to the base to form a rabbet about 3 in. (75 mm) wide.

2 Screw the base and the second piece together, leaving the 3 in. (75 mm) rabbet.

3 Cut a right-angled triangle from fairly thick plwood, with adjacent sides 8 x 8 in. (200 x 200 mm). The accuracy of the

right angle is critical, so plane it carefully. 1 in. (25 mm) plywood would be good for this piece, or you could laminate some thinner stuff.

4 Trim 1⁹⁄₁₆ in. (40 mm) from the triangle tip.

5 From the underside, drill and countersink four ³⁄₁₆ in. (4 mm) clearance holes in the base piece to allow screws up into the triangle.

6 Clamp the triangle in place in the center of the shooting board, with the trimmed point in line with the edge of the rabbet. Use a miter or combination square to check that both edges of the triangle are at 45° to the edge of the rabbet.

7 When it is accurately fitted, drill ¹⁄₁₆ in. (2 mm) pilot holes through the clearance holes into the base. Glue and screw in place, checking for 45°.

Checking end for 45°

Checking rail for 45°

Sawing the top and bottom rails apart

Block in vise acts as stop

MAKING A BOX MITER SHOOTING BOARD

To form long miters by hand, such as would be used in box construction, you need a long miter shooting board. This differs from an ordinary shooting board (see pages 48–49) inasmuch as the plane is held at 45° to the cut, running on a ramp that engages with the plane at each edge. It is important that the shooting board is accurate, because you can't cut accurate joints on an inaccurate board! The board we are making will accommodate a miter approximately 13 in. (330 mm) long, and is designed for a plane with a 2⅜ in. (60 mm) blade. For a plane with a 2 in. (50 mm) blade, the endpieces should be reduced in width to 1¾ in. (44 mm).

1 Prepare a 15¾ x 15¾ in. (400 x 400 mm) baseboard from ¾ in. or ⅝ in. (18 mm or 15 mm) birch plywood. Also cut out the secondary board from ½ in. (12 mm) birch plywood to 13⅛ x 14 ¾ in. (333 x 375 mm). Make sure that the edges are square.

2 Plane a 45° angle on one of the narrow edges of the secondary piece, making sure it remains square to the long edges. Then plane a ³⁄₁₆ in. (4 mm) flat on the sharp edge.

3 The endpieces are 1³⁄₁₆ x 2 in. (30 x 50 mm) hardwood — I used beech. In the original, the endpieces did not extend to the end of the baseboard. It would be tidier if they did. Prepare a piece at least 27⁹⁄₁₆ in. (700 mm) long. At 14¾ in. (375 mm), mark a 45° line across the width with a miter square (the point of the angle being at 14¾ in./375 mm).

4 Saw the miter and trim both pieces on a miter shooting board. Use a miter square to check that the miter is correct.

5 Prepare the wood for the top and bottom rails as one piece. This is 16⁹⁄₁₆ x 2¾ x 1 in. (420 x 70 x 25 mm). Mark a 45° degree line on the end, ¾ in. (20 mm) from one edge. Now set a marking gauge to extend the line down either side. Saw lengthwise down this miter, following the gauged lines to give two angled rails. You may have to turn the piece halfway down.

6 The long sawn cut will be pretty rough. Plane it straight and smooth, checking regularly that you are maintaining the 45° angle. Butting the piece up to a block clamped in the vise helps with holding the awkward shape.

Shooting flat on end of endpiece

The flats on the end and bottom rail will fit together like this.

Bottom rail

Top rail

End rail

Checking bottom rail square with end

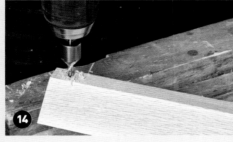

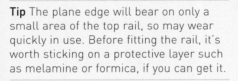

Tip The plane edge will bear on only a small area of the top rail, so may wear quickly in use. Before fitting the rail, it's worth sticking on a protective layer such as melamine or formica, if you can get it.

Must be flat along here

7 Trim both rails to 15¾ in. (400 mm).

8 Plane a ³⁄₁₆ in. (4 mm) flat on the mitered edge of the rails.

9 Also trim a ³⁄₁₆ in. (4 mm) flat on the ends of the endpieces.

10 Do a final check that all your angles are accurate before assembly.

11 Mark lines ⅝ in. (15 mm) from both long edges of the baseboard and ¾ in. (20 mm) from one of the short edges, then drill and countersink ³⁄₁₆ in. (4 mm) diameter holes at the positions shown in the photograph.

12 Clamp the bottom rail in position on the short edge of the baseboard, drill ⅛ in. (2.5 mm) pilot holes and screw in the rail.

13 Clamp the endpieces in position. The angle between the bottom rail and the endpiece miter should be 90°. If it's not, investigate what is wrong. The pieces may need trimming to length. Pilot drill and screw the endpieces in position.

14 On the top rail, drill and countersink ³⁄₁₆ in. (4 mm) screw holes at ⅜ in. (10 mm) back from the miter and ⅝ in. (15 mm) from the end.

15 Position the top rail on the end rails and check that the angle of the rail is continuous with the miter on the endpieces; adjust if necessary.

16 When everything is satisfactory, clamp the rail in place and pilot drill and screw it in place.

17 Drill and countersink ³⁄₁₆ in. (4 mm) screw holes in the secondary board, as illustrated, and position it between the endpieces. Check the alignment of the angle on the board — it should form a continuous face with the endpieces and be in line with the angle on the top rail. Pilot drill and screw it in place.

18 Finally, to aid stability in use, you could screw a batten on the underside at one end, depending on whether you are right- or left-handed. When in use, this would butt up to the edge of the bench.

Tools needed

Marking knife

Miter square and engineer's square or combination square

Tenon or carcass saw

Specialized long miter shooting board

Jack plane

Block plane

Bevel-edged or paring chisel

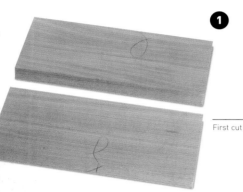

First cut

Turn the piece in the vise for second cut.

Tip: One problem with sawing the miter in the vise is damaging the bench top with the saw — a thin piece of plywood or MDF on the bench will help to protect it.

The ends roughly sawn shy of the line

The end planed to the line

CUTTING A BOX MITER BY HAND

1 Prepare the pieces — the face side and face edge should be on the inside and top edge. In this example, the pieces are 4 x $^{15}/_{16}$ in. (100 x 23 mm).

2 Mark the position of the miters with a knife and a square across the face side.

3 Mark the position of the miters across the edges with a miter or combination square.

4 The miter is likely to be too high to cut in a miter sawing box, so it will need to be done freehand — sawing either vertically in the vise from both sides or horizontally using a bench hook. You don't need to worry too much about accuracy — just stay on the waste side of the line.

5 Put the pieces on the long miter shooting board, and plane the miter until you have a clean face on the marked line.

6 Place the joints together and check the fit. Some can be "tweaked" carefully with a block plane to adjust the fit. Otherwise, return to the shooting board. If the problem remains, it may be worth checking your shooting board for accuracy.

7 The miter will need reinforcing in some way. If the components are quite thick, this could be done with biscuits, dominoes, a loose spline or veneer keys (see next page).

ADDING VENEER "KEYS" FOR STRENGTH

Adding veneer "keys" to a miter joint helps reinforce the joint and also provides a decorative element. For this you need a saw that cuts a kerf of the same thickness as the veneer available. A dovetail saw usually gives a kerf about the same as standard veneer (1/32 in./0.06 mm). If your saws are too wide, you could cut your own thicker keys. If too narrow, try sanding the veneer.

Fitting the keys

1 Glue up the assembly using the method suggested for box miters (see pages 248–57). If it's quite tall, you may need two ratchet clamps or to use wide miter clamping blocks.

2 When the assembly has fully cured, remove it from the clamps and mark a pencil line less than the thickness of the parts from the corner on each face (e.g., if the side thickness was 1/2 in./12 mm, you may mark a line 7/16 in./11 mm either side of the corner). This indicates the sawing depth.

3 Mark the positions for the keys and square to the previously marked lines — this is a matter of judgment. In this example, the outer ones are about 3/8 in. (10 mm) from top and bottom, and at about 1 in. (25 mm) intervals. The lines can either be square or you could angle them to give a dovetail effect, which I have done here.

4 Place the joint sideways in the vise with the corner uppermost. With the chosen saw, saw down the lines to the depth line.

Try to keep the cut straight so that the bottom is flat for the splines to fit to.

5 Prepare the veneer keys oversized — they will be inserted with the grain running across the corner.

6 Check the fit and adjust if necessary. There can sometimes be a high spot in the middle of the saw cut, which stops the splines from sitting down into the kerf. Cut a slight concave curve in the edge to allow for this.

7 Work glue into the saw kerfs and insert the keys.

8 When the glue has set, trim off the excess veneer with a sharp chisel. Pare it away, working from the outside inward, then sand smooth.

Dowel joint

Dowel jointing is the strengthening of a simple butt joint, using dowels that locate in holes in either piece. A persistent problem with dowel joints is the need for absolute accuracy in locating and drilling vertically. The biscuit and domino jointer provide a technical response to these problems, which means that the dowel joint is falling out of use in the home workshop. However, if you prefer not to use a jointer, various doweling jigs and aids are available. Here are a couple of low-cost options.

Tools needed

Miter square or combination square

Tenon or carcass saw

Jack plane

Miter shooting board

Vise

Awl

Depth stop accessory or masking tape

Drill

Spur point bit

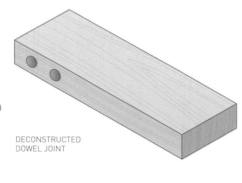

DECONSTRUCTED
DOWEL JOINT

USING DOWEL POINTS

Dowel points are metal dowels that can be inserted into previously drilled dowel holes. A point on the end of the dowel is used to mark the location to drill the matching dowel holes. In this example, we will form a corner joint in pieces 3⅛ in. (80 mm) wide by ¹⁵/₁₆ in. (23 mm) thick, then a central "T" joint. On one piece, the dowels will be inserted into the end of the piece (the endpiece); on the other, the dowel holes will be on the face side (the facepiece).

Corner dowel joint

1 Prepare the pieces with face side and face edge — when jointed, the faces should be adjacent. On the endpiece, the end must be flat and true, so it's worth shooting it on the shooting board.

2 Place the endpiece in the vise and use an awl to mark the dowel positions in the end, ⅝ in. (15 mm) from either edge and central in thickness.

3 Select a spur point bit to match the dowel diameter you are using. Set the drilling depth. This is calculated depending on the length of the dowels and the thickness of the pieces. See calculation in the panel, right, as a good rule of thumb.

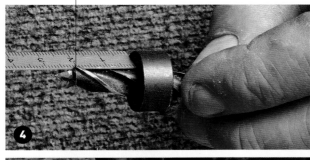

Measure to the end of the drill flute, not the tip of the spur.

Don't press down until you are sure the piece is aligned correctly.

Marks left by pins

Scrap wood

Butt the square up to the faces. Check that the face edges are aligned.

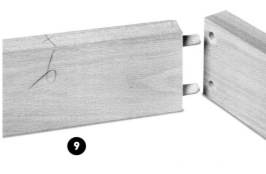

4 To set the depth, you can use a depth stop accessory or wrap masking tape around the drill bit. Measure to the end of the drill flute, not the end of the central spur.

5 Drill for dowels at the marked locations — the spur on the drill should locate in the points marked by the awl. Concentrate on drilling square with the end.

6 Insert dowel points into the holes.

7 On the bench top, butt the facepiece up to a piece of scrap wood to act as a stop. Then invert the endpiece and position it against the stop, with the face edges aligned. Press down so that the points indent the face.

8 Adjust the drill stop to the new depth and drill in the marked locations.

9 Insert the dowels in the endpiece and try the joint together.

DRILLING DEPTH CALCULATION
For the endpiece
Dowel length + ¼ in. (6 mm) – thickness of facepiece
e.g., 1⁹⁄₁₆ in. (40 mm) + ¼ in. (6 mm) – ¹⁵⁄₁₆ in. (23 mm) = ¹⁵⁄₁₆ in. (23 mm)

For the facepiece
Facepiece thickness – ¼ in. (6 mm) = ¹¹⁄₁₆ in. (17 mm)

"T" DOWEL JOINT

Here, the same endpiece is used as described in the "Corner dowel joint" sequence (see pages 174–75), but it is located 6 in. (150 mm) in from the end of the facepiece.

1 Mark the endpiece position on the face with a pencil line; mark arrows on to show which side of the line the piece will sit.

2 Clamp a straight-edged piece of scrap wood onto the marked line. With the dowel points in position, locate the endpiece against the clamped piece and, with face edges aligned, press the piece down to mark the dowel locations.

3 Set the depth stop and drill at the marked points.

4 Test the joint for fit.

Straight edge piece aids location

2

3

Arrow shows that the endpiece sits this side of the line.

1

4

Clinic

Most difficulties with this method derive from inaccurate drilling. If the dowels are slightly misaligned, the joint will not go together or it will be twisted. Even if the holes are aligned correctly, if they are not square with the faces, the joint may still not fit properly.

Using a spur point bit helps with alignment, but in woods with a strong grain pattern, the drill can be deflected from its position. Using a drill press can help with alignment and also with drilling vertically.

Offset caused by inaccurate drilling

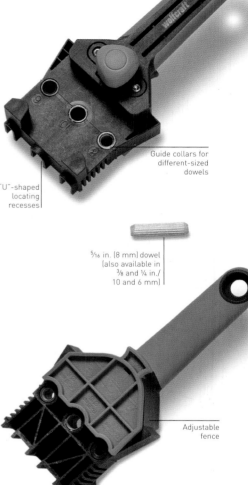

Guide collars for different-sized dowels

"U"-shaped locating recesses

⁵⁄₁₆ in. (8 mm) dowel (also available in ³⁄₈ and ¼ in./ 10 and 6 mm)

Adjustable fence

USING A DOWELING JIG

Using a doweling jig can overcome many of the problems with using dowel points. There are many different doweling jigs on the market, of varying quality and price. One such is the Wolfcraft Dowel Master jig, which is used in this demonstration.

The jig consists of a plastic housing pierced by three metal collars of ¼, ⁵⁄₁₆ and ³⁄₈ in. (6, 8 and 10 mm) diameter. When the jig is located, the collars guide the appropriate drill vertically. Fixed stops on one face of the jig help to locate the holes centrally on

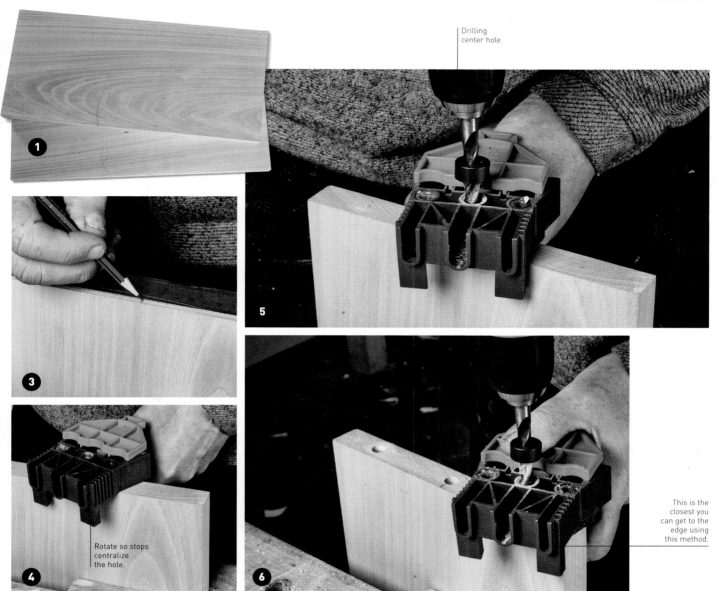

Drilling center hole

Rotate so stops centralize the hole.

This is the closest you can get to the edge using this method.

different thicknesses of board. On the other side is a sliding stop to aid positioning on the ends of the boards.

Here, the dowel master is used to create a corner and then a "T" joint, using 15/16 in. (23 mm) thick boards. For this thickness, the dowel master uses 3/8 in. (10 mm) diameter dowels.

Corner dowel joint

1 Prepare the pieces with face side and face edge; when jointed, the face sides should be on the inside and the face edges aligned. In this example, the pieces are 9 13/16 in. (250 mm) wide by 15/16 in. (23 mm) thick.

2 Set the drilling depth on a 3/8 in. (10 mm) spur point bit. The depth is calculated as for dowel points (see page 175), but you need to add 1 in. (25 mm) for the thickness of the jig — so the depth would be 1 7/8 in. (48 mm).

3 Make a center line 4 15/16 in. (125 mm) from the edge on the end of the endpiece.

4 Place the jig on the end, with the 3/8 in. (10 mm) hole over the center line, and turn it until the fixed stops bear against the sides of the board. This should centralize the dowel hole across the thickness.

5 Drill the dowel hole.

6 Move the jig until the fixed stop is just on the edge of the board, turn to centralize it and drill.

CONTINUED ▸

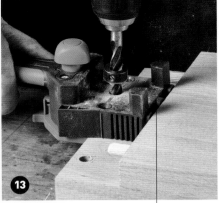

³/₈ in. (10 mm) dowel recess over central dowel

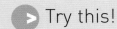

Try this!

> Using this method means that the closest the end dowels can come to the edge is 1⁹/₁₆ in. (40 mm) for ³/₈ in. (10 mm) dowels. In some circumstances (narrow pieces, for instance), it is useful to drill closer to the edge. This can be done by locating the jig on a dowel inserted in the center hole and moving the sliding stop up to the edge. The jig could then be moved closer to the edge, but still be central in the thickness.

Setting sliding stop to dowel position

7 Move the jig to the other end and repeat.

8 Fit dowels in the holes.

9 The holes can now be drilled in the facepiece. First, place the jig on one of the dowels in the endpiece and locate the sliding stop against the board face (see "Try this!" above).

10 Place the facepiece on the bench, with the face side uppermost. Then place the endpiece on top, face side down and with the face edges aligned.

11 Place the jig on the end of the facepiece, with the ³/₈ in. (10 mm) "U"-shaped locating recess over the central dowel. Move the endpiece back until the sliding stop can press against the end of the facepiece. Clamp the boards in place.

12 Set the drill depth stop to 1¼ in. (32 mm).

13 The three dowels in the endpiece determine the position of the holes in the facepiece. Place the jig on the end of the

facepiece, with the ³/₈ in. (10 mm) locating recess over one of the dowels and the sliding stop against the end. Drill the first hole, then repeat for the other two dowels.

14 The joint can now be assembled.

"T" dowel Joint

For the "T" joint, drill the endpiece as described in Steps 3–8 of "Corner dowel joint," pages 177–78.

1 Now place the facepiece, face side up, on the bench and mark the center line of the joint.

2 Mark another line 1⅝ in. (41 mm) from the center line (the manufacturer's instructions say 1⁹⁄₁₆ in. (40 mm), but I have found 1⅝ in. (41 mm) to be more accurate for my jig — it may be worth checking this on yours).

3 Clamp the endpiece on top, with the face edges aligned and the end on the 1⅝ in. (41 mm) mark.

4 Slacken the locking screw and remove the sliding stop.

5 Place the jig flat on the surface, with the end butted up to the end of the endpiece and the ⅜ in. (10 mm) locating recess over a dowel. Drill with the depth stop at 1¼ in. (32 mm).

6 Repeat for the other two dowels.

7 The joint can now be assembled.

Biscuit jointing

The biscuit jointer was developed mainly to aid jointing man-made boards in modern cabinetwork. It is also very useful for alignment when edge-jointing solid boards. When using the jointer for cabinetwork, setting out is very important because it is easy to end up with biscuit slots in the wrong place. While marking out, we will try to indicate simply but unambiguously how the parts are oriented.

Tools needed

Biscuit jointer

Clamp

Vise

Router

Jack or longer plane

Primary fence can rotate through to 90°.

Adjusting the primary fence

SETTING UP THE JOINTER

There are two main settings: the depth of cut and the fence position.

Depth of cut — this is usually determined by a turn knob, close to the base. There are a number of settings, but the three you are interested in are those for the commonly found biscuits — 0, 10 and 20. The 20 is the largest and is used for most cabinetwork, if the boards are thick enough, while the 10 is smaller and used for thinner boards. The zero is smallest and is useful for board alignment when edge-jointing and for very thin cabinetwork.

Fence setting — the jointer will have a hinged primary fence, plus an auxiliary fence that can slide onto the primary. If the primary is hinged down, the center of the biscuit slot should be ⅜ in. (10 mm) from the top surface. The auxiliary fence can be adjusted to give a center from zero up to about 2 in. (50 mm). Generally, you are aiming to biscuit the center of the board, but the primary fence is usually used for boards from ¾–⅞ in. (18–22 mm). In use, the fence rests on the "reference" surfaces — i.e., the surfaces you are trying to line up.

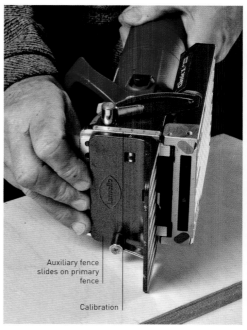

Auxiliary fence slides on primary fence

Calibration

Adjusting the auxiliary fence

Set the depth stop to the biscuit size.

Adjusting the depth of cut

Primary fence in down position parallel to slot cutter

0

10

20

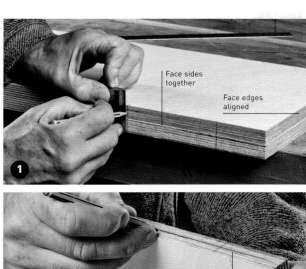

Face sides together

Face edges aligned

1

3

Line shows where biscuit slots should be cut, helping to avoid confusion later on.

Bottom piece

2

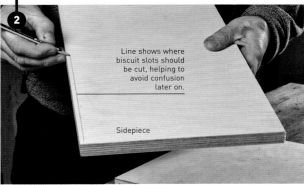

Line shows where biscuit slots should be cut, helping to avoid confusion later on.

Sidepiece

2

5

Note the overhang. If the piece doesn't overhang, there is a danger of the jointer resting on the bench surface and giving a false cut.

> ## Try this!

> Having the fence flat on the surface is critical. It helps to establish this if you give the jointer a slight shake before plunging. This helps you to feel the jointer "sit" on the corner. Then concentrate on keeping the forward pressure horizontal.

BISCUITING A CORNER JOINT

Let us imagine jointing a cabinet bottom into a sidepiece using ¾ in. (18 mm) thick pieces. Both pieces have been cut out and face side and face edge marked. The face edges will be at the back of the cabinet and the face sides on the inside.

1 Lay the pieces on the bench with the face edges together, the face sides facing each other and the ends to be jointed aligned. Mark the ends with the position of the biscuit centers, about 2⅜ in. (60 mm) from the edge and 8 in. (200 mm) apart.

2 The biscuit slots will be in the end of the bottom piece, but in the side of the sidepiece. To avoid confusion, it is worth marking this with a rough line. When cutting the biscuit slots, always check that you are cutting into one of these notation lines.

3 You may need to extend the biscuit center lines to the bottom face of the bottom board.

4 Set up the jointer, depending on the board thickness. Here, I've used the primary fence to give biscuits slightly off center.

5 Clamp the bottom board on the workbench, face side down, and offer up the jointer so that the fence is on the bottom face and the base is against the end. It is very important that the fence is quite flat on the reference surface when cutting the slot, so press down firmly on the fence. Switch on, align the indicator arrows on the jointer with the marked center, push the jointer body forward and then let it spring back. Use a fairly positive motion — don't snatch, but also don't dwell in the cut.

CONTINUED ▶

The fence will always sit on the surfaces that are to be lined up.

Packing piece provides additional support.

8

9

10

6 Repeat this for the other center marks.

7 Now for the sidepiece. Place it in the vise with the jointing face (face side) out.

8 Cutting the slots for the sidepieces is a little more tricky, because you have to balance the fence on the narrow end of the board. This can be made easier by clamping a backing piece level with the edge, thus extending the surface. You can now rest the fence on the end and joint into the side.

9 To fit the joint, insert appropriate biscuits into the slots in the end of the bottom piece.

10 Then offer them up to the sidepiece. There is a little lateral tolerance available to accommodate inaccurate markings.

Clinic

The bottom is not aligned with the bottom of the side
The fence has probably drifted off one or both of the reference surfaces when jointing, causing an offset. Measure the slot positions and you will probably find the culprit. Glue in a cut-down biscuit; when the glue is dry, flatten off with a block plane and then recut.

The joint will not close up
You're using the wrong size biscuit! Or you may not have plunged to the full depth.

Step here shows biscuit slots out of line.

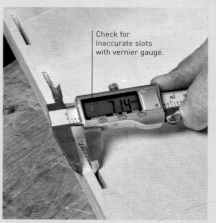

Check for inaccurate slots with vernier gauge.

Cut-down biscuits

Flattening inserted biscuits with block plane

Arrows indicate which side of the line the shelf will be — so which side to biscuit.

3 After marking biscuit location, indicate the bottom face with arrows.

4 Arrows on shelfpiece point at line on sidepiece.

5 Keep base flat on surface.

6

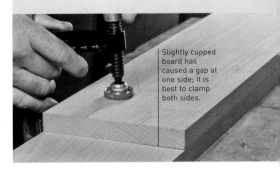

7 Location is usually easier with biscuits in the end than in the face.

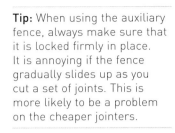
Tip: When using the auxiliary fence, always make sure that it is locked firmly in place. It is annoying if the fence gradually slides up as you cut a set of joints. This is more likely to be a problem on the cheaper jointers.

Clinic

The shelf does not sit on the marked line
It could be upside down!

Perhaps you did not align the end of the shelf correctly when clamping the pieces together for jointing.

Another possibility is that the shelf was not flat on the side. If you clamped on just one side, it may have raised up a little on the other side, causing misalignment. It's best to use clamps on both sides.

Slightly cupped board has caused a gap at one side; it is best to clamp both sides.

BISCUITING A SHELF

Parts can be jointed up to about 2 in. (50 mm) from an edge using the auxiliary fence. Here is a method for jointing a crosspiece where the fence cannot be used — a shelf onto a side, perhaps. This method uses the flat face of the jointer as a reference surface. This should give a biscuit slot with a center ⅜ in. (10 mm) from the reference.

1 Cut the pieces and mark the face side and face edge, as before.

2 On the sidepiece, mark with pencil and square the position of the shelf on the face. This is not the center line, but either the top or the bottom edge. Indicate with arrows on which side of the line the shelf will sit.

3 On the shelf, mark the ends with the biscuit positions, as before. It's worth marking them with arrows pointing to the bottom face; this aids orientation later on.

4 Lay the shelfpiece on the sidepiece, with the end aligned with the marked shelfline and the face edges aligned. Make sure that the arrows on the shelf ends are pointing appropriately, depending on whether you are aligning with the top or bottom of the shelf position. Imagine the shelf hinging on the line of the sidepiece. In this example, I marked the bottom of the shelf on both pieces. Clamp them firmly to the bench.

5 Place the jointer with the flat face on the sidepiece, so that you can joint into the end of the shelf. Aligning the arrows on the jointer with the marks on the shelf, cut slots at the marked positions.

6 Turn the jointer around so that it is standing vertically with the flat face against the shelf end, so that it joints into the side. There should be center lines on the end; align the jointer with these and joint down into the side (you may have to bring the lines around from the end onto the top face to enable alignment).

7 Assemble the joint — imagine the shelf hinging up into position on the marked line on the side.

Insert glue into biscuit slots.

You only need to glue one edge, but biscuit slots should be glued on both.

Clinic

Steps between boards There are two possible reasons for this — either the fence has drifted up from the surface when jointing, or the fence has slipped sometime in the process. Glue in a biscuit, trim off and recut.

BISCUITING AN EDGE JOINT

When gluing up edge-jointed boards for wide panels, the glue can act as a lubricant, and this makes it very difficult to get the joints flat. Using biscuits overcomes this problem. With modern glues, reinforcement is not really needed if the joint is perfect; the biscuits are simply for alignment.

1 Plane the edges to a good joint (see pages 150–52), lay the boards out on the bench and mark the biscuit positions across the boards at about 18 in. (450 mm) intervals, with the outer ones about 2⅜ in. (60 mm)

from the final edge. (Be careful about this if you will be cutting the board later — you don't want biscuits showing at the ends.)

2 Depending on the thickness of the board, set either the primary or auxiliary fence, so that the biscuit center is approximately in the center. Then set the depth. As edge joints have a good gluing surface, you don't need very large biscuits; zeros are good enough for alignment.

3 Cut slots in the marked positions. Take extra care to make sure that the fence is perfectly flat on the surface.

4 Insert the biscuits to test fit before gluing.

Gluing the joint

Do a test run before gluing the joint.

1 Apply adhesive in the biscuit slots. I use a special glue dispenser for this. This is available in a set from online retailers.

2 Apply adhesive to one edge.

3 Clamp up and check for level. If you used the correct amount of glue, there should be only a bead along the joint, not large drips and dribbles.

Tools needed
Domino jointer

Domino jointing

If you have used a biscuit jointer, you will recognize the shape and method of the domino jointer. The domino can be used in exactly the same manner as the biscuit jointer (see pages 180–84). However, there are a few features that make it more versatile and a stronger joint than the biscuit. The domino can be used in a wider range of furniture applications than the biscuit, especially as a substitute for mortise and tenon joints.

Adjustment for size of domino
Dominoes come in many different thicknesses and lengths. To change the thickness of the mortise for the dominoes, you need to change the cutter. To do this, release the body from the plunge mechanism, then unscrew the cutter using the spanner provided.

The depth of the mortise The depth can be changed using the small toggle on the side of the plunge mechanism. Because the domino jointer can cut deeper than the biscuit jointer, be more careful about checking the depth of cut to make sure that you do not go all the way through the piece.

The domino has a single fence that can be tilted; the hinge is locked using the lever on the left. The fence can also be moved vertically to adjust the distance of the domino from the top surface. The lever on the right unlocks it. There is a calibration on the left, but also a stepped sliding spacer that sets for the center of standard-sized boards.

The width of the mortise This can be adjusted using the turn knob on the top of the body. In the first position, the mortise is a snug fit widthwise. The two further positions create wider slots, which allow some leeway when assembling, as long as one pair of slots is kept standard for location.

Fence height calibration

Stepped sliding spacer

Hinge lock lever

Height lock lever

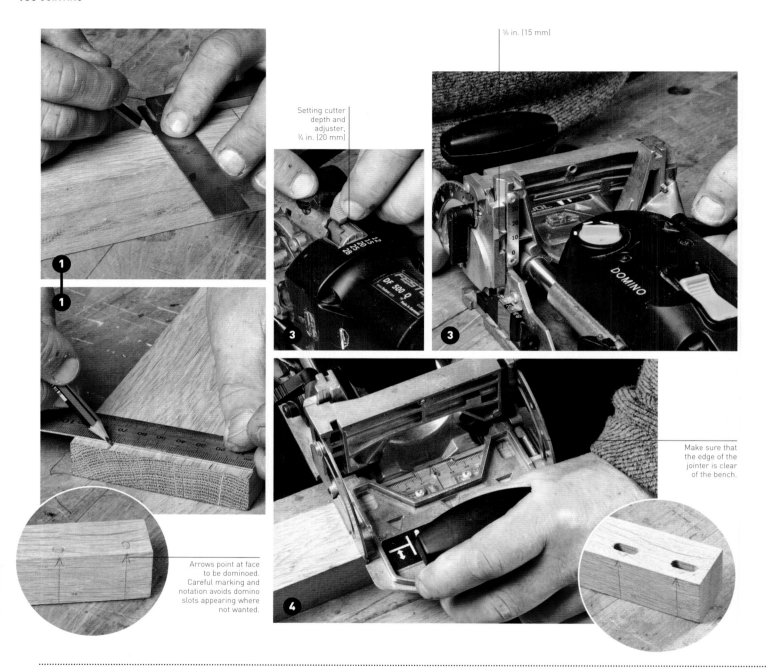

⅝ in. (15 mm)

Setting cutter depth and adjuster, ¾ in. (20 mm)

Make sure that the edge of the jointer is clear of the bench.

Arrows point at face to be dominoed. Careful marking and notation avoids domino slots appearing where not wanted.

JOINTING AN OFFSET RAIL

To illustrate what the domino jointer can do, we will joint an offset rail. Often you want a rail to be set back from the upright — a rail to a table leg, for instance. In this example, we will joint a 3⁹⁄₁₆ x ¾ in. (90 x 20 mm) rail into a 1¾ in. (45 mm) square-section leg with a ³⁄₁₆ in. (5 mm) setback, using ⁵⁄₁₆ x 1⁹⁄₁₆ in. (8 x 40 mm) dominoes.

1 Mark the domino positions on both the leg and the rail, ¾ x 2¾ in. (20 x 70 mm) from the top end. The lines on the leg should be on the adjacent face to where the mortise will be cut. Mark the face to be dominoed with arrows. The lines on the rail will be on the outside face.

2 Set up the jointer with a ⁵⁄₁₆ in. (8 mm) cutter set to a snug fit.

3 Set the fence to ⅝ in. (15 mm) and the depth of cut to ¾ in. (20 mm).

3/8 in. (10 mm)

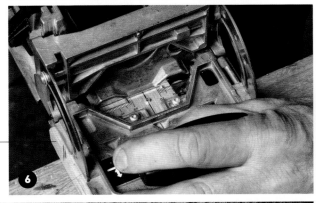

Overhang is important.

Dominoes in rail ends first

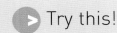

> Try this!

> Dominoes are a very snug fit into the standard slots — so snug, in fact, that they are difficult to remove after a dry run. It's useful to have a set of dominoes that have been thinned slightly for use in dry runs. You can create these by sanding or taking a couple of shavings with a block plane. Stain the dry-run dominoes with a bright color so that they don't get mixed up with the standard ones.

4 Now mortise into the leg at the marked positions. The action is very similar to biscuiting (see pages 181–84).

5 Lower the fence by the amount of the offset — 3/16 in. to 3/8 in. (5 mm to 10 mm).

6 Domino the ends of the rails.

7 Fit the dominoes into the end of the rail.

8 Assemble the joint.

THE ASSEMBLED JOINT

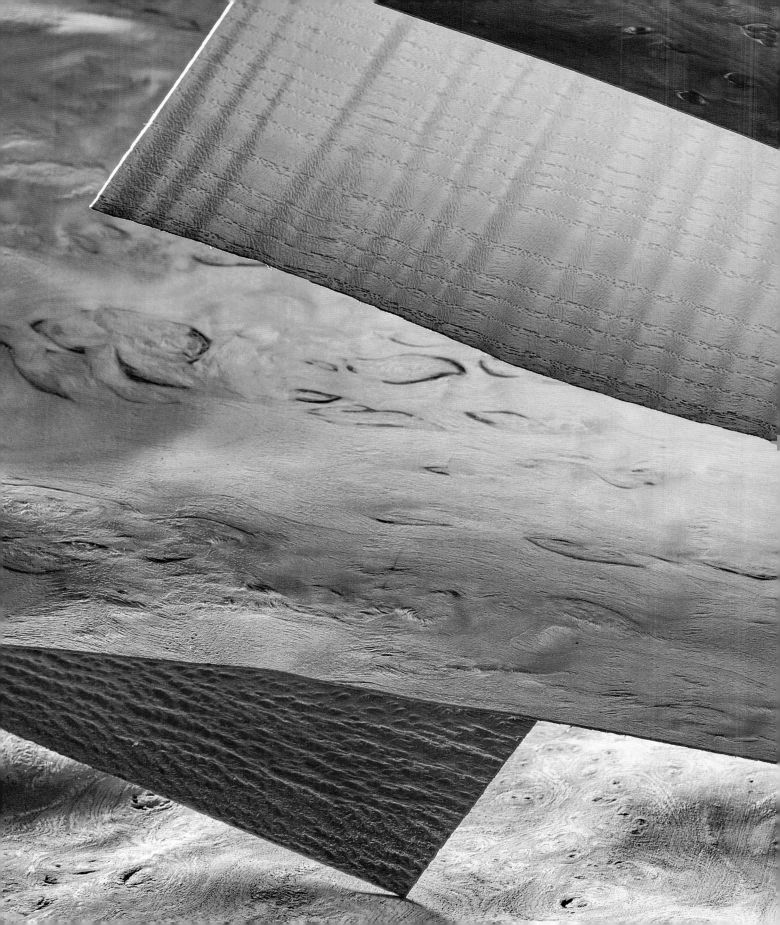

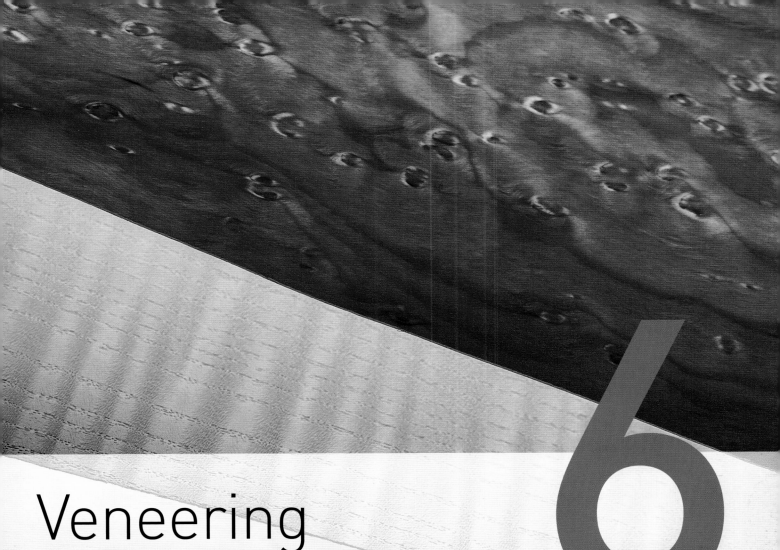

Veneering

In the 20th century, veneering acquired a bad name because it became associated with cheap, mass-produced furniture. However, veneering has a long and venerable history, and many designs by acclaimed furniture maker Thomas Chippendale depended on the technique. Veneers have a number of advantages for the woodworker. On a practical level, they make the most of a scarce resource and provide stability, because they can be bonded to man-made boards. Aesthetically, veneers are usually cut from logs with the most attractive figure, allowing you to achieve the decorative effect of an exotic species without the expense of using solid wood. They are also wonderful for pattern creation, because they can be cut and jointed to create striking symmetry.

Choosing veneers

Veneer is produced by slicing selected logs to a standard thickness, usually of 0.02 in. (0.6 mm). However, thicker veneer — known as constructional veneer — is also available, in thicknesses ranging from 0.06 in. to 3/16 in. (1.4 mm to 5 mm). These constructional veneers are usually used for laminating curved forms.

In the cutting process, the logs are either sliced across the grain or placed between rotating centers and rotary cut, rather like a huge lathe. The figure on sliced veneers will vary depending on the grain orientation. When cut at right angles to the annual rings, known as **quarter cut**, the figure is straight and regular; when cut obliquely to the annual rings, known as **crown cut**, it is more wavy and arched. Rotary-cut veneers are not usually decorative, except for certain

unusual figures such as bird's eye maple and masur birch. Rotary cutting is suited to producing very wide veneers useful for plywood production.

Burl veneer is specially sliced from the bulbous burls that grow on the side of the tree, while **crotch veneer** is from the meeting of trunk and branches at the crown. So both types are usually smaller than standard sliced veneers.

Veneer can be bought from specialized suppliers, although they are often

reluctant to deal in individual leaves. If you can, it's best to select your veneer in person, but most suppliers are fairly good at interpreting your needs if you cannot visit and need to order by phone. If you have problems sourcing small quantities, look at online sellers and marketplaces such as eBay.

Veneer is available as individual leaves, as half bundles (12 or 16 leaves) or as bundles (24 or 32 leaves). It is much more economical to buy veneer in half or whole

QUARTER-CUT VENEER

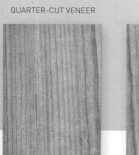

CROWN-CUT VENEER

BURL VENEER

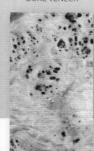

CROTCH VENEER

bundles, as the price per square foor (or meter) is much greater for individual leaves — often more than double.

Crown- and quarter-cut sliced veneers are fairly straightforward to source. Good-quality burl and crotch veneers can be more difficult to find — they will often have blemishes such as cracks and ingrown bark.

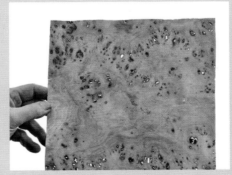

When selecting burl veneers, hold a leaf up to the light to see if it has any holes or cracks in it. Some holes are acceptable, but if it's too pockmarked, you will have a lot of work to do before applying a finish.

SELECTION OF VENEERS

Quarter-cut veneers

1 Ripple ash

2 Lebanon cedar

3 Brown oak

4 Sycamore

Burl veneers

5 American walnut burl

6 Elm burl

7 Vavona burl

8 European walnut burl

Crown-cut veneers

9 Pear

10 Birch

11 Oak

12 Olive ash

Preparing veneers

When working with solid wood, you need to prepare the wood prior to actually making anything, and this is also the case with veneer.

FLATTENING VENEERS

Some veneers, especially burl and crotch veneers, are prone to distortion. Often this is so bad that it is impossible to lay or work the veneer, and so it must be flattened before use. How does one know when a veneer needs flattening? If, when you press on a buckle, the veneer distorts locally, then it needs flattening. Alternatively, you can check in both directions with a 6 in. (150 mm) rule — if there are gaps under the rule greater than ⅛ in. (3 mm), it should be flattened.

There are a couple of different methods that you can use for flattening veneers. For a short-term method, you can simply wet the veneers and clamp them between boards, interlaced with newspaper to aid drying. Replace the paper at intervals of approximately four hours until dry. Using this method, the veneer will return to a buckled state over time, so it must be cut and laid before it starts to buckle again.

A more long-term method can be used to flatten any number of veneer leaves in a stack. Here, the veneers are sandwiched between sheets of paper, with a layer of porous plastic or fiberglass mesh to prevent the veneer from sticking to the paper. This mesh is the kind used by gardeners and can be easily obtained from garden centers.

Stir well, because the ingredients don't mix easily.

Apply liberally (this is brown oak burl).

If there are any gaps over ⅛ in. (3 mm), the burl needs to be flattened.

FLATTENING A STACK OF VENEER

1 Mix together two parts PVA glue, three parts water, one part glycerin and one part denatured alcohol.

2 Liberally apply this mixture onto both sides of each veneer leaf with a brush or roller, and allow any surplus to soak in or run off. Leave for approximately 10 minutes.

3 Lay a double sheet of newspaper or lining paper on an MDF or plywood board. Cover this with a layer of fiberglass matting or fine-mesh netting.

4 Lay a veneer leaf on the matting.

5 Repeat a layer of matting or net, then add more newspaper. Continue this sequence of paper/matting/veneer/matting/paper.

6 Repeat this for each leaf of veneer to be flattened, then finally complete with a second MDF board.

7 Clamp the boards with "C" or "F" clamps at about 6 in. (150 mm) intervals. For badly buckled boards, apply a moderate pressure to start with, progressively increasing it over a couple of hours. This prevents cracking from flattening too quickly. For only moderately buckled leaves, full pressure can be applied immediately.

8 For the first 24 hours, you'll need to replace the paper with dry (dry it out on a radiator) around three times. In the second 24 hours, the mesh can be discarded and the paper renewed a couple of times. Maintain pressure throughout.

9 At the end of the second day, the veneers should be flat and dry enough to use. If you use them too early, the moisture content will be too high and the veneer may move after laying.

CUTTING VENEERS

Veneer can be cut easily with a scalpel — I find that a Swan Morton 10a surgical scalpel cuts best. You can cut individual leaves or stack them up to cut all at once. If you want to cut cross-grain through a whole bundle, it is possible to saw them. Veneer saws are available for this, or you could also use a Japanese dozuki saw (see page 23).

CUTTING VENEER WITH A SCALPEL

1 To make a cut, place a metal straight edge on the line on the side you are keeping (worked piece) and press down hard with splayed fingers.

2 Position the scalpel at the start of the cut, with an angle between the blade and veneer of about 45° and slightly tilted away from the edge. The tilt compensates for the sharpening bevel of the blade, so the cut edge should be square. Draw the blade down the edge.

3 If you are cutting across the grain, there is a danger of pulling the grain away as you cut to the back edge. To avoid this, rock the blade down to sever the fibers vertically rather than across.

4 It may take more than one pass to cut through the veneer. Repeat the cut until you see the waste "spring" away from the cut. If you are cutting a stack of veneers, you will need many more passes. It is important to keep the straight edge in place until cutting is complete.

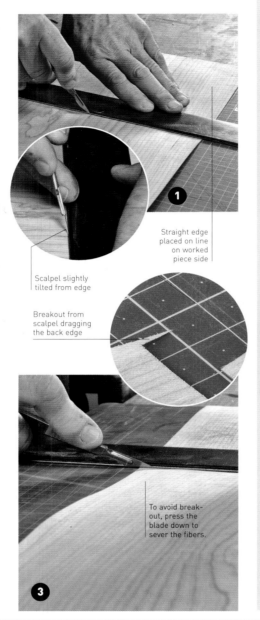

Straight edge placed on line on worked piece side

Scalpel slightly tilted from edge

Breakout from scalpel dragging the back edge

To avoid break-out, press the blade down to sever the fibers.

Clinic

Line of cut is not straight This can be one of two issues.

On coarse-grained woods, such as oak, the veneer can easily split along the grain in front of the cut when cutting with the grain. If the grain runs at an angle to the cut you are making, there is a tendency for the cut to follow the grain, giving an uneven edge. In this case, it is better to cut in the other direction, across the grain angle. This is a similar situation to planing with or against the grain.

Grain direction

Cutting in this direction may lead to an uneven cut.

Cutting this way will give a smoother cut.

Using a scalpel against a straight edge can be difficult, and the scalpel can sometimes drift away. Counter this by very slightly turning the blade toward the edge, so that the pressure of the cut pushes it into the edge. However, this method does not work on coarse-grained woods unless you observe the point above.

SAWING VENEER

1 Lift the leaves you want to cut and slip a batten of approximately 2 x 1 in. (50 x 25 mm) underneath. Clamp a similar batten on top, on the line you want to cut.

2 Now saw through the layers of leaves, using the batten to guide the saw. Take care to avoid breakout at the back edge.

Clamping a half bundle prior to sawing

Cutting with a Japanese dozuki saw.

Jointing veneers

Often you may have to joint veneer, either to make it wide enough for the panel or for decorative purposes. Making a selection and choosing the orientation of veneers for jointing is called matching.

The way in which veneers are matched has a big impact on the appearance of the finished panel. A number of different methods of composition can be used to create different veneer effects, but the most common matchings are as follows:

Slip matching Consecutive leaves are jointed side by side as they rise from the bundle. This works well for quarter-cut veneers where the figure is straight.

Book matching Alternate leaves are flipped over so that there is symmetry either side of the joint. Interesting patterns can be created by book matching crown-cut and burl veneers.

Random The matching here is done by eye, selecting for the best appearance and often to distribute blemishes in the veneer that would be obvious when slip or book matched. This is not used much as a decorative effect (not shown).

Quartered or four-way match Four leaves are book matched to give symmetry in two dimensions. Burls are particularly suited to quartering, because their wild grain gives some beautiful symmetries.

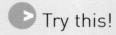 Try this!

> When you get a new bundle or half bundle of veneers, number them to make sure that you use consecutive veneers when jointing. This is especially important with burls.

SLIP MATCHING

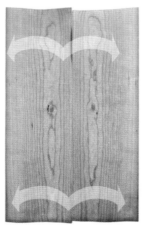

BOOK MATCHING

QUARTERED OR FOUR-WAY MATCH

Veneers are not usually jointed straight from the scalpel, because the edges need further dressing to create a perfect joint. In the workshop, you should use a shooting board and then fix the joint using veneer tape. This is a thin, gummed paper tape — the gummed side is lightly wetted before application and contracts very slightly on drying, which helps to pull the joint together. Some veneer tapes have perforations down the center to aid seeing the joint, but in this example we are using unperforated tape.

Shooting works better on multiple edges. Sometimes you will only have one joint to cut, but if you are veneering a number of doors, for example, it's better to do this as a stack rather than individually. The more layers there are, the more stable they are under the plane.

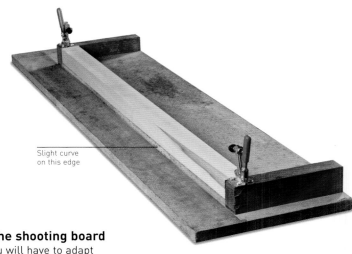

Slight curve on this edge

Adapting/making the shooting board

For veneer jointing, you will have to adapt your shooting board or make a new one. The leaves need to be compressed their whole length. This is best done using a slightly curved clamping strip and toggle clamps. The strip should be approximately 1½ x 1½ in. (35 x 35 mm) in section and a little longer than the veneers you want to joint.

Plane a very slight convex curve on the bottom. Fit a pair of toggle clamps to the shooting board, so that they can bear on the ends of the clamping strip.

JOINTING SLIP-MATCHED OR BOOK-MATCHED VENEERS

1 Cut the line of the joint with a scalpel. On slip-matched joints, the position of the line is not so critical, as long as it is along the line of the grain. For book matching, choose the line you want to match along and mark the position at either end of the top leaf. Now line up the other leaves underneath, so that the figure in each leaf is aligned.

2 Cut through the stack along the line. After cutting, there should be symmetry along the joint when the leaves are opened out.

3 Tap the leaves on the bench top to get them true along the cut line, and lay them on the shooting board with just a fraction overhanging. Pushing them against a plane laid on the board can help with alignment.

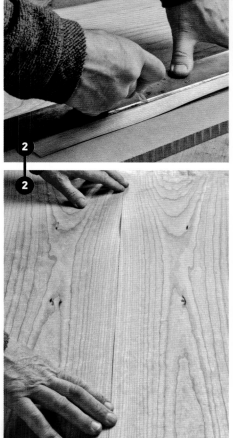

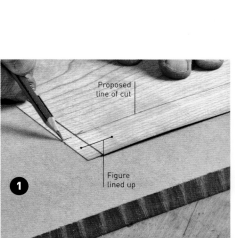

Proposed line of cut

Figure lined up

Fine shaving
is removed.

You should be able to feel
and see a single face when
all leaves are being cut.

Tape stretch | Veneers
pushed
together | Pressure
down on
tape

4 Lay the clamping strip, convex side down, on the edge of the stack with just a little protruding underneath, and press home the toggle clamps. The whole length of the stack of veneers should be compressed.

5 Make sure that your plane is very sharp and finely set, then plane the protruding edge of the stack. Try to add bias pressure at the front of the plane, at the start of the cut and at the back at the end. This helps to stop a curve from forming on the edge.

6 Keep checking the edge of the stack — initially, it will be evident that some edges are not being planed, but slowly a single,

flat surface will appear, showing that all the edges are being cut.

7 Take the veneers off the board and put the joint together. If the joint is good, it can be taped (see "Clinic" on page 201 for further advice if the fit is poor).

8 Start with approximately 3 in. (75 mm) long strips of tape across at either end. Lick or wet the gum and press the tape down on one side of the joint. Then stretch the tape across the joint and press it down on the other side. While doing this, you should also be forcing the edges together — it takes some coordination!

9 With the ends taped, apply tape similarly at 4 in. (100 mm) intervals.

10 Add one strip lengthwise. The joint should be flat, with no overriding of the leaves.

Matching quartered panels

Due to the effect of grain direction, veneers can have different refractive qualities, depending on the angle from which you view them. This should be balanced when arranging a quarter match. The grain will also change progressively as you move through a pack, so by organizing the panels correctly, you can keep the grain change in adjacent panels to a minimum.

Number and mark the front (f) and back (b) of consecutive leaves in the pack of four (i.e., 1f, 1b, 2f, 2b, etc).

You will have previously decided where the axis of your match will be, perhaps using mirrors as described below right.

Open out leaves 1 and 2, hinging on the long axis — this may mean flipping leaf 1 either left or right, so the numbering will be either 2f and 1b or 1b and 2f.

Open out 3 and 4 along the same axis, turning leaf 3 in the same direction as you turned leaf 1.

Then flip leaves 3 and 4 over (rotating on the horizontal axis). You should now have either:

| 2f and 1b | or | 1b and 2f |
| 4b and 3f | or | 3f and 4b |

This may seem complicated, but following this method means you limit the jumps in grain between quarters and that the refractive qualities are balanced.

JOINTING QUARTER-MATCHED VENEERS

When making a quarter match, you are essentially book matching in one dimension and then book matching this first match in the other dimension. So in describing jointing a quarter match, I am also showing how to book match.

Matching burl and crotch veneers requires more care, because the patterns are strong and any inaccuracy is more evident. A mirror is a useful aid in deciding where to make the match. Even better is two mirrors stuck together with tape so that they can be hinged. By positioning these mirrors on the veneer at right angles, you can see what a quartered match around that point would look like.

Check mirrors are at 90° before marking axes.

Use a veneer pin to locate and align features in the leaves.

1

1

Marked axis of the quartered joints

2

2

3

4

Clamp the rule if you are worried about it moving.

5

---

1 Decide the axes around which the match will be made by moving the mirrors around the veneer held at 90°. Check the mirrors are at 90° to each other and mark the axis of the chosen position.

2 For a quarter match, you will have at least four consecutive leaves — perhaps eight or more if you are jointing more than one matching panel. The leaves need to be in a stack for cutting. To precisely align the leaves, find a feature in the burl and push a veneer pin through it in each successive leaf, and then repeat at another point. To prevent the pins from dropping out, it can be useful to lightly tap them into the surface you are cutting on.

3 You need to keep this alignment for cutting, either by taping along an edge or stapling on an edge that will be cut away. Once it's taped or stapled, you can remove the pins.

4 Cut the long edge first. Place the pack on a cutting mat and a metal straight edge along the line of cut. If you are not confident you can keep the straight edge steady, clamp it at either end. Make the cut with a sharp scalpel. It may take a number of strokes — keep going until you are through all of the leaves, and resist the temptation to move the rule to see how you are doing!

5 Place the leaves on the shooting board and shoot them as described in Steps 3–10 on pages 196–97.

CONTINUED ▶

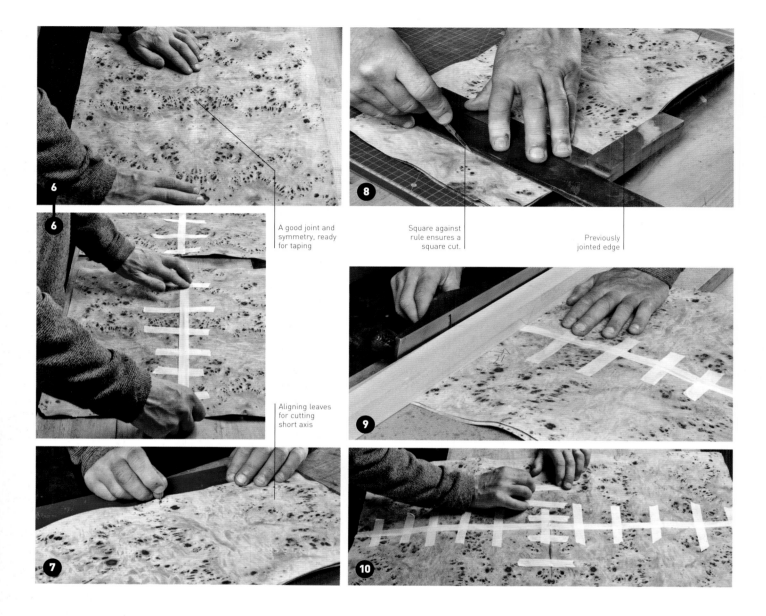

A good joint and symmetry, ready for taping

Square against rule ensures a square cut.

Previously jointed edge

Aligning leaves for cutting short axis

6 You will have to disassemble the pack to check the fit of the joint. Align the pieces so that there is symmetry, and check the joint for fit. If it's successful, tape them up as shown in Steps 8–10 on page 197. Keep in mind the ordering of the leaves described in "Matching quartered panels" (see page 198).

7 Fold the two pairs of veneer along the veneer-taped edges and stack them to cut the short axis. Keep the taped edges

together, but slide them until the burl features are lined up (you can use the veneer pin method again; see Step 2).

8 Return to the cutting board and cut the short axis at 90° to the taped edges.

9 Open up the leaves and put them on the shooting board to lightly shoot the short axis.

10 Remove from the board, and if the joint is good, tape the short axis.

11 You should now have a quartered panel, with the grain pattern symmetrical around the two axes. The lines of cut on the axes should meet at the center, and all the tape should be on one side.

Clinic

The joint meets in the middle but not at the edges There are two main causes for this:

If you don't apply differential pressure at the start and end of the cut, there is a danger of forming a convex edge. Think of the pressure as an infinitesimal twisting forward at the start of the stroke and backward at the end.

The problem can be corrected on the shooting board by taking stopped cuts in the center and then extending the length of the cut progressively, aiming for a final clean cut the full length.

Another reason for a bad joint can be angling of the veneers on the shooting board. If they are protruding slightly more at the front, the plane sole is slightly angled and the back end of the plane can foul on the edge of the board, lifting the blade away from the cut at the start.

Veneers protruding too far from the shooting board

The joint meets at the edges but not in the middle This is less common and less likely to be due to planing technique. It can be caused by the following issues:

• The veneers protrude too far from the edge of the shooting board, so they flex away from the plane as the cut is made, usually at the start or end of the cut. Try to limit the amount of overhang.

• If you are planing only a couple of leaves, they can be quite flexible on their own. Add some spare leaves to the pack to bulk it up and stabilize it.

• Check the pressure from the clamping strip — flexing can arise from a lack of compression of the pack of veneers.

Uneven gaps in the joint This is usually because the edge has not been planed enough, resulting in odd unplaned sections.

Overlapping joint after taping This could be because the joint is not true, it was not meeting at the edges, or the middle sections overrode each other as the joint was taped. The other cause could be overzealous compression of the joint — stretching the tape and pushing the joint together too much. Overlapping joints can lead to problems after pressing with cleaning up the overlaps and bad adhesion where the top veneer is not in contact with the substrate.

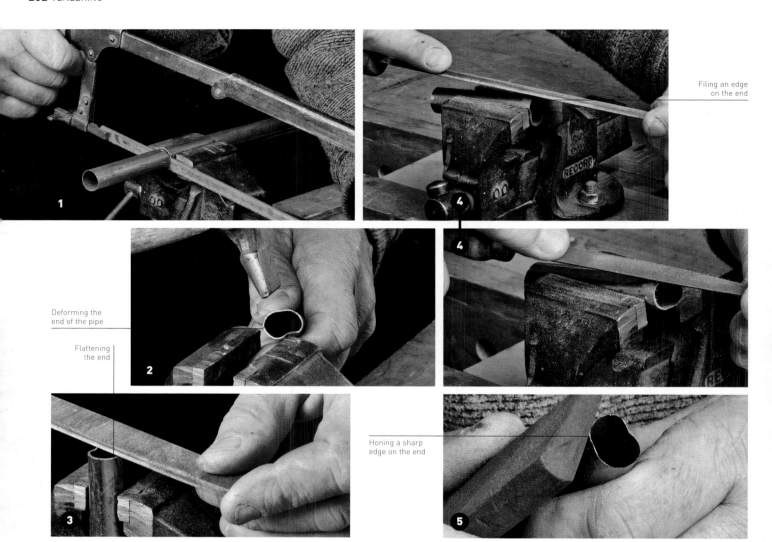

Filing an edge
on the end

Deforming the
end of the pipe

Flattening
the end

Honing a sharp
edge on the end

PATCHING VENEERS

It is possible to patch veneer to remove
blemishes, but this only works on burl or
other irregular-grained veneers where the
patch is lost in the chaotic grain pattern —
the irregular profile helps to break up the
line of the patch. Patching is often needed
on burls, because they frequently have
holes and blemishes in them. On regular
grain, the patch tends to stick out like a
sore thumb. You can purchase veneer
punches for patching — irregular-shaped
hollow tubes with sharp edges that chop
out a section of veneer and cut a new piece
to replace it. Veneer punches are quite
expensive, so you may wish to make
your own.

MAKING A VENEER PUNCH

1 Obtain some thin-walled steel tube
approximately ¾ in. (20 mm) in diameter.
Cut to about 4 in. (100 mm).

2 Using a vise and hammer, bend the
profile out of shape.

3 File the end flat.

4 Then file the edges so that they are
sharp, but keep the end flat across. You
will need a selection of different files to
follow the contours of the punch.

5 Finally, hone with a slip stone.

THE FINISHED VENEER PUNCH

Looking for areas to patch

Carefully push out the patch with a pencil.

Punching overlapping patch

Inserting second patch

Patch being inserted

USING A VENEER PUNCH

1 Select the area you wish to patch — this is aided by holding the leaf up to the light.

2 Position the punch and strike firmly with a hammer or mallet. Carefully lift the punch away from the veneer — a plug of veneer should be removed inside the punch, leaving an irregular hole in the veneer.

3 Select a suitable area from a piece of waste veneer, preferably with the grain oriented in the same direction as the original, so that the reflection will be correct when finished, and punch a new patch. Push out the plug of veneer from the punch with a pencil end.

4 Place the patch into the previously punched hole. The patch can be held by spearing it with a scalpel. Fix with veneer tape.

5 When you turn the leaf over, the patch should be level, with no gaps around it.

6 Sometimes the area to patch may be larger than the punch. You can overcome this by overlapping the patches. Punch out the first area, patch it, and then punch out and patch an area that overlaps the first.

7 Deciding which blemishes need patching and which can be filled later is a matter of judgment!

THE COMPLETED PATCHES

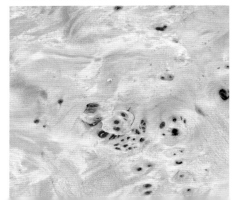

Preparing the substrate

The very best substrate for veneering is MDF, because it's stable, cheap and takes adhesive easily. Birch plywood is also good for veneering, but isn't quite as stable as MDF.

The edges of both MDF and birch plywood boards are not very attractive, so they are usually lipped or edged in some way if they are going to be on show. Depending on the effect you want to achieve, the panel can either be lipped prior to veneering or after, or it can be framed by a wider edging.

These different methods each have advantages and disadvantages:

Lipping prior to veneering This is more discreet, and the panel seems more like a solid piece. However, the veneer running right to the edge can be damaged more easily, and there can be a danger of the lipping being "telegraphed" through the veneer if there was differential movement between substrate and lipping.

Lipping after veneering In this case, the veneer edge is protected, but the lipping is more evident, especially where it runs across the grain.

Framing This is a different approach entirely. Instead of trying to keep the lipping discreet, it is wider and turned into a feature to frame the panel, sometimes with inlay on the joint between panel and edging. The edging joint will usually be reinforced, with biscuits perhaps, while lipping does not need reinforcement.

Edge banding, which uses an iron-on adhesive edging strip, can also be used. This is useful when working with pre-veneered MDF panels. However, the top corner of the edged panel is usually quite delicate. For workshop-veneered panels a more robust lipping is preferable.

NARROW LIPPING AFTER VENEERING

FRAMING

Lipping on right is quarter sawn, so is more stable than on left.

HOW TO LIP A PANEL

1 Prepare the lipping about ³⁄₁₆ in. (4–5 mm) thick and ¹⁄₆₄ in. (0.5 mm) wider than the panel. It is better if the lipping is quarter sawn (the annual rings at right angles to the long sides), because this means it will move less with humidity changes.

2 Now prepare the panel square and to size, allowing for the thickness of the lipping.

3 The lipping can either be overlapped at the ends or mitered on a miter shooting board. In this example, we are overlapping.

4 If you are overlapping the lipping, you will have to apply it in two stages. First apply

MDF soaks up glue, so spread fairly generously.

Get a good stretch on the tape as you wrap it around.

Press plane down on panel to avoid rounding.

Checking for rounding of edge.

Tip: Mitered lipping must be applied in one process, because the miters are trimmed prior to gluing.

---

the lipping on two opposite edges, with some overhang at either end. Spread glue on the edges and place the lipping on.

5 Hold the lipping in place with masking tape at intervals of approximately 2 in. (50 mm). The tape can give quite a positive pressure if you stretch it — press it down on one face of the panel and stretch it over and around to the other face, always keeping it under tension. As you are taping, check that the lipping is overhanging or at least level with the face on both sides.

6 When the first pieces are glued, trim off the ends and plane level with the edge, using a block plane.

7 Apply the second set of lipping as before.

8 When the glue has set, trim off the overhanging lipping and peel away the masking tape.

9 The lipping must be leveled to the surface of the panel. Do this with a block plane or, if there is not much overhang, coarse sandpaper with a sanding block. Take care not to round the edge at all. For good adhesion, the surface should be flat right to the very edge — this is important!

10 Check regularly that the edge is not being rounded.

11 Once the panel is lipped, rough up the surface by rubbing with coarse abrasive paper (60 grit, perhaps) on a sanding block.

Tip: There can be problems holding a lipped panel in the vise before the lipping is planed level. The vise grips the lipping but not the panel, placing undue stress on the lipping. This can be countered by sticking blocks on the vise faces (with double-sided tape), so that the blocks bear on the panel rather than the lipping.

Laying the veneer

You need to be organized when laying the veneer — there are a number of elements involved, and you don't want to get halfway through the process and find something is not ready.

Generally speaking, when laying veneer on a panel, it should be done on both sides so that it is in balance. If you veneer on one side only, the panel is likely to bow. Usually there will be a decorative and a nondecorative face. For instance, a veneered tabletop may have a quartered burl on the top (the face veneer), but only an irregularly marked veneer on the reverse (the balancer veneer).

As with most gluing operations, preparation is crucial. It's important to make sure that you have everything ready before you start spreading the glue.

We will be describing two pressing methods — caul pressing and vacuum pressing. Veneer can also be laid using hot animal glue and a veneer hammer, but we will not be covering this.

CAUL PRESSING

For this, prepare two boards (cauls) at least ¾ in. (18 mm) thick, just a little longer and wider than the panel to be veneered. If the panel is more than 16 in. (400 mm) wide, you also need to prepare pairs of cross bearers made from pine or other cheap wood of approx. 2 x 3 in. (50 x 75 mm). It can be useful to do a test run so that all the clamps are set to the correct dimension.

Preparing the cauls

1 You will need bearers at approximately 10 in. (250 mm) intervals along the length. Plane a slight convex curve, about ¹⁄₁₆ in. (2 mm), on the inner edge — this will make sure that pressure works from the center outward. Mark the curved edge to aid with orientation when clamping up.

2 Pressure will be applied with clamps at the ends of the bearers. Make sure you have enough clamps of the right size — "F" clamps are best.

Mark centers on edges.

Pressing the veneers

You should now have two jointed veneer sheets (two face sheets if both sides of the panel are decorative, or one face sheet and one balancer), with one side clear and the other taped. If some tape has mysteriously appeared on the other side, very lightly dampen it with a cloth, leave for a few minutes and then peel it away. Do not over-moisten or else the veneer will curl up.

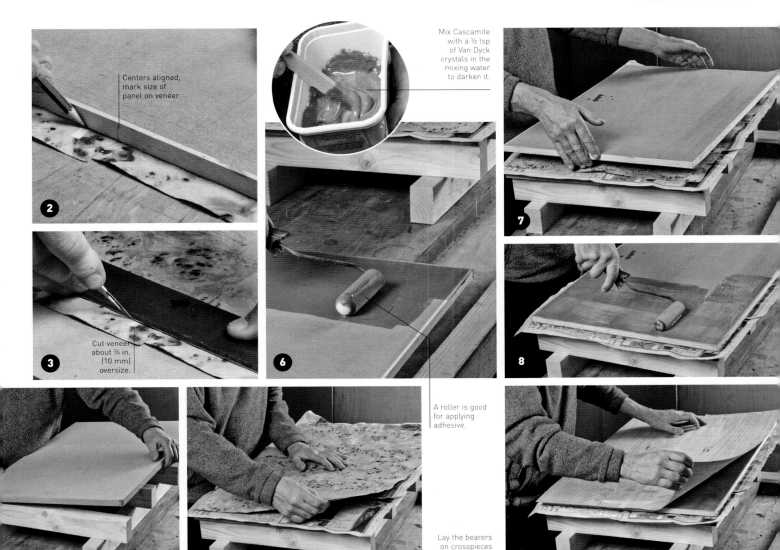

Mix Cascamite with a ½ tsp of Van Dyck crystals in the mixing water to darken it.

Centers aligned, mark size of panel on veneer

Cut veneer about ⅜ in. (10 mm) oversize.

A roller is good for applying adhesive.

Lay the bearers on crosspieces to make it easier to apply clamps.

1 If the veneer has been book or quarter matched, mark the axes on the substrate so that the sheet can be correctly aligned. Take the marks down the side of the board, because this is where you will be sighting it.

2 Mark all around the outside of the base on the veneer with a pencil.

3 Trim the veneer sheets about ⅜ in. (10 mm) oversize.

4 Lay two support pieces at right angles to the four bearers. Place a caul on the bearers.

5 Lay a sheet of paper on the caul, then lay the top veneer on this, tape side down.

6 Apply glue to one surface of the panel. You can spread the glue with a brush, but a foam paint roller is quicker and gives a more even coverage. The best adhesive for veneering is a urea-formaldehyde (UF) resin powder glue (such as Cascamite), because it is waterproof, sets glass hard and can be colored. Otherwise, a good waterproof PVA (D3 or above classification) is okay. Aim for a layer of glue that is about as thick as a very heavy coat of latex paint.

7 Invert the panel onto the veneer and check that it is centralized. If it's a quartered veneer, align the joints with the center marks on the edge of the panel.

8 Spread glue on the back of the panel.

9 Lay the balance veneer on top of this and smooth it down onto the surface.

10 Quickly place a sheet of paper over this, followed by the second caul. If you are not quick, you can have problems with the veneer curling up as it absorbs moisture from the glue.

Tip: Urea-formaldehyde glue can be colored by adding pigment to the mixing water. Van Dyck crystals work well for oak and poplar burl.

CONTINUED ▶

Curved side down

Apply clamps from the center outward.

Clamps should be well tightened.

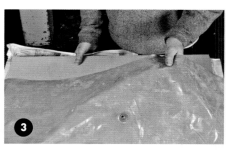

Breather fabric allows the air to be sucked from the whole bag.

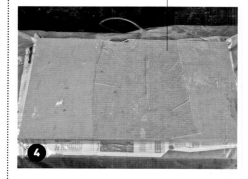

Centers should be aligned.

If you are cautious, you could apply further clamps along the edges.

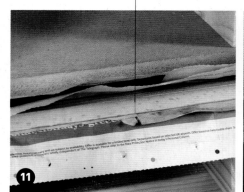

Vacuum pressing

With this method, the piece to be veneered is placed in a plastic or latex bag and the air is sucked out using a vacuum pump so that atmospheric pressure of up to about 15 lb per square inch (15 kg per square centimeter) presses the veneer.

1 Sandwich the veneered panel between two sheets of paper, then two boards slightly oversize, with the edges slightly rounded to avoid puncturing the bag. These boards can be quite thin, because the bag will press over the whole surface.

2 It can be difficult to check alignment once the panel is in the bag, but taping at the edges of the veneers can help with this.

3 Slide the "sandwich" of boards into the bag.

4 A breather fabric is supplied with the bag — position this so that air can be sucked from the sandwich to the pipe connector. Check the veneer alignment, then seal the bag and switch on the pump. Soon you should see the bag compressing around the sandwich and the vacuum dial rising. About 0.7 to 0.8 bar is enough. Drying time is the same as for caul pressing.

11 Recheck that the veneer is correctly aligned on the substrate by sighting the edge markings.

12 Place the remaining bearer's curved face down on the caul and apply pressure. Start clamping from the middle out. You may need an assistant so that balanced pressure can be applied at either end of the bearer. You can apply additional clamps at the edges between the bearers.

13 When all clamps are tightened, check the alignment because it may have slipped.

14 If using Cascamite, the panels should be left pressing for about five hours; for PVA, about two hours should suffice.

Use a batten to lift the end of the panel.

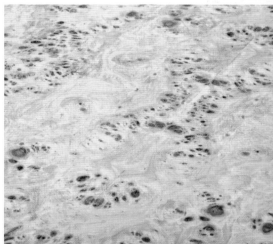

THE FINISHED RESULT

CLEANING UP THE VENEERED PANEL

Leave veneered panels for at least 12 hours after pressing for the adhesive to cure before cleaning them up.

1 You will have some veneer overhanging the edge of your panel. Use a scalpel to remove this. Place the panel on a cutting board and slightly elevate one edge.

2 Press down hard on the opposite end and trim the lower veneer on that edge, running the scalpel against the board edge. Avoid cutting right to the back, because this may cause breakout. Instead, make a second cut from the other direction.

3 Repeat for the other edges.

4 Plane the edges lightly with a block plane.

5 Then sand in a slightly downward direction to remove any excess glue and to give a slight rounding to prevent the veneer from being pulled away.

6 Use a damp cloth to lightly moisten the veneer tape.

7 After a few minutes, peel away the tape — you may have to repeat the moistening until the tape comes away easily, but try not to wet the veneer too much.

8 The panel may need sanding vigorously to clean up any bleed-through and to level joints. Start with 120 grit, then 180, using abrasive paper and block or a random orbital sander. Veneer can be sanded quite vigorously without cutting through it, but don't use a belt sander on it!

Clinic

Veneer lifting at edge

Veneer lifting

Veneer lifting

Veneer lifting

VENEER NOT STUCK DOWN

There are a number of reasons for this:

• It can be a problem along edges, especially if they slope away slightly due to overzealous planing of the lipping.

• Inadequate pressure at the edges — when caul pressing, add some extra clamps between the bearers.

• Edges are delicate until the overhang is cut away and the corner slightly rounded, so do this as soon as possible — otherwise the edges could lift while you are working on the panel.

• Sometimes the veneer may lift in the center — this usually occurs with burls, probably due to localized thinning of the veneer, which means that the area was not under pressure when laid.

• Veneers overlapping at a joint can also cause this problem, the overlapping veneer not being in full contact with the substrate. It can be worth slightly hinging the joint as you lay it on the substrate and feeling if it is fitting together properly. The overlap can be scraped or sanded away after the area has been glued down.

• The veneer was wet too much or too soon after laying, making it bubble.

• Sometimes contamination of the substrate with wax or oil may cause bad adhesion.

• Incorrect mixing of Cascamite or using degraded PVA. PVA can lose its properties if it is exposed to low temperatures.

Identifying raised areas Raised areas should be found and dealt with before sanding; otherwise there is a danger of sanding through the bubbled area.

You can detect raised areas of veneer by tapping with the back end of a pencil. The bubble will sound different even if it's not noticeable visually.

Ironing down lifted areas One remedy for raised veneers is to iron down the lifted areas. This works best with PVA glue — Cascamite is not so responsive to the iron. To iron down a bubble or lifted edge, place a sheet of paper over it and apply pressure locally with an iron on a fairly hot setting. Move the point of the iron around over the lifted area, checking occasionally to see if it has stuck down.

Regluing lifted veneers

Lifting veeneer with a scalpel

Adding the Superglue

Taping the joint

If the glue does not respond to the iron, an additional adhesive will be required. At the edge, Superglue or polyurethane glue can be used. Lift the loose area and introduce the glue — thin Superglue is good, because it creeps into the area via capillary action. The veneer can be taped down to provide pressure.

Slitting the veneer

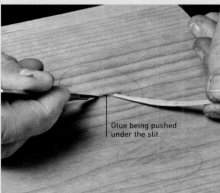

Glue being pushed under the slit

Clamping the piece

Away from the edge, the veneer can be slit with a scalpel along the grain and the glue injected or pushed under. This works better on burls, where the cut will be lost in the pattern; on straight-grained veneers, the cut may be evident. If a clamp cannot reach the area, a heavy weight may keep it down.

ADHESIVE BLEED-THROUGH

Often the glue will show through the veneer where it has seeped through. This often happens with burls because of their erratic grain. It is not usually obvious after sanding burls, but on light-colored standard veneers, it can be unsightly. For these, avoid glues that will dry dark, such as some of the Titebond glues, and do not spread too thickly.

THE FINISHED REPAIRS

Finishing

When you add a finish to a project, the grain, color and texture of the wood are brought out, giving the piece character and vibrancy. In this chapter, we will look at the three stages of finishing: surface preparation to create a clean smooth surface for the final finish; staining and coloring; and how to apply three different finishes — an oil finish, sanding sealer with wax finish and acrylic lacquer.

Finishing tools and materials

There are a number of specialized tools and materials required for the three stages of finishing.

SURFACE PREPARATION

Abrasive paper [1]
Aluminum oxide is best in grades of 100–180 for surface preparation and 400 or 500 for between coats.

Sanding block [2]
Usually sandpaper is wrapped around a cork block. This provides a flat sanding surface to keep the prepared surface flat. When sanding with a sanding block, it is economical to tear the sanding sheet into three across the short dimension. Fold the sheet into three, lay a steel rule along the fold and tear against this. The thirds can be wrapped around the block and moved around as they become worn.

Steel wool [3]
This can be used for working moldings, etc. The coarser grades are useful in restoration for stripping old finishes. The finest grade (0000) can be used for burnishing the final coat of a finish. Steel wool must not be used on oak or other tannin-rich woods — steel particles can cause black spots in the wood.

Webrax or Scotch-Brite [4]
These are abrasive-impregnated nylon pads that are good for working moldings and curved surfaces, and also for burnishing the final coat. We will use the fine grade pads (they are graded by color — fine is gray).

Iron (not shown)
An ordinary domestic iron can be used for steaming out dents.

Plug cutter (not shown)
A hollow cutter for cutting plugs for filling drill holes.

Two-part filler [5]
A quick-setting filler consisting of the filler and a hardening catalyst.

Wax filler [6]
Colored wax stick that is used for filling minor defects. Supplied in a large range of colors.

CLEANING

Tack cloth [7]
A fine cloth impregnated with a tacky resin. Use this for cleaning off dust prior to finish application.

Dusting brush [8]
A specialized brush that is used by decorators for final dusting prior to applying the finish.

Mineral spirits (not shown)
Mineral spirits can be used to clean contaminated surfaces and thin oil-based stains and finishes.

APPLICATION

Applicator pads [9]
These felt or foam pads are used for lacquer application and are available in various sizes.

Polishing mop [10]
A very soft, hair brush that is used for applying finishes, especially those that are spirit based.

Foam paint roller and tray (not shown)
Useful for applying oil-based finish.

Earth pigments [11]
Pigments created from naturally occurring minerals can be used for coloring fillers and finishes.

Stains [12]
Stains can be defined by the solvent used. Oil-based stains use a naphtha solvent — they are slow drying, so are good for staining large areas. Spirit stains have an alcohol solvent — they are quick drying and can be mixed with shellac finishes. Water-based stains are water soluble. The Van Dyck crystals that we will be using are water based.

Finishes (not shown)
Many different finishes are available — we will be dealing with three different types. It is important that your finish is compatible with any stain used.

Denatured alcohol (not shown)
Used to thin spirit stains and finishes.

The finished patch

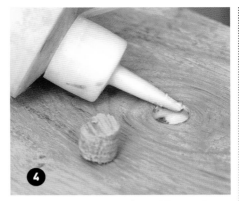

Rub with fine abrasive.

stand, because the plug cutter is difficult to start freehand.

4 Lever the plug out of its hole and glue it into the hole in the workpiece, broken end up.

5 Tap it home with a hammer, making sure that the grain is in line. Leave it raised above the surface.

6 When the glue has set, plane and scrape the plug back to the surface and sand to a smooth finish.

SMALL CRACKS AND DINGS IN THE SURFACE

These can be dealt with using wax filler. The wax filler should be matched for color very carefully — the best time to do this is after the first coat of finish has been applied, because the finish may change the color of the wood but not the filler. When filling knots and ingrown defects, as in this illustration, match the filler to the color of the knot rather than the color of the grain.

1 If a match cannot be achieved, it is possible to mix the different colors by melting them in a teaspoon over a flame (take care, though, because they are flammable). Earth pigments can also be mixed in to change the color.

2 Very thin cracks can be filled by rubbing the stick of wax filler across the crack.

3 Scrape off the excess, then lightly rub with fine abrasive.

4 Larger defects can be filled by picking a piece off the stick with a putty or pallet knife and forcing it into the crack.

5 Then scrape off the surplus with the edge of the tool.

6 Follow this with fine abrasive and block. If the wax is too hard, you can soften it by kneading it between your fingers.

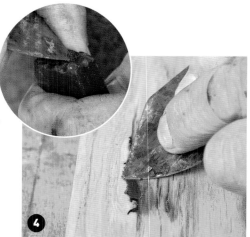

GLUING UP COMPONENTS

It may seem strange to have gluing up in the finishing chapter, but the way you glue up will have a big effect on the finish, possibly causing dents, dings and glue marks. Once the surfaces are prepared, you can glue the parts together. Most beginners use too much glue, leaving a lot of squeeze-out to deal with.

1 Apply glue sparingly in the mortise. Avoid getting it on the face around the mortise.

2 Add a thin smear of glue to the tenon.

3 Make sure to use adequate clamping blocks.

4 Protect parts with scrap pieces if you need to use a mallet.

Use clamping blocks.

Protect your piece with scrap wood.

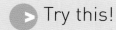

> ## Try this!

> For cabinetwork, apply the finish to the inside surfaces before glue up. This makes application and sanding between coats easier. The joint areas should be carefully covered with masking tape.

GAPS AROUND JOINTS

These gaps should be treated in the same way as surface cracks (see page 219). However, it can be difficult to get the wax filler into gaps in corners.

1 Trim a thin piece of wax from the stick with the edge of a putty knife or a chisel and work it into the gap, applying pressure into the corner.

2 Scrape off any surplus with a chisel.

Staining

Personally, I prefer to apply finishes to bring out the natural color and grain of the wood without staining. However, there are many different techniques for staining — some use chemical processes to change the color, such as fuming with ammonia to give a rich dark honey color to oak; others use pigments or dyes to create the color change. We do not have space to cover all the different types available, so we will look at using one in particular.

STAINING WITH VAN DYCK CRYSTALS

Van Dyck is a wood stain popular for aging oak, but it can be used to darken other woods. It's a water-based stain created by dissolving roasted walnut skins (Van Dyck crystals) in boiling water. You may wish to use latex or acrylic gloves when applying this stain to avoid staining your fingers.

1 As Van Dyck is water based, it will raise the grain when it is applied. To avoid this, wet the surface with a damp cloth and allow to dry, then rub down lightly with 180 grit. Repeat this until wetting does not raise the grain any more. This should be done for all water-based stains and finishes.

2 Mix a dessert spoonful of crystals with a cup full of boiling water in an open-top container and stir until dissolved. Test the color on a piece of scrap wood. If the color is too strong, it can be diluted with water; add more crystals to darken.

3 When you're happy with the color, dip a rag into the stain and wipe it on the surface of the piece. Try to work so that you are always wiping up to a still-wet edge. Be fairly generous, then wipe off any excess.

4 Avoid spilling water on the surface until the finish is applied, because this will show as splash marks.

Try this!

> When applying stains and finishes, decant them into an open-topped container. This allows you to get the cloth well into the liquid so that you get plenty on the surface. For oil-based stains and finishes, make sure to use a metal container, because oil is a solvent and a plastic container will melt.

> A dash of ammonia in the Van Dyck solution helps the stain to bite more deeply into the pores of the wood.

Finish application

There are many different types of finish with many different properties.
The chart below lists just some of those available that can be easily
applied in the home workshop.

Finish	Base	Build/sheen	Color change	Application	Comments
Danish oil	Oil	Low/Low	Some darkening	3–4 coats with brush, rag or roller, wipe off excess.	Simple, if time consuming, to apply. Very resilient. Patch finishing and touching up possible.
Hard wax oil	Oil	Low/Low	Little darkening	2–3 coats with brush, rag or roller, wipe off excess.	Similar to Danish oil, slightly more build but more resilient. Patch finishing and retouching possible.
Wax polish	Wax	Low/Medium	Little darkening	Apply with cloth or steel wool/ Webrax.	Not resilient. Soaks in unless surface sealed. Easy to restore.
Acrylic lacquer	Water	High/Matte to gloss available	No darkening but dulls color on some woods	3–4 coats with pad. Burnish afterward.	Hard wearing but difficult to retouch or patch finish. The high build can detract from the tactile quality of wood.
Polyurethane varnish	Oil	High/Matte to gloss available	Darkens and can yellow with age	2–3 coats with brush.	Very hard wearing. Long drying time can be a problem in dusty workshop. A bit plasticky.
French polish	Spirit	Very high/Sheen can be controlled from satin to gloss	Depends on type of polish used	Number of coats applied with cotton rubber to build up, then shining with spirit. Sheen level determined by burnishing.	Difficult to apply and not resilient, but finish gives a lovely deep luster. Can look plasticky if overdone.

On the following pages, you will find the
method for applying three finishes:
• An oil finish, such as Danish oil or a
  hard wax oil.
• A simple shellac sanding sealer and
  wax finish.
• A water-based acrylic lacquer.

If you are using a stain, it is important to
consider its compatibility with a finish.
The basic rule is to avoid using a finish
and stain with the same base. For
example, don't use Van Dyck crystals
with an acrylic lacquer, because they are
both water based. Van Dyck crystals work
well with Danish oil (oil based) or shellac

polish (spirit based). Always test stain
and finish together on a piece of scrap
wood beforehand.

Tip: Do not leave oil finish rags in a pile in the workshop. They can self-combust due to the heat of oxidation.

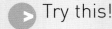 **Try this!**

> Use a foam paint roller to apply the oil on large surfaces, such as a table top. The roller and tray can be stored in a plastic bag to prevent drying out.

> Applying the last coat with gray Webrax or 0000 steel wool helps to soften and burnish the previous coat and enhances the final finish.

After the final coat has hardened, adjust the sheen by burnishing with steel wool or gray Webrax with wax polish.

> If you have a random orbital sander with Velcro pad fitting, attach Webrax to it for the final burnishing with the speed low. This can also be done when buffing with a duster, as long as you use a few layers of duster.

Clinic

Problems usually arise from preparation issues.

Slight marks across the grain, about 4 in. (100 mm) wide This is due to errors when using the belt sander. The sander was running when applied to the surface and the front wheel dug into the surface. Scrape and sand locally, then reapply the finish.

Scratches evident in the surface If these are straight scratches across or diagonal to the grain, it's a sanding technique problem. Always sand with the grain. If the scratches are in small circles, it's likely to be a problem with the orbital sander — a deficient sander and clogged sanding disk. Scrape and sand locally, then reapply the finish.

Finish is sticky This is usually because the surplus was not fully removed, or possibly the surface was contaminated with wax. If it's the former, try rubbing down with mineral spirits with 0000 steel wool or Webrax. The latter may require stripping and cleaning the surface with a dewaxer or mineral spirits.

APPLYING AN OIL FINISH
Oil finishes (such as Danish oil and hard wax oil) are easy to apply and usually fairly resilient. They are low build (meaning they don't form layers on the wood surface), so the finished surface still has the tactile quality of the wood. Avoid using oil-based finish on the interior of cabinets due to the odor. Hard wax oil is my "go to" finish.

1 Prepare the surface as described previously (see pages 216–20) and remove any dust with a tack cloth or dusting brush. If the finish is in a narrow-topped container, decant some into an appropriate open-topped one.

2 Apply the oil fairly liberally with a cloth, brush or foam paint roller in the direction of the grain. Leave for 20 minutes or so.

3 Thoroughly rub off any surplus oil, using a clean rag or kitchen roll. Be rigorous about this, because any excess oil can remain tacky. Allow to dry for around eight hours.

4 Lightly de-nib with 400–500-grit abrasive or gray Webrax.

5 Apply another coat as before. Hard wax oils will require two or three coats, while Danish oil may need three or four.

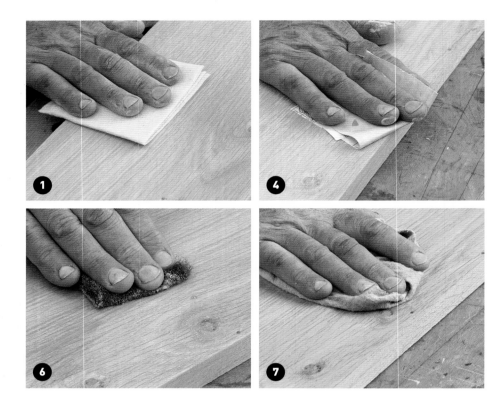

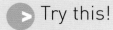 Try this!

> When sanding by hand without a block, use sandpaper torn into three and fold it over twice. The three layers work together so that they don't slide around when rubbing.

> When you've finished applying the sealer, rinse the mop in denatured alcohol, then squeeze it out, shape it and allow to dry. It will dry stiff, but will soften up quickly (in about 20 minutes) when steeped in spirit.

> You can tell when the shellac is dry, because it leaves a talc-like powder when you sand it.

APPLYING A SHELLAC SANDING SEALER AND WAX FINISH

Beeswax is a traditional finish that produces a wonderful patina on antiques. However, when applied directly onto new wood, it quickly disappears into the surface, requiring repeated application over a long period. Applying a spirit-based shellac sanding sealer prior to wax application can help with this, because it limits the amount of absorption. The finish is not very resilient and will not withstand heat or alcohol. Use a wax paste rather than an aerosol. Avoid waxes with added silicone. Most modern waxes have a synthetic microcrystalline wax base — these are more durable than traditional beeswax finishes and less prone to finger marking.

1 Prepare the surface as described previously (see pages 216–20), and clean off any dust with a tack cloth or dusting brush. Shake and decant the sealer into an open-topped container.

2 Use a fine-hair (such as zorino, a combination of badger, skunk and squirrel hair) polishing mop to apply the sealer. Dip the mop into the sealer, then rub off on the edge of the container.

3 Apply the sealer with long, light strokes with the grain. On large flat surfaces, try to drift the mop onto the surface at the start of the stroke, so that you don't work it against the leading edge. Then continue off the surface at the trailing edge. This prevents dribbles at the leading edge as the mop is dragged over it. Work in overlapping strokes to keep the edge wet. Allow the sealer to dry for approximately an hour.

4 De-nib with 400–500 grit or use Webrax on moldings. The sealer produces a fine dust when sanded and gives a very fine surface.

5 Remove the sanding dust with a tack cloth or dust brush and repeat the application of sealer.

6 Allow the sealer to cure overnight and then lightly rub down. Apply the wax using 0000 steel wool or gray Webrax, working with the grain.

7 Leave a very thin film of wax on the surface to harden for about four hours,

Clinic

Dry patches in the finish You may have sanded through the finish. The area should be cleaned with mineral spirits to remove any wax, allowed to dry and then sealer applied again. If this does not work, you may have to scrape off and start again. This is likely to happen on high points, so your initial preparation may not have leveled adequately.

Dribbles and runs at the edges These arise from mopping technique. It is possible to pare off the worst runs with a sharp chisel and then sand back.

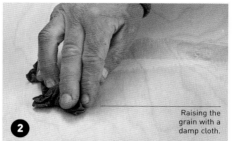

Raising the grain with a damp cloth.

The surface will be powdery.

Clinic

The same surface preparation and edge run errors can occur as above Runs may be dealt with as above, but it is not easy to refinish locally with acrylic, so the whole surface may need to be refinished.

The surface has streaks of a different sheen The finish has not been rubbed down sufficiently, so applicator marks remain; the lower marked areas have different sheen to the sanded areas. Try sanding again, starting with 500 grit and working through.

Dry areas in the finish You may have sanded through the finish. Sand again with 500 grit to key the surface, then apply a couple more coats of lacquer. Then take a lighter touch with the abrasive in that area.

APPLYING AN ACRYLIC LACQUER FINISH

While oil and wax finishes are low build, leaving little or no coating on the surface, acrylic lacquers are a high-build finish and they are film forming. This has advantages and disadvantages — the layer can be worked with fine abrasives to burnish it to a very fine finish, but the tactile nature of the wood is lost. This does not matter so much on close-grained woods, such as maple, that are very smooth anyway, but on open-grained woods, such as oak, it may be an issue. Acrylic lacquer is resilient but any scratches will be evident in the high build, and it's difficult to refinish locally as you would on low-build finishes. Acrylic is an excellent finish for cabinet interiors where odor can be an issue.

Acrylic finishes tend to "kill" the color on woods such as cherry and walnut, while they have little darkening effect on light woods. For this reason, they are good finishes for light, closed-grain woods, such as maple, birch plywood and sycamore, but less so for other woods.

Acrylic lacquer is available with different levels of sheen, from matte to full gloss.

For large surfaces, such as panels and tabletops, use a paint pad for application, but make sure it's high quality because cheaper ones can shed fine hairs into the finish. For smaller surfaces and for getting into corners, foam applicators are good. Paintbrushes tend to leave striated brush marks in the finish.

1 Prepare the surface as described previously (see pages 216–20). Clean off any dust with a tack cloth or dusting brush.

2 Raise the grain by dampening the piece and sanding back with 180 grit, until the grain will no longer rise.

3 Stir or shake the finish and then decant it into an open-topped container. Charge the applicator with finish. With larger paint pads, you may need to rub off some finish on the side of the container.

4 Using a fairly light pressure, draw the pad across the surface, working with the grain. Try to avoid dribbles by not drawing the pad across the leading edge (see "Applying sanding sealer," Step 3, previous page). On large surfaces, work methodically from the far side, keeping a wet edge. Aim for an even film on the surface without flooding it. Store the finish container and applicator in a plastic bag to prevent drying between coats.

5 The lacquer will dry fairly quickly (1–2 hours) and can then be de-nibbed with 400–500 grit. When the finish is dry enough, it will form a talc-like powder without clogging the paper.

6 Use a sanding block and sand until any applicator marks are gone — you could use 320 grit, but finish with the finest grit.

7 Apply the next coat and repeat until you have added three or four coats. The final coat could be thinned slightly to reduce applicator marking.

8 Allow the finish to harden for 12 hours or so. You can now work on it to achieve a fine surface — on larger surfaces, you could use a random orbital sander. Start with 500-grit aluminum oxide paper or, for an even smoother surface with slight sheen improvement, use gray Webrax or abrasive foam pads, working through 1,000, 2,000 and 4,000 grit until you are satisfied with the finish.

Projects

8

The following five projects are designed for you to hone your skills. The shelf project uses prepared redwood (PSE), which you should be able to source from a local supplier, and the workshop cabinet uses birch plywood, but for the other projects you will have to prepare the wood from the sawn state. It's worth searching for somewhere that will cut and plane the parts for you. You will notice that the cutting lists for projects using solid hardwood specify rough-cut and final dimensions. The rough-cut dimension is the minimum size for the part when it is in the sawn state; some wastage has been added to allow for planing and final squaring of the ends. Board thickness is the standard board size from which the part can be thicknessed.

PROJECT: Breadboard with knife

This project is a good test of your sawing and edge-jointing skills. This simple but striking design works best if there is a contrast between the board and the knife handle. Make the board from a close-grained wood to aid cleaning and hygiene. In this example, the bread knife has a black handle, so I would suggest using maple, sycamore or beech (beech is probably the easiest of the three to obtain), which are close-grained, light-colored woods.

Y ou may have to amend the dimensions to accommodate the knife you want to use. Here, the knife has a 5⅛ in. (130 mm) long handle and a blade that is 8¼ in. (210 mm) long and 1 in. (25 mm) wide. The project can also be adapted for cheese or vegetable chopping boards.

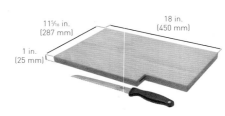

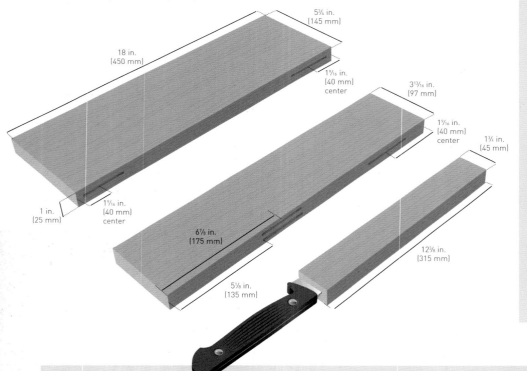

Tools + materials list

Power tools

Biscuit jointer

Router

¼ in. (6 mm) router bit with long shank

Chop saw (optional)

Edge tools

Planes: jack plane, block plane

Cabinet scraper (optional)

Saws

Handsaw, preferably rip

Crosscut backsaw (if no chop saw)

Measuring and marking

24 in. (600 mm) steel rule

Square

Marking gauge

Clamping

Two clamps with at least 12 in. (300 mm) capacity, preferably bar clamps

Various

Shooting board (if no chop saw)

Materials

Bread knife

Maple, sycamore or beech as per cutting list

5 no. 10 biscuits

Waterproof adhesive

Food-safe oil finish, plus cloths for application

Cutting List

DESCRIPTION	QUANTITY	Rough cut			Final dimension		
		MIN. CUT LENGTH	MIN. CUT WIDTH	BOARD THICKNESS	LENGTH	WIDTH	THICKNESS
Board	2	18¼ in. (455 mm)	6 in. (150 mm)	1 in. + (25 mm +)	18 in. (450 mm)	5¾ in. (145 mm)	1 in. (25 mm)

Method

1 Plane the boards to thickness and width, then edge-joint them as described on pages 151–52.

2 Biscuit the joint with centers 1⁹⁄₁₆ in. (40 mm) from the ends, and glue and clamp up.

3 When the glue has set, clean up the surfaces. Check for flatness and establish face side and edge.

4 Mark a gauge line all around, 1⅞ in. (47 mm) from the face edge.

5 Saw down the gauge line with a sharp handsaw, preferably sharpened rip style.

6 With a crosscut backsaw or chop saw, cut a piece off the end of the cut piece that is the same length as the knife handle; in our example, this is 5⅛ in. (135 mm). If using a backsaw, you may need to clean up the end with a shooting board.

7 Plane the cut edges flat and square to form an edge joint, as shown on pages 151–52. Try to do this in as few shavings as possible. When the joint is glued, the cut line will be invisible.

8 When the joint is true, mark centers 1⁹⁄₁₆ in. (40 mm) from the ends and use the biscuit jointer to cut for no. 10 biscuits. At the non-handle end, the biscuit can be in the center. At the handle end, have two biscuits with centers, ³⁄₁₆ in. (5 mm) from the top and bottom surfaces.

9 Set up a handheld router with a ¼ in. (6 mm) long shank. Use this to rout a groove in the edge of the cut-off piece, long enough and deep enough for the knife to fit in. In the example, I made it 8¹¹⁄₁₆ in. (220 mm) long and 1⅜ in. (35 mm) deep; the extra depth is to allow for the width of the handle.

10 To make the cut, mark a line across at the start position. Starting on the line, rout the groove using progressively deeper cuts. Support will be needed at the handle end to stop the router from dropping off the end.

11 Glue and clamp the cut piece back onto the main board and check for flatness. Use a waterproof adhesive, because the board may be washed occasionally. Be sparing with the glue — you don't want too much squeeze-out into the knife slot.

Sawing off the section for the knife holder

Planing the edge joint for the knife holder

Routing a groove for the knife blade

The knife should fit in the slot with the handle below the edge.

12 The piece has been left over-width while jointing — now you can cut it to final width. There should not be much to take off, so it may be easiest to do with a plane rather than saw a narrow piece. The ends can also be trued up, either by planing in the vise, working from the outside inward to avoid breakout, or on a shooting board.

13 Round over or chamfer the corners slightly with a block plane.

14 Clean up with a jack plane and, possibly, a cabinet scraper. Sand down, then apply a finish. I would recommend a food-safe oil finish — those based on paraffin oil are good.

See also

Marking and measuring page 66

Sawing (by hand) pages 70–72

Chop and sliding compound miter saws pages 89–92

Biscuit jointing pages 180–83

Grooving and rabbeting page 104

SKILL LEVEL: **EASY TO MODERATE**

PROJECT: Skeleton shelves

The minimalist design of these shelves is enhanced by the absence of visible fixings. This is achieved by machining out a recess in the back edge of each shelf that fits over a batten screwed to the wall. Made from easily obtainable redwood (pine) in standard width and thickness, you should be able to buy the wood ready planed. Before starting, make sure that the wall is flat. If it's too uneven, it may be difficult to mount the shelves without gaps between them and the wall.

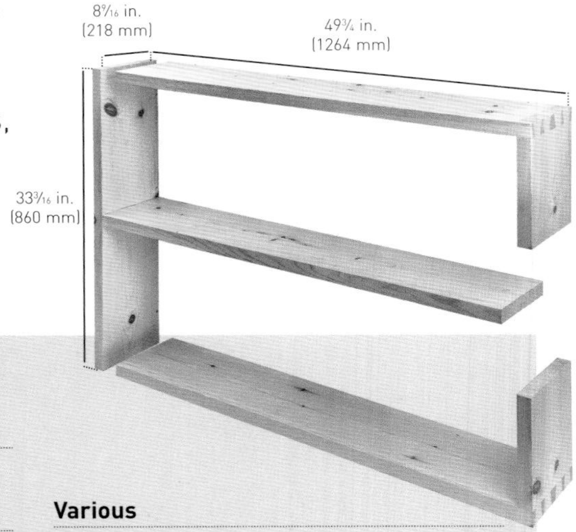

Tools + materials list

Power tools
- Chop or miter saw (optional)
- Router and router table (optional)
- $\frac{5}{8}$ in. (15 mm) or smaller straight flute router bit
- SDS or hammer drill for hanging shelves if onto a solid wall
- Masonry drill bit suitable for screw anchor used
- Cordless drill
- $\frac{1}{8}$ in. (4 mm) twist bit
- Countersink
- Orbital sander (optional)
- $\frac{3}{8}$ in. (9 mm) or similar board
- Level

Edge tools
- Jack plane
- Set of bevel-edged chisels
- Hand router (if no electric router)

Saws
- Handsaw (if no chop/miter saw)
- Dovetail or other backsaw
- Coping saw

Measuring and marking
- Large square
- Cutting gauge
- Marking knife
- Sliding bevel or dovetail template
- Dividers
- Mortise gauge

Clamping
- Two or more bar clamps with at least $51\frac{3}{16}$ in. (1300 mm) capacity

Various
- Mallet
- Brushes and containers for applying finish
- Forstner bit $1\frac{1}{8}$ in. (28 mm) diameter
- Drill
- Shooting board (if no chop saw)
- Dovetail pin marking jig (optional)
- Dovetail routing jig (optional)

Materials
- Redwood as per cutting list
- Screws and anchors for fixing strips to wall
- Water-based acrylic lacquer and applicators
- Abrasive 180 grit
- PVA glue

Cutting list

		Final dimension		
DESCRIPTION	QUANTITY	LENGTH	WIDTH	THICKNESS
a Top shelf	1	$47\frac{1}{4}$ in. (1200 mm)	$8\frac{9}{16}$ in. (218 mm)	$1\frac{1}{4}$ in. (32 mm)
b Middle shelf	1	$38\frac{3}{16}$ in. (1224 mm)	$8\frac{9}{16}$ in. (218 mm)	$1\frac{1}{4}$ in. (32 mm)
c Bottom shelf	1	$47\frac{1}{4}$ in. (1200 mm)	$8\frac{9}{16}$ in. (218 mm)	$1\frac{1}{4}$ in. (32 mm)
d Left-hand end	1	$33\frac{3}{16}$ in. (860 mm)	$8\frac{9}{16}$ in. (218 mm)	$1\frac{1}{4}$ in. (32 mm)
e Right-hand end	2	$10\frac{5}{8}$ in. (270 mm)	$8\frac{9}{16}$ in. (218 mm)	$1\frac{1}{4}$ in. (32 mm)
f Top and bottom fixing strip	2	$41\frac{11}{32}$ in. (1050 mm)	$\frac{9}{16}$ in. (14 mm)	$\frac{9}{16}$ in. (14 mm)
g Middle fixing strip	1	$29\frac{1}{8}$ in. (740 mm)	$\frac{9}{16}$ in. (14 mm)	$\frac{9}{16}$ in. (14 mm)
h Left fixing strip	1	$27\frac{15}{16}$ in. (710 mm)	$\frac{9}{16}$ in. (14 mm)	$\frac{9}{16}$ in. (14 mm)
i Right fixing strip	2	$7\frac{7}{8}$ in. (200 mm)	$\frac{9}{16}$ in. (14 mm)	$\frac{9}{16}$ in. (14 mm)

WOOD SELECTION

Redwood of this width and thickness should be available from any good woodyard. PSE (planed square edge) wood dimensions can be confusing. We are using pieces 8⁹⁄₁₆ x 1¼ in. (218 x 32 mm), but you should ask for the standard size 8⅞ x 1½ in. (225 x 38 mm). This is because the standard size is the size it was originally sawn to. When the wood is subsequently planed, about ¼ in. (6 mm) is lost in both dimensions to end up as 8⁹⁄₁₆ x 1¼ in. (218 x 32 mm).

Good woodyards should let you select boards. Look for straight pieces with no cupping or twisting across the boards and as few knots and surface cracks as possible. You could ask the yard to cut to length, but it may be better to get the pieces overlength and trim to size yourself; then you have more control over accuracy and grain selection.

Redwood is prone to movement. A board that is flat one day can be cupped the next. Limit humidity changes. If your workshop is damp, don't leave the wood out there — bring it in between sessions. Before starting the project, you could keep the wood for a few weeks in the room where the shelves will be, then plane out any unevenness. Avoid hanging the shelves over a radiator.

See also

Marking and measuring page 66

Using backsaws page 71

Chop and sliding compound miter saws pages 89–92

Planing page 58

Finishing, acrylic page 225

TOP AND BOTTOM DOVETAIL LAYOUT

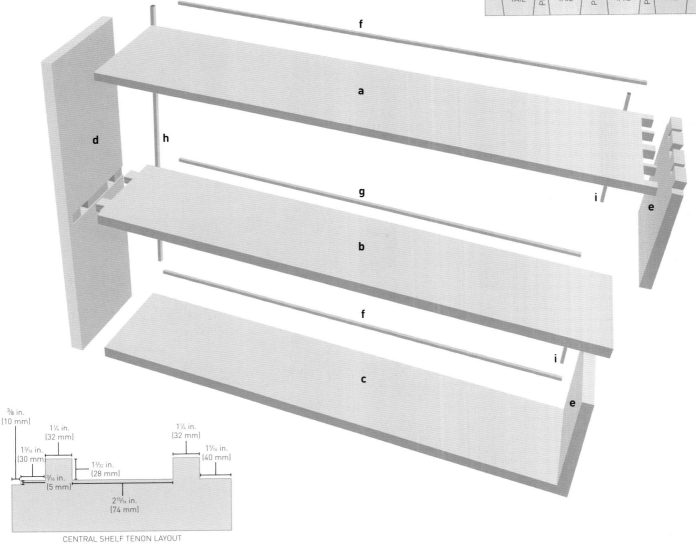

CENTRAL SHELF TENON LAYOUT

Method

Shelf parts

1 Cut the shelf parts to length. An accurate chop or miter saw is good for this; otherwise use a sharp, crosscut handsaw. If you use a handsaw, you will have to shoot the ends on a shooting board. If your chop saw is not accurate, you may also have to shoot the ends. Support the long end of pieces sticking out beyond the board.

2 Establish face side and face edge on each piece — the face edges at the back with face sides inward; on the middle shelf have the face side uppermost. It's worth checking the edges. Don't rely on the machined planing. Mark the corner pairs you will be dovetailing 1 and 2.

Dovetails

3 See pages 153–61 for details on marking and cutting dovetails. Start marking out the dovetails by setting the cutting gauge to the thickness of the shelves and gauging around the end of each piece. Put the shelf pieces to one side.

4 In the photograph and plan, you can see that I have introduced variation in the dovetail widths to add interest to the joint. Lay out a similar spacing on the end of your pieces and square across with a knife. This

is a softwood, so the dovetails have a slope of 1:6. With a knife and suitable template or sliding bevel, mark the slope down to the cutting gauge line. Mark the waste.

5 These are quite chunky dovetails, and you may find sawing them difficult with a small dovetail saw. Do some trial cuts in some offcuts. If it's difficult, try a larger backsaw Do some practice cuts anyway. These dovetails will be on show for many years to come, so practice will pay off.

6 When you are ready, cut the dovetails as described on page 154.

7 Marking the pins will be a challenge. The pin piece is long, so will stick up when in the vise. This is where the pin-marking jig described on page 157 comes into its own. Clamp the jig onto the face side of the sticking-up pin end, so that the side fence is against the face edge and the end is level with the top. Lay the tailpiece face side down, with the face edge against the fence and the end aligned with the outside face of the pin piece.

8 Mark the pin positions with a knife, and square them down to the cutting gauge line. Mark the waste and saw the pins. Roughly cut away the waste with a coping saw, then chop and pare down to the cutting gauge line. Although redwood is

The tail spacings are varied to give visual interest.

The pin-marking jig is really useful because the tailpiece is high above the bench.

Marking and chopping the through mortise and tenon

The shelf is dadoed about ¼ in. (5 mm) into the sides, with two tenons extending through the side and wedged from outside. The dado is mainly to give crispness in the jointing between vertical and shelf. The shoulder between the tenons is likely to be a little uneven, but the dado will hide this.

1 Mark out the position of the dado on the face side of the vertical. Use a marking knife, being very careful that the width of the dado is the same as the shelf width. With a sharp pencil, extend the dado lines around to the outside face and the edges. The lines should meet up.

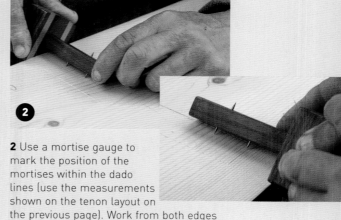

2 Use a mortise gauge to mark the position of the mortises within the dado lines (use the measurements shown on the tenon layout on the previous page). Work from both edges for this, because the outer mortise is too far from the face edge to gauge accurately. For accuracy in positioning the tenons, cut the mortises first, and then mark the tenon positions from them.

a softwood, it can be difficult to cut. Your chisels need to be very sharp. Working with a slight sideways slicing action can also help. The dovetail routing jig described in Chapter 5 (see pages 159–60) could be used here.

9 After a little fettling, your dovetails should be complete. Now mark and chop the through mortise and tenons (see panel, below).

Support strips
11 Rout the recesses in the back of the shelves for the support strips. This is most easily done as a stopped cut on the router table, though you could do it handheld as well (see pages 104–105 and 125). If you don't have a ⅝ in. (15 mm) cutter, use a smaller diameter one and take a cut from both sides of the board. If taking two cuts, the cut is cleaner and safer if you set to cut on the side farthest from the router fence.

12 Drill and countersink ⁵⁄₃₂ in. (4 mm) holes through the face of the board into the recess at centers ¼ in. (7 mm) from the back of the board, 4 in. (100 mm) from the ends and at 12 in. (300 mm) intervals. Arrange that these holes will be in the face that is least exposed — under the bottom shelf and on top of the top shelf, perhaps.

13 Make up some support strips in redwood, ⁹⁄₁₆ x ⁹⁄₁₆ in. (14 x 14 mm) in section (allowing ¹⁄₃₂ in./1 mm wiggle room). Drill and countersink ⁵⁄₃₂ in. (4 mm) holes, 2 in. (50 mm) from either end and at 12 in. (300 mm) intervals.

14 Clean up all shelves and uprights, either with a finely set very sharp plane or with an orbital sander. The corners can be slightly arrised (lightly rounded at the outer edges), but avoid doing this at the joints.

Assembly
15 Finish the inside surfaces before glue-up, so that you don't have to sand into the corners. Mask off the joints and apply three coats of acrylic lacquer (see page 225). Because it's a water-based finish, the grain will rise after the first application and need cutting back thoroughly — or you could raise the grain prior to application (see Step 1, page 221).

16 You are now ready for clamping up. Clamping the dovetail joints will need a clamping strip with cutouts, so that the pressure is exerted only on the dovetails (see top right). Do a dry run first to see that the joint closes up fully and is square. If the joint is nice and tight, you should only need to clamp against the tails, not in the other

Clamping strip

Tails clamped up with cutout clamping strip and checked for square.

direction. When you are happy, apply glue to the sockets between the tails. Gluing on the shoulders or on the faces of the tails has no strength and just adds to squeeze-out.

3 Start by establishing the center of the mortises on both sides by drawing diagonals. Mark the center with an awl. Drill out the waste with a forstner bit that is slightly smaller than the mortise. Drill halfway from both sides to avoid breakout.

4 With the piece on the bench, chop away the waste. Work progressively back to the lines with the chisel at right angles to the grain, until you engage with the cut line. (You should knife the pencil line locally on the outside edge.) Avoid cutting right through to the other side, because this may cause breakout. Angle the chisel slightly to avoid undercutting. When you have cut to the line, put the piece in the vise and pare horizontally to remove

the hump between the two cut lines. You could clamp a piece of waste at the back to support the grain should you slip and pare out the back. Check that all faces are square.

5 Now cut the ¼ in. (5 mm) deep dado, either with the electric or hand router (see pages 144–50).

CONTINUED ▶

17 Before gluing up the tenons, cut some wedges. It's a nice touch if the wedges are in a contrasting wood — perhaps a dark wood, such as walnut. The wedges should be about 1⅜ in. (35 mm) long, tapering from 1/16 in. (1.5 mm) up to 5/32 in. (4 mm), and 1¼ in. (32 mm) wide.

18 Dry run clamp the mortise and tenon with clamps at either edge. Check for square and also that the side is flat. It may have bowed from the pressure at either edge. If so, you may have to make up curved clamping bearers so that the pressure is distributed right across the board. Do not pit the wedges on the dry run. When everything is okay, apply glue to the mortises and the dado. When the joint is properly clamped, tap in the wedges — you want them to appear the same thickness when the end is cleaned off, so tap them in progressively and evenly. Don't drive one home fully before the other.

19 When the joints are set, clean them up with a sharp plane. For the tenons, trim off the protruding wedges first. When planing the dovetails, work from the outside in to avoid breaking out the grain at the ends.

20 Apply finish to the remaining unfinished areas.

21 The shelves are supported by narrow strips fastened to the wall. It is useful to fix the shelves to a thin board first, then use the board as a template for drilling the strips.

22 Lay out the shelf parts on a piece of ⅜ in. (9 mm) MDF. Make sure that the top shelf is parallel to the top of the board. Mark the positions of the parts. Remove them and fix the support strips appropriately, 5/16 in. (8.5 mm) from the edge of the shelf or upright. You should now be able to place the shelves over the support pieces and check everything is fitting well and parallel with the top edge of the board. Number and remove the support pieces, making sure that the drill holes for the pieces went right through the board.

23 An assistant may be needed for this part. Offer the board up to the wall and use a level to check that the top edge is horizontal. Mark the location of a couple of the screw holes through the board. Drill and insert anchors at the marked locations, and screw the board to the wall. Mark the other screw locations and remove the board. Now the screw holes can be drilled and anchored, and the support strips screwed to the wall.

24 Offer the shelves up to the support strips and screw into the strips through the holes at the back of the shelves.

Apply glue to the mortise sides.

Tap the wedges home evenly. Don't worry about squeeze-out — you will be planing later.

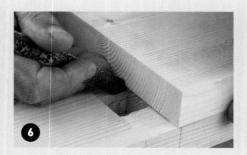

6 Now the tenons. Make the tenons 1/32 in. (1 mm) overlength, so that they can be trimmed off after glue-up. Use a cutting gauge to mark the shoulder line of the tenons, 1 1/16 in. (28 mm) from the end (assuming that the end of the shelf is square). Put the side on the bench, face side uppermost, then put the shelf on top and carefully align the face edges. Mark the

⅜ in. (10 mm)

1 5/16 in. (33 mm)

mortise positions accurately with a knife onto the shelf end, and square around to the cutting gauge lines.

7 Mark the dado notch at the front. This will be 1 5/16 in. (33 mm) from the end and ⅜ in. (10 mm) from the front, non-face edge. Mark the waste.

8 With the shelf upright in the vise, make the vertical saw cuts for the tenons and the dado notch. This is complicated by the length of the shelf, which will be sticking up above the vise, so there will be some vibration when sawing.

Decorative end joints — dovetails (top) and mortise and tenon (above).

9 Saw the two shoulders at the front, taking particular care over the notch shoulder because this will be visible after assembly. Also saw the back shoulder.

The completed tenons, showing the dado notch at the front

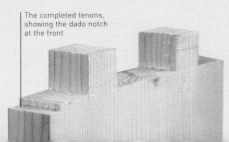

10 Use a coping saw to roughly remove the waste between the tenons. Chop and pare back to the cutting-gauge lines. Although they are not dovetails, you could use the dovetail waste removal jig described in Chapter 5 (see page 161) for removing the waste between the tenons.

11 The tenons will splay out when they are wedged. Open out the mortise slightly on the non-face side to allow for this. Mark knife lines ³⁄₃₂ in. (2 mm) above and below

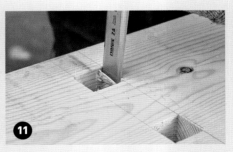

the mortises, but do not extend beyond the mortise width. Pare back to these lines with the chisel angled so that the mortise is slightly wedge shaped.

12 Use a marking gauge to mark each tenon with two lines, ¼ in. (5 mm) from the top and bottom faces of the shelf. Saw down these lines to the tenon shoulders with cuts parallel to the faces. These cuts are to receive the tenon wedges on glue-up. This finishes the jointing.

SKILL LEVEL: **MODERATE**

PROJECT: Oak side table

15¾ in. (400 mm)   31½ in. (800 mm)

33⅛ in. (840 mm)

The clean lines and gently curving rail of this table make it an elegant design. This can be enhanced by careful grain selection so that the faces of the legs have unity and there is continuity of figure in the top. Although it was designed as a side or hall table, the design can be altered to fulfill other functions, reducing the height to 15¾ in. (400 mm) for a coffee table or increasing the width and making the height 29½ in. (750 mm) for a writing table.

Tools + materials list

Power tools
Biscuit joiner

Orbital sander (optional)

Belt sander (optional)

Jigsaw (optional)

Chop saw (optional)

Circular saw (optional)

Router preferably with ½ in. (12 mm) collet

⅜ in. (10 mm) pocket hole cutter (or other long reach cutter)

¹⁄₁₂ in. (12 mm) bearing-guided straight flute

1⅜ in. (35 mm) tenon cutter or similar wide cutter

Router table

Edge tools
Planes: jack plane, block plane

Cabinet scraper

Bevel-edged chisels, various sizes

Mortise chisel ⅜ in. (9 mm or 10 mm) (if cutting mortise by hand)

Spoke shaves

Saws
Crosscut backsaw

Tenon saw (optional; you could use the crosscut saw)

Bow saw (if no jigsaw)

Handsaw (preferably rip)

Measuring and marking
Engineer's square

Small combination square (optional)

Miter square or sliding bevel

Marking knife

Marking gauge

Mortise gauge

Vernier gauge (optional)

Steel rules: 12 in. (300 mm), 36 in. (1 meter)

Clamping
Two bar clamps with at least 33⁷⁄₁₆ in. (850 mm) capacity

One other clamp with at least 20 in. (500 mm) capacity

One pair small toggle clamps

Various
Shooting board

Sanding block

Mallet

Materials
Oak as per cutting list

Screws for fitting toggle clamps

6 no. 10 biscuits

PVA glue

Abrasives 120, 180 and 400 grit in sheet, disk or belt form, depending on sanding method used

Danish oil or hard wax oil, plus cloths for application

Eight "L"-shaped expansion plates (stretcher plates) and fixing screws

Cutting List

DESCRIPTION	QUANTITY	Rough cut			Final dimension		
		MIN. CUT LENGTH	MIN. CUT WIDTH	BOARD THICKNESS	LENGTH + TENON	WIDTH	THICKNESS
a Top boards	3	31⅞ in. (810 mm)	15¹⁵⁄₁₆ in. (145 mm)	1 in. (25 mm)	31½ in. (800 mm)	15¾ in. (140 mm)*	¾ in. (20 mm)
b Legs	4	32¹¹⁄₁₆ in. (830 mm)	1⅞ in. (48 mm)	2 in. (50 mm)	32⁹⁄₃₂ in. (820 mm)	1¹¹⁄₁₆ in. (43 mm)	1¹¹⁄₁₆ in. (43 mm)
c Front rail	2	29 in. (736 mm)	3¾ in. (95 mm)	1 in. (25 mm)	28⁹⁄₁₆ in. (726 mm)	3¹⁷⁄₃₂ in. (90 mm)	¾ in. (20 mm)
d Side rail	2	13¼ in. (336 mm)	3¾ in. (95 mm)	1 in. (25 mm)	12¹³⁄₁₆ in. (326 mm)	3¹⁷⁄₃₂ in. (90 mm)	¾ in. (20 mm)

*15¾ in. (140 mm) is not strictly the "final" dimension, because the top is trimmed to size after glue-up.

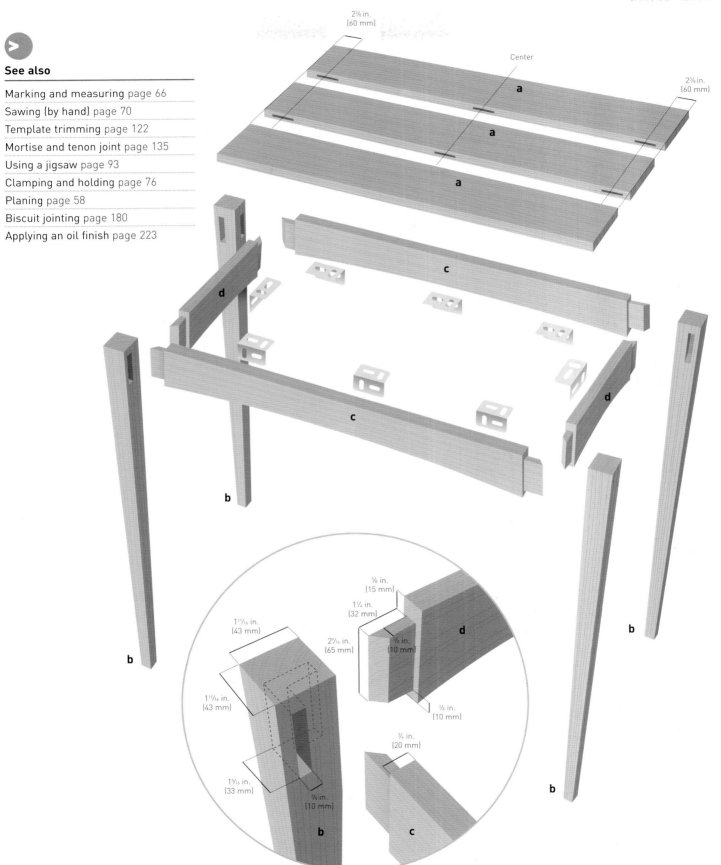

2³⁄₈ in.
(60 mm)

Center

a

a

a

2³⁄₈ in.
(60 mm)

c

d

c

c

b

b

d

b

b

1¹¹⁄₁₆ in.
(43 mm)

1¹¹⁄₁₆ in.
(43 mm)

1⁵⁄₁₆ in.
(33 mm)

³⁄₈ in.
(10 mm)

b

2⁹⁄₁₆ in.
(65 mm)

⁵⁄₈ in.
(15 mm)

1¼ in.
(32 mm)

³⁄₈ in.
(10 mm)

d

³⁄₈ in.
(10 mm)

¾ in.
(20 mm)

c

Method

Start by preparing the parts according to the cutting list. Establish face side and face edge on the legs and rails. The boards for the top will be oversize; the table is cut to final size after glue up. It's good if you can select the wood for the legs so that the annual rings run diagonally across the section. This makes the figure similar on each face. If the rings are parallel to a face, the figure will vary from face to face and look untidy. It's also beneficial if the boards for the top can come from a single plank, which will give a better match for figure and color.

Legs and rails

1 The legs and rails will be oriented with the faces on the inside and with face edges at the top on the rails. Now mark the set of joints (see panel, below).

2 Cut the mortise and tenons using either of the methods in Chapter 5 (see pages 135–43). If you are routing the joints, you don't need to mark out all of them — mark just one joint and use this to set up the router. All the joints can be cut at this setting.

3 The joints will probably need a little adjustment to fit. Number the joints so that you can reassemble them correctly. This

Mark the line of the miter at 45°.

need not be complicated — just number the legs 1–4, then number the tenons that fit the numbered legs. Good face side and edge notation helps here. Do the marking at the tops of the legs and rails, because you are less likely to lose them up there.

4 You will find that the tenons will not fit fully into the mortises; they meet in the middle. The ends need mitering. With a miter square, or a sliding bevel set to 45°, mark the line of the miter on the end of the tenon and square it down the tenon cheeks (make sure that you have the miter facing toward the face side — that is, inward).

5 Saw the miter with a backsaw or chop saw.

Try this!

> Working a curve on the bottom of the rails using hand tools.

Use a long steel rule to mark the curve. The rule can be located against clamps fixed at the bottom corners of the rail. Flex the rule up until the desired curve is achieved (in the example, the height of the arc is ¾ in./20 mm for both long and short rails), then mark the arc with a pencil. I find a truer arc is found if you flex it at two points offset from the center, rather than flexing just at the center. Unless you have very unusual anatomy, you may need an assistant for this job.

Use a bow saw or jigsaw to cut the curve just a tad shy of the line.

Clean up the curve with spoke shaves. See page 65 on using the spoke shave. You may just about be able to work the long rail with a flat-bottomed spoke shave, but the short one will need a convex-bottomed shave. You can check whether the curve is symmetrical by marking the curve on a board and then turning the rail over to see if the curves match up.

Marking a set of joints

1 Put the legs together, with the faces all facing into the middle.

2 Open the legs out along the horizontal joint.

3 Align the ends and clamp the legs together, then mark the mortise position in pencil at the top end, ⅝ in. (15 mm) and 3⅛ in. (80 mm) from the end.

4 Put the legs back together, then open them

out on the vertical joint and mark the mortise on these faces.

5 Clamp the rails together in pairs, with the ends aligned. Using a marking knife, mark the length of the tenons across the top edge at either end at 1⁵⁄₁₆ in. (33 mm).

6 Square the tenon-length knife marks right around each rail.

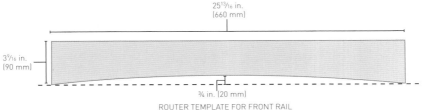

25¹³/₁₆ in.
(660 mm)

3⁹/₁₆ in.
(90 mm)

¾ in. (20 mm)

ROUTER TEMPLATE FOR FRONT RAIL

6 Having done all the jointing, start shaping the pieces. The golden rule is always complete any jointing before you start shaping, if possible. Regular-shaped pieces are easier to work than irregular.

7 Start by working the curve on the bottom of the rails. You can use a router and template for this, but if you want to do it by hand, see the "Try this!" panel, opposite.

8 Make the templates in ⁵/₈ in. (15 mm) MDF or birch plywood. Form the curve using a flexed steel rule and spoke shaves as in the "Try this!" panel, opposite. Make the template about 2 in. (50 mm) longer than the rail. This will give room to run the cutter in before hitting the wood. The template should also be wide enough to fit toggle clamps to hold the workpiece — about 7¹/₁₆ in. (180 mm). The curve could be formed using a trammel (see pages 111–13 on trammel routing), but the radius for the larger curve is 109 in. (2,733 mm), so would require a very long trammel; the smaller curve is only 17¹/₁₆ in. (433 mm), so it is a little more manageable.

9 Fit toggle clamps to the template. They should be fitted to blocks about ⁵/₈ in. (15 mm) thick screwed to the template from

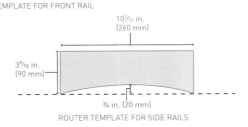

10³/₁₆ in.
(260 mm)

3⁹/₁₆ in.
(90 mm)

¾ in. (20 mm)

ROUTER TEMPLATE FOR SIDE RAILS

below. A piece of abrasive stuck rough side up at the clamp position will stop the workpiece from moving under the clamp.

10 Position the workpiece on the template so that the corners just meet the curve. Mark the curve with a pencil. Cut just shy of the curve with a bow or jigsaw.

11 Fit a bottom-bearing guided straight flute cutter in the router table. A ½ in. (12 mm) diameter cutter would be good. Adjust the cutter so that the bearing hits the template and the cutter the workpiece. See template trimming on page 122.

12 Trim the curve, being careful to feed with the workpiece to the left of the cutter when feeding forward. For the side rail, you will need to cut part of the way, then flip it to avoid breakout (see "Clinic," page 122).

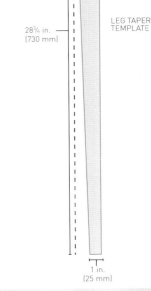

1¹¹/₁₆ in.
(43 mm)

LEG TAPER
TEMPLATE

28¾ in.
(730 mm)

1 in.
(25 mm)

7

8

9

10

7 Set the mortise gauge to the width of the chisel you will be using to chop the mortises.

8 Centralize the mortise gauge on the rail and mark the tenon width.

9 Reset the gauge stock without disturbing the pin setting, so that the outer pin is

1⁵/₁₆ in. (33 mm) from the stock. Mark the mortise width, working from the face.

10 Finally, set a marking gauge to mark the width of the tenon, ⁵/₈ in. (15 mm) and 3¹/₈ in. (80 mm) from the face edge.

Use a template to mark the taper on legs.

Use a handsaw to rip the legs.

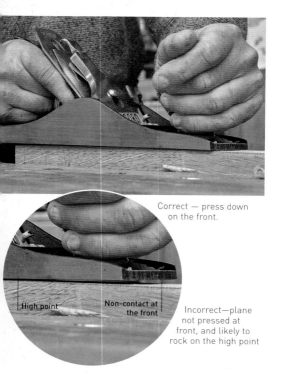

Correct — press down on the front.

High point   Non-contact at the front

Incorrect—plane not pressed at front, and likely to rock on the high point

13 Now to taper the legs. The taper should start just below the rail. Make a template in ¼ in. (6 mm) MDF or plywood, 28¾ in. (730 mm) long and tapering from 1 in. (25 mm) to 1¹¹⁄₁₆ in. (43 mm). Use the template to mark the taper on the legs, locating the narrow end of the taper against the bottom end of the leg. The taper is on the inside edge of each leg, so the waste will be at the bottom end of the face side and edge of each leg.

14 Use a handsaw to rip down the taper on each inside face of all the legs. You will have to re-mark the taper on the sawn face for the second cut. Use a tapered offcut to help with holding in the vise for the second cut.

15 Clean up the sawn edge with a jack plane. If holding the leg in the vise for planing, use a tapered offcut for packing. Planing the taper can be difficult at the point where the taper meets the face at the top of the leg. The plane chatters as it rocks on the high point caused by the change in direction. At the start of the cut, apply pressure to the front of the plane to force it to cut on the tapered surface.

16 You are likely to be planing from the top of the leg downward. The flat at the top of the leg, where the shoulders of the rail sit, must be kept flat, so avoid bringing the taper so far up the leg that it interferes with this surface.

17 Clean up and sand all surfaces, and also very lightly round the corners of the legs and lower edges of the rails (known as arrising). Be careful to preserve your joint numbering marks.

18 The legs and rails are now ready for assembly (see "Clamping and holding," pages 76–77, and "Gluing up components," page 220).

19 When the glue has set, do a final clean-up of any glue squeeze-out.

Tip: The golden rule of gluing up is always to do a dry run. So assemble without glue and check that the joints go together well and that the tops of the legs are level with the rails. This saves finding mistakes when there is glue all over the place. Also, check the diagonals to make sure they are square, then glue and clamp up. The stress-free option is to glue up the ends first, then when they have set, complete the assembly. This also requires fewer clamps.

The top

20 The boards for the top should be jointed and biscuited as described in the sections on edge-jointing on page 151, and biscuiting on page 180. Set the outer biscuits 2⅜ in. (60 mm) from either end, with one in the middle; no. 10 should do. Dry run the glue-up and check for level. Glue when you are happy with the joints.

21 When the glue for the top has set, plane one edge true and trim the other edge to width with a handsaw (or jack or circular saw). Plane off the saw marks.

22 Plane one end square, either freehand in the vise (being careful to plane from the outside inward to avoid breakout) or with a shooting board. Mark off the length with a rule and square, and trim to length. If there is not much to remove, you could plane it; otherwise, saw and plane.

23 Hand plane or belt sand (120 grit) the top and bottom to level, then finish sand the top and edges (180 grit). Arris the corners slightly.

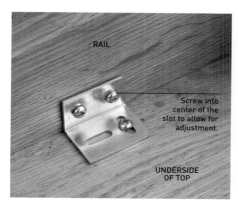

RAIL

Screw into center of the slot to allow for adjustment.

UNDERSIDE OF TOP

Expansion or stretcher plate allows the top to move.

24 The top is fixed to the rails using "L"-shaped expansion plates (also known as stretcher plates) — three on the long edges and one in the middle at either end. These plates are used because the top will expand and contract across the grain, depending on humidity (perhaps $1/8$ or $3/16$ in./3 or 4 mm between winter and summer). Screwing through the slots in the plates that run across the grain will allow for this expansion and contraction. Depending on the plates, use $5/8$ in. (15 mm) no. 8 (or equivalent) screws. You will need to pilot drill for the screws ($3/32$ in./2.5 mm diameter). Use masking tape on the drill to indicate depth. An alternative to expansion plates is wooden "buttons"; see "Try this!" below.

25 Danish oil or a hard wax oil is best for finishing oak (see page 223). Finishing is easier with the top removed.

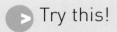 Try this!

> An alternative fixing method would be a wooden "L"-shaped "button" that fits into a slot routed in the inside of the rail.

PROJECT: Workshop cabinet

This simple cabinet is designed to hold and organize essential woodworking tools and materials so that they are easily accessible. The doors and drawers are opened using finger cutouts — a simple but elegant method in minimalist furniture. This size of cabinet should be able to hold a good-sized set of tools, but can be adjusted to suit. The top shelf is narrow to allow tools such as chisels and screwdrivers to be hung on the back of the doors for easy access. You can amend the dimensions to your setup.

See also

Stepped cuts page 123

Marking and measuring page 66

Chop and sliding compound miter saws
    pages 89–92

Using a circular saw pages 86–89

Biscuit jointing pages 180–184

Acrylic lacquer page 225

Construction is almost entirely using biscuits, although dominoes could also be used. The method of construction is the same as would be used in kitchen and other fitted cabinets, making this project a good introduction to this form of cabinetwork. Accuracy in marking out, cutting and checking square is essential. The emphasis is on using power tools on this project; it could be made with hand tools, but it would be hard work.

9¹⁵⁄₁₆ in. (250 mm)

40¹³⁄₁₆ in. (1036 mm)

24⁷⁄₁₆ in. (620 mm)

Tools + materials list

Power tools
Drill, preferably on a stand

1⅜ in. (35 mm) drill bit

Biscuit jointer

Router

Router table

Router cutters:
    ¼ in. (6 mm) straight flute or
        grooving cutter
    1 in. (25 mm) straight flute
    ¹⁄₁₆–³⁄₃₂ in. (2–3 mm) rounding-over
        cutter
    Large 45° cutter (optional)

Orbital sander (optional)

Track saw or other power saw (optional
    but difficult without)

Level for fitting to a wall

Hammer or SDS drill if you are hanging
    the cabinet on a solid wall

Edge tools
Jack plane

Block plane

Saws
Crosscut handsaw

Measuring and marking
Pencil

Steel tape measure

36 in. (1 meter) rule

12 in. (300 mm) rule

4 in. (100 mm) engineer's square

8–12 in. (200–300 mm) engineer's square

Clamping
Six bar clamps with at least 48 in.
    (1200 mm) capacity

Two "F" or "C" clamps with at least 4 in.
    (100 mm) capacity

Various
Sanding block

Materials
Birch plywood and beech as per
    cutting list

2 pairs of 110° overlay clip-on concealed
    hinges with plates and fixing screws

No. 20 biscuits

Adjustable shelf pegs (optional)

120-, 180- and 400-grit sanding sheets

180-grit disks for sander

Clear satin acrylic lacquer, cloths and
    applicators for finish application

Masking tape

PVA glue or similar

Appropriate fixings for the wall

Cutting list

DESCRIPTION	QUANTITY	Final dimension		
		LENGTH	WIDTH	THICKNESS
a Top	1	$39^{3}/_{8}$ in. (1000 mm)	$9^{27}/_{32}$ in. (250 mm)	$^{23}/_{32}$ in. (18 mm)
b Bottom	1	$39^{3}/_{8}$ in. (1000 mm)	$9^{27}/_{32}$ in. (250 mm)	$^{23}/_{32}$ in. (18 mm)
c Sides	2	$24^{13}/_{32}$ in. (620 mm)	$9^{27}/_{32}$ in. (250 mm)	$^{23}/_{32}$ in. (18 mm)
d Bottom shelf	1	$39^{3}/_{8}$ in. (1000 mm)	$8^{21}/_{32}$ in. (220 mm)	$^{23}/_{32}$ in. (18 mm)
e Middle shelf	1	$39^{3}/_{8}$ in. (1000 mm)	$6^{1}/_{2}$ in. (165 mm)	$^{23}/_{32}$ in. (18 mm)
f Adjustable shelf (optional)	1	$39^{11}/_{32}$ in. (999 mm)	$6^{1}/_{2}$ in. (165 mm)	$^{23}/_{32}$ in. (18 mm)
g Back	1	$23^{19}/_{32}$ in. (599 mm)	$39^{31}/_{32}$ in. (1015 mm)	$^{1}/_{4}$ in. (6 mm)
h Side packers	2	$3^{15}/_{16}$ in. (100 mm)	8 in. (203 mm)	$^{1}/_{4}$ in. (6 mm)
i Divider	1	$3^{15}/_{16}$ in. (100 mm)	8 in. (203 mm)	$^{23}/_{32}$ in. (18 mm)
j Drawer front	2	$19^{3}/_{8}$ in. (492.5 mm)	$3^{15}/_{16}$ in. (100 mm)	$^{19}/_{32}$ in. (15 mm)
k Drawer side	4	8 in. (203 mm)	$3^{15}/_{16}$ in. (100 mm)	$^{19}/_{32}$ in. (15 mm)
l Drawer back	2	$17^{7}/_{8}$ in. (454 mm)	$3^{15}/_{16}$ in. (100 mm)	$^{19}/_{32}$ in. (15 mm)
m Drawer bottom	2	$18^{9}/_{32}$ in. (464 mm)	$7^{27}/_{32}$ in. (199 mm)	$^{1}/_{4}$ in. (6 mm)
n Door	2	$24^{13}/_{32}$ in. (620 mm)	$20^{11}/_{32}$ in. (517 mm)	$^{23}/_{32}$ in. (18 mm)
o Cabinet cleat	1	$39^{3}/_{8}$ in. (1000 mm)	$2^{7}/_{8}$ in. (73 mm)	$^{23}/_{32}$ in. (18 mm)
p Wall cleat	1	$35^{7}/_{16}$ in. (900 mm)	$2^{3}/_{8}$ in. (60 mm)	$^{25}/_{32}$ in. (20 mm)

All parts are birch plywood, except for the wall cleat, which can be any wood. I used beech. Cut the pieces so that the surface grain direction is running in the length dimension.

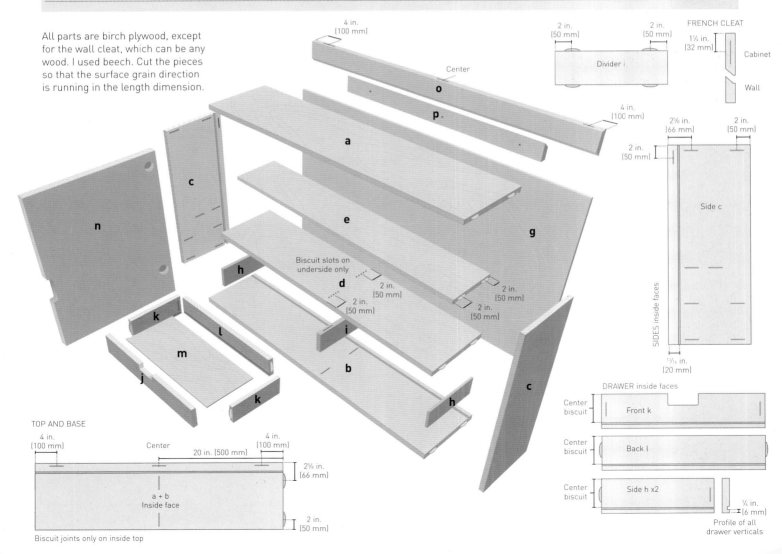

Method

Carcass

1 Prepare the parts for the carcass according to the cutting list. It is important that the edges are clean and true. This is difficult to achieve with a crosscut handsaw. You would need to cut slightly oversize, then plane to final size, making sure that the edges are square. A track saw makes this job much easier, but you must still be sure that all edges are square. The board edges as supplied are usually not crisp and accurate enough, so must be trimmed or planed true. For the drawer components, keep the parts in longer lengths and slightly wider than needed. Form the groove for the bottom ¼ in. (6 mm) wide by ¼ in. (6 mm) deep, as described in Step three. It's expedient not to cut the parts to size yet, because the drawer openings may not turn out as planned. Leaving the drawers uncut gives some wiggle room. For small components, it is good practice to cut the groove in longer lengths and then cut to length. Leave cutting the doors to size until later; again, this leaves room for adjustment.

2 Mark face side and face edge on the components. Face sides will be on the inside or facing up on shelves, with face edges at the back.

3 Rout the groove ¼ in. (6 mm) wide and ⁵⁄₁₆ in. (8 mm) deep in the face sides of the top, bottom and sides. Use a straight flute cutter, either handheld or on the router table, or a side-cutting grooving cutter on the router table. Make a test cut on a piece of scrap wood to check the fit against the back panel. If it is too tight, make the first cut, then adjust and test against the scrap until the fit is good, then make the second cut. See "Biscuit jointing," below.

Drawer dividers

4 The divider between the drawers is fitted in a similar way to the shelves. Place the bottom and the bottom shelf on the bench, with the face edges meeting and the ends aligned. The bottom will be face side up; the shelf will be face side down. Mark across the position of one edge of the divider, and mark with arrows which side of the line the divider will sit. Separate the pieces, and biscuit the joint in the same way as the shelves. The divider will be against an

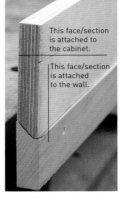

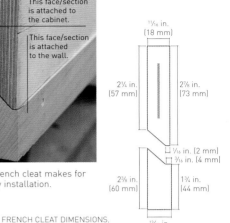

A French cleat makes for easy installation.

FRENCH CLEAT DIMENSIONS.

insert in the groove for the bottom joint, but just aligned with the back edge for the top joint.

French cleats

5 The cabinet is fitted to the wall using a method known as French cleats. This consists of a piece with an inward-angled edge attached to the cabinet, and a piece with a reverse of this angle fixed to the wall. The two pieces hook together when the

---

Biscuit jointing carcass and shelves

1 Stack the top, bottom and sides, with the face edges and ends aligned. Mark the biscuit centers down the end of the stack, 2 in. (50 mm) from the non-face edge and 2⅝ in. (66 mm) from face edge. Turn the stack around. Then reposition so that the other ends are aligned and mark them. As a little reminder for later, roughly pencil in the line of the biscuit positions on the ends of the top and bottom and the inside face of the sides. Some jointers have additional lines offset from the center line. These can be used to biscuit a set distance from the edge without having to mark up. We'll use these for biscuiting the shelves. On the jointer shown, the lines are offset 2 in. (50 mm).

2 Biscuit the corners for no. 20 biscuits, making sure you cut into the previous rough markings. The fence will be on the non-face side of the top and bottom and on the ends of the sides.

3 Now to joint in the shelves. The bottom shelf extends the full depth of

Roughly mark to show the biscuits will be on the ends.

Roughly mark to show the biscuits will be on this face.

Biscuit the top and bottom with fence on outside (non-grooved) face.

Biscuiting the side

cabinet is hung. The step in the angle on the wall cleat and the flat on the cabinet piece are intended to prevent the cleat from being levered away from the wall by a heavy cabinet. This makes for fairly easy installation, with some lateral adjustability.

6 Create the two cleats as shown in the diagram, left. Use 45° cutters on the router table. The step in the wall cleat is difficult to make by hand; you could make it in two parts, planing the angle on a ⅝ in. (16 mm) wide piece, then gluing and clamping on a ³⁄₁₆ in. (4 mm) wide piece for the step.

7 Mark the biscuit centers on the cabinet top and sides and the cleat, then biscuit the joint as follows. There is a ¹⁄₁₆ in. (2 mm) gap between the back edges of the cabinet and the back of the cleat. This is formed by positioning the jointer against the back groove. Place an offcut from the back panel into the back groove, then biscuit (four size 20 biscuits) vertically into the top and sides at the marked positions, with the base of the jointer against the inserted offcut. Rotate the primary fence down, and biscuit into the top and ends of the cleat with the fence on the side with the angled edge.

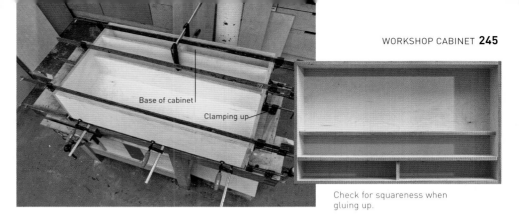

Check for squareness when gluing up.

Assemby

8 Clean up and sand all surfaces, lightly rounding (arrising) the outer edges. Try to retain the face markings in unobtrusive areas, so that you know how the parts go together, especially the shelves.

9 Dry run the assembly. I would suggest working from the bottom up. Fit a side to the bottom, then fit the back panel into the formed "L" shape. Next, add the divider, then the bottom shelf and now the other side. Carefully turn the whole thing onto one side. Angle up the top side, and position the middle shelf, top and cleat. Carefully place the cabinet so that the back is resting on three clamps. Put another three clamps on top and tighten. You will also need "C" or "F" clamps — a wide one for the divider and

small ones for the the cabinet cleat. The edge of the cleat will be delicate, so be gentle with the clamping here. Don't forget to use clamping blocks to protect the work. Check that all joints close up and that the diagonals are equal. Clamping up is always easier with an assistant.

10 Apply the finish to the interior surfaces now, because it's easier to sand flat surfaces than to work into corners. Sand between coats. I would suggest an acrylic lacquer on light-colored birch plywood. Before applying, cover the joints with narrow strips of masking tape, so you don't get finish in the biscuit holes. See page 225 on acrylic lacquer.

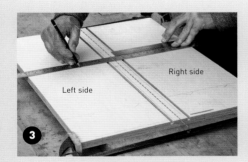

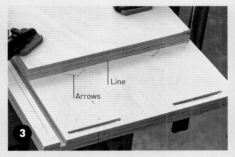

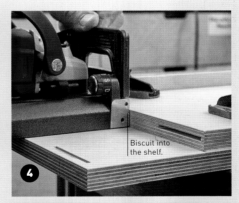

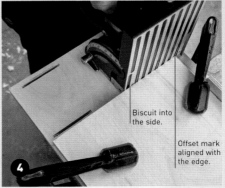

the cabinet interior; the upper shelf is narrower to allow for tools to be hung on the inside of the doors. Both shelves butt up to the back panel. Place the sides together, side by side, with the face edges together, face sides up and the ends aligned. Mark the position of the top edge of both shelves across both faces, 5⅜ in. (136 mm) from the bottom. Mark arrows pointing down on both lines to show the eventual position of the shelf.

4 Place a side on the bench with the grooved side uppermost, and insert an offcut of the back panel into the back groove a little way up from the marked shelf. Place the appropriate shelf face side

down on the side, with the face edge against the insert and the end aligned with the shelf line, so that the arrows on the side are showing. With the jointer base flat on the side, joint into the end of the shelf, with the offset marks on the jointer fence aligned with either edge. Then turn the jointer so that the base is against the end of the shelf and joint into the side — again, with the offset marks aligned with the edges.

Hinge fitting

1 You are using 110° opening overlay hinges. The drilling positions for these may vary depending on the manufacturer. It may be possible to find the specification online; otherwise you may have to establish them by trial and error. For most hinges, the large hinge hole in the door is 1⅜ in. (35 mm) diameter and ⅝ in. (15 mm) deep, with a center ⅞ in. (22.5 mm) from the door edge.

2 Test drill a hole at this position in an offcut and fit the hinge into the hole. Check that it's square and mark the position of the retaining screw holes.

3 Offer the fitted hinge up to another scrap piece and mark the position of the hinge

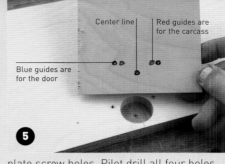

plate screw holes. Pilot drill all four holes and screw the hinge in place.

4 Check the hinge action. Will the door open without fouling at the corner? Does the edge of the door align with the side of the cabinet (the hinge should have an

---

11 Now you can glue up. Use PVA or similar in the biscuit holes and a small bead of glue in the back panel groove. Don't overdo the adhesive. Check for squareness.

Doors

12 Fit the doors before making the drawers. Depending on which hinges you use, the doors may limit the size of the drawer openings, so the doors should be hung first. See panel on hinge fitting, above.

13 Cut the doors to fit, then form 3¹⁵⁄₁₆ in. (100 mm) finger holds on the inner edges of the doors. To do this, put the doors together and mark the cutout positions clearly to avoid later confusion. The cutouts are formed on the router table using stopped cuts with a 1 in. (25 mm) cutter (as described on page 123). Set the width of cut to ¾ in. (20 mm) and clamp on start and end stops. The holes are offset downward, so the start stop should be 16⅝ in. (422 mm) from the outfeed side of the cutter and the stop stop 11¾ in. (298 mm) from the infeed side. To avoid burn marks, make staged cuts, raising the cutter about ¼ in. (6 mm) between cuts and reducing the cutter speed a couple of notches. Adjust the speed further if there are burn marks after the first cut. Burn marks are reduced if you do not hesitate at the start and end of the cut. If you do get burn marks, sand them away with 120-grit sandpaper wrapped around a dowel.

14 Fit the hinges as shown above.

15 Clean up and sand the doors and any exterior surfaces not yet finished. On the doors, a light rounding all around would look good. Do this with a ¹⁄₁₆–³⁄₃₂ in. (2–3 mm) radius bearing-guided rounding-over cutter, either handheld or on the router table, or use a block plane and sanding block.

16 Once sanded, apply finish to those areas not previously done.

Drawers

17 The drawers are of fairly simple construction — no dovetails here! There are packing pieces at either side of the drawer openings — these restrict the opening to allow the drawer to slide out without fouling on the door if it doesn't open clear from the side. You must decide on the width of this packing, depending on the opening position of the door with your hinges. Once the packing has been fitted, you can establish the width of the drawer. This should be about ¹⁄₃₂ in. (0.5 mm) less than the opening, allowing for a nice sliding fit. The width of the drawer will define the length of the front and back pieces.

18 If you followed good practice in Step 1, the sides, front and backs should already be grooved for the drawer bottom. The groove will define the face side and face edges, the face side facing inward with the face edge uppermost. Stack all the drawer components with face edges aligned and mark a center line down either end at 2 in. (50 mm).

19 Now roughly mark the biscuit positions. On the sides at the front, they will be in the end; at the back, they will be on the face side. Keep in mind that the sides are paired, so the back biscuit marking will be on the left on two pieces and on the right on two. On the back, the biscuits will be in the ends. They will be in the face side of the front pieces. The illustration above right shows this clearly.

20 Joint all pieces appropriately using the auxiliary fence (see page 180) set to ⁵⁄₁₆ in. (7.5 mm) and depth to no. 20. Remember that the fence should always sit on the

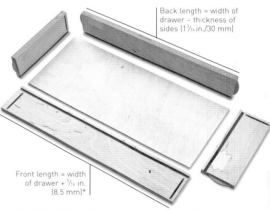

Back length = width of drawer – thickness of sides (1³⁄₁₆ in./30 mm)

Front length = width of drawer + ⁵⁄₁₆ in. (8.5 mm)*

*The ⁵⁄₁₆ in. (8.5 mm) is because the front spans half of the divider between the drawers, with a ¹⁄₃₂ in. (1 mm) gap.

Make sure that the packing clears the open door.

Packing piece

adjusting screw for this)? Is there a gap between the back of the door and cabinet (again, the hinge has some limited adjustability)? Amend the drilling positions if you can't get the correct configuration.

5 When you have the correct configuration, make up a template using the established hole positions in a thin material (I used $1/16$ in./1.5 mm plywood), with a center line and $1/16$ in. (2 mm) holes through which you can mark the drilling positions.

6 When you have established the drilling pattern, mark center lines 2 in. (50 mm) and $17^{29}/32$ in. (480 mm) from the top of the cabinet and the door. Use the template to mark the drilling pattern at those positions. As a precaution, before drilling, check that there is room for the hinge plate on the cabinet side at this position — it may clash with the bottom shelf. Drill appropriately and trial fit the doors using the adjusting screws to get the final fit.

Marking hinge drilling position

faces you want to be aligned when the joint is assembled. The one exception to this rule is the front, where the drawers meet in the center — the fronts overlap the ¾ in. (18 mm) central divider by $11/32$ in. (8.5 mm). Set the fence to $21/32$ in. (16 mm). Remember that the fronts are paired left and right.

21 Fit the ¼ in. (6 mm) drawer bottom. You can now check the fit of the dry-assembled drawers. Some adjustment can be made by planing the side packing pieces if it looks as

if the drawer may be tight, but this can be left until after gluing up.

22 The drawer fronts have finger cutouts for opening. Form these in the same way as the doors, with start and stop blocks 12 in. (300 mm) from the cutter.

23 Clean up and sand the parts. You can apply finish before gluing up.

24 Drill and countersink the wall cleat along its center, 3 in. (75 mm) from either end and centrally with the countersinks on the non-angled side. Offer it up to the wall so that the flat at the bottom of the angle is $3^9/16$ in. (90 mm) from the proposed top of the cabinet. Check that it's level. Mark through the holes with an awl or screw points, then drill for screw anchors suitable for no. 10 screws. Screw the cleat to the wall and slide the cabinet down onto it.

SKILL LEVEL: **DIFFICULT**

PROJECT: Memory box

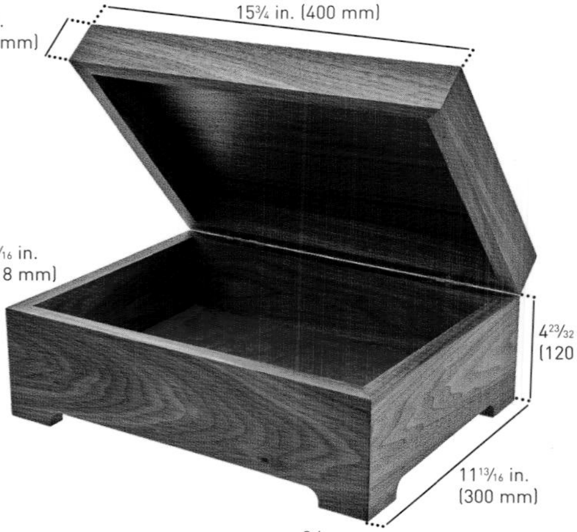

Boxes are a great way to develop your woodworking skills. You can use various jointing techniques, such as splined, keyed miter, dovetail or finger joints for the corners. You can also decorate the box in different ways with carving, veneer and inlays. The other advantage of boxes is that, being small, you don't need much workshop space to make them and they are cheap on materials.

Tools + materials list

Power tools

- Chop or compound miter saw (optional)
- Router
- ¼ in. (6 mm) straight flute cutter
- ¾ in. (18 mm) straight flute cutter
- 1/16 in. (1.5 mm) slitting cutter on a long arbor
- 3/32 in. (1.8 mm) or less straight flute cutter
- 1 in. (25 mm) cutter
- Router table (optional)

Edge tools

- Set of various size bevel-edged chisels
- Jack plane
- Scalpel

Saws

- Crosscut backsaw
- Rip-sharpened tenon saw (if not using a slitting cutter)

Marking and measuring

- Engineer's square, preferably about 8 in. (200 mm)
- Steel rule, at least 24 in. (600 mm)
- Vernier gauge (optional)
- Marking gauge (preferably two)

Clamping

- Approximately eight "C" or "F" clamps (if you are not using strap clamps)
- Pair of strap clamps (optional)
- Six or more quick clamps (optional)

Various

- Box miter shooting board
- No. 2 small slotted posidrive screwdriver
- Pair of mirrors hinged (optional)

Materials

- Wood and veneer as per cutting list
- One pair solid brass 2½ in. (63 mm) butt hinges
- Piece of suede or faux suede, at least 15¾ x 11 13/16 in. (400 x 300 mm)

Cutting list

			Approx. rough cut		
DESCRIPTION	QUANTITY	WOOD TYPE	MIN. CUT LENGTH	MIN. CUT WIDTH	BOARD THICKNESS
a Front/back	2	American walnut	16⅛ in. (410 mm)	6⅞ in. (175 mm)	1 in. (25 mm)
b Side	2	American walnut	12 3/16 in. (310 mm)	6⅞ in. (175 mm)	1 in. (25 mm)
c Top	1	MDF	11 7/32 in. (285 mm)	¼ in. (6 mm)	
d Bottom	1	MDF or plywood	11 3/32 in. (282 mm)	¼ in. (6 mm)	
e Top veneer	4	Burl oak veneer	7⅝ in. (194 mm)	5 ¾ in. (146 mm)	0.02 in. (0.6 mm)
f Balance veneer	1	Walnut	15¼ in. (387 mm)	11 5/16 in. (287 mm)	0.02 in. (0.6 mm)
g Inlay	2	Boxwood stringing	39 in. (1,000 mm)		1/16 in. (1.8 mm) square
h False bottom	1	Birch plywood or MDF	14 9/16 in. (370 mm)	10⅝ in. (270 mm)	1/16–3/32 in. (1.5–2 mm)

Cut and prepare front, back and sides as a single length approximately 59 x 6¾ x ¾ in. (1,500 x 172 x 18 mm).
Boxwood stringing for inlay comes in 39 in. (1 meter) lengths to be cut to fit.

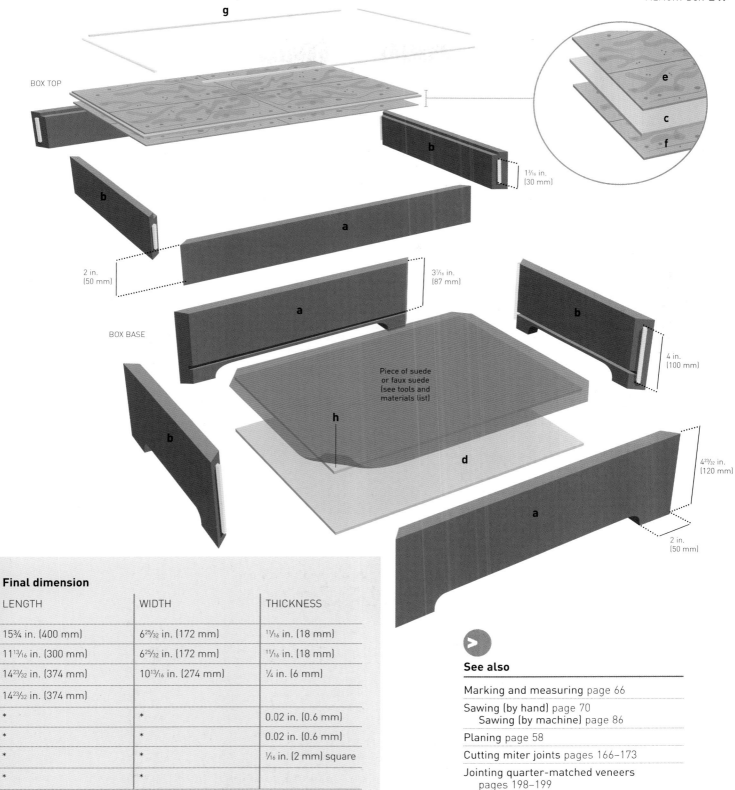

BOX TOP

BOX BASE

g

b

b

a

b

a

a

b

b

a

d

e

c

f

1³⁄₁₆ in.
(30 mm)

2 in.
(50 mm)

3⁷⁄₁₆ in.
(87 mm)

4 in.
(100 mm)

Piece of suede
or faux suede
(see tools and
materials list)

h

4²³⁄₃₂ in.
(120 mm)

2 in.
(50 mm)

Final dimension

LENGTH	WIDTH	THICKNESS
15¾ in. (400 mm)	6²⁵⁄₃₂ in. (172 mm)	1¹⁄₁₆ in. (18 mm)
11¹³⁄₁₆ in. (300 mm)	6²⁵⁄₃₂ in. (172 mm)	1¹⁄₁₆ in. (18 mm)
14²³⁄₃₂ in. (374 mm)	10¹³⁄₁₆ in. (274 mm)	¼ in. (6 mm)
14²³⁄₃₂ in. (374 mm)		
*	*	0.02 in. (0.6 mm)
*	*	0.02 in. (0.6 mm)
*	*	¹⁄₁₆ in. (2 mm) square
*	*	

* Trimmed as appropriate during making

See also

Marking and measuring page 66

Sawing (by hand) page 70
Sawing (by machine) page 86

Planing page 58

Cutting miter joints pages 166–173

Jointing quarter-matched veneers
pages 198–199

Stopped cuts on router table page 123

Applying an oil finish page 223

This box is designed for holding documents and objects of a sentimental value. You can change the dimensions and interior configuration depending on its intended use — perhaps a jewelry or collector's box. The internal dimensions of this design mean it can take letter-size sheets. In this example, the main wood is American walnut, while the top is a quartered burl oak veneer with a boxwood inlay around the edge. Burl oak contrasts well with the walnut.

When making boxes, I like the grain to run unbroken around the outside, although there has to be a discontinuity at one corner. Select the wood from a single board, chosen so that there is attractive grain at the front of the box and along the sides. I prefer walnut sap free; others like the variation provided by the lighter sapwood. Boxes of this design are made as a single piece, the lid being cut off after gluing. This ensures a perfect fit between top and bottom.

Method

Veneering the top

It may seem premature to start the job by veneering the top panel, but early on in the jointing, the box parts need rabbeting to receive the top, and a more accurate fit is possible if the top panel has already been veneered.

1 The top features a quarter-matched burl veneer. Select your veneer and match and joint it as described in Chapter 7, pages 190–91 and 195–203. It's crucial that the axes of the quartering are central. To make sure of this, mark centers on the edge of the board to be veneered. When the veneer is laid, the axes of the quartering must align with the centers. If the veneer or the clamping boards overhang a long way, it can be difficult to spot these positions, so keep the margins narrow. As the panel is small, the quartered burl and balancer can be laid by sandwiching them between ¾ in. (18 mm) plywood or MDF clamping boards and clamping with "C" and "F"

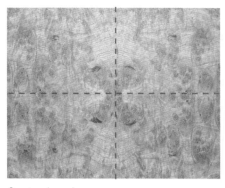

Quartered panel

clamps (see Chapter 7, pages 76–79). If possible, use a urea-formaldehyde glue such as Cascamite, which sets glass hard so there is no danger of the joints opening. If the burl has small holes in it, you could add pigment such as Van Dyck crystals to the glue via the mixing water. After laying, trim off the overhanging veneer and set the panel aside. Check for any adhesion problems and iron them down if possible.

Side

Front

Side

Back

The grain aligns around the front, back and sides of box.

Making the spline/jig

This jig may be useful in other situations, so it's worth making it so that it can take thicker pieces if necessary.

1 Miter the ends of two pieces of ¹¹⁄₁₆ in. (18 mm) MDF or plywood for the top and bottom boards. Check that the mitered ends are square with the sides.

2 Prepare two side pieces with mitered ends.

3 Drill and countersink ³⁄₁₆ in. (4 mm) diameter holes in the top and bottom boards at the positions shown. The countersinking should be on the mitered side.

4 Position and clamp the two side pieces onto the bottom board, as shown in the photograph. The mitered ends of the side piece and the board should form a 90° angle. Pilot drill and screw on the side pieces.

5 Position, clamp and screw the top board, as shown. Again, the angle between the miter on the bottom board and the side pieces and top board should be 90°.

6 Screw a piece underneath, as shown. This is just to hold the jig in the vise at an appropriate angle, so any scrap piece will do as long as it can locate firmly in the vise.

7 In use, the workpiece is offered up so that the mitered face is level with the top surface, the router fence bears against the bottom board mitered face and the top board face supports the router base.

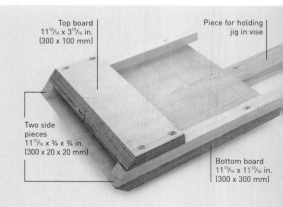

Top board
11¹³⁄₁₆ x 3¹⁵⁄₁₆ in.
(300 x 100 mm)

Piece for holding jig in vise

Two side pieces
11¹³⁄₁₆ x ¾ x ¾ in.
(300 x 20 x 20 mm)

Bottom board
11¹³⁄₁₆ x 11¹³⁄₁₆ in.
(300 x 300 mm)

Mitering the corners

If you are mitering the corners by hand, it's worth re-reading the sections on box miter joints in Chapter 5, page 172.

2 Prepare the parts for the box front, back and sides as a single board. Mark out the position of the parts along the length of the board so that the grain will run around the box when it is constructed. This should be just an approximate layout at the moment, with about ⅝ in. (15 mm) allowance for cutting between each piece. Check and mark the face side and face edge on each piece before cutting; the face side should be on the inside, with the face edge at the top.

3 You could groove for the bottom and rabbet for the top while everything is in one length. However, there's the possibility of breakout when planing the miters, so leave this until later. If using the chop saw, you could groove and rabbet now.

4 Cut out the parts. This is straightforward if you have a compound miter or chop saw. Set the tilt on the saw to 45°. Take two test cuts and check that the two together form a right angle. Make the cut proper when you are ready. Use a stop to make sure that the paired parts are equal length. If you are hand cutting, rough cut the mitered corners or just cut square across and rely on the shooting board to remove most of the waste. If rough mitering, mark the line of the miters, then saw just shy of the line with a crosscut backsaw. Whichever method you use, the face of the miters should be facing the face side; check this before sawing.

5 If the miters were rough cut, trim them on the box miter shooting board (see page 170). Check that the paired parts are equal length.

Reinforcing the miters

The miters on their own will not be strong enough — they need reinforcing. My preferred method is to rout grooves for splines in the miter faces. Another method is to fit veneer keys across the corner as described in Chapter 5, page 173. If you do use keys, make up a test miter so that you can check your technique before going at the real thing.

6 There are two spline positions, one for the lid and another for the base. Mark for the groove position on the miter faces. If you line up the mitered ends with the face

Shoot the miters.

Mark the spline positions.

Check miter is level with top of jig.

Routing spline grooves

Cut splines to width, minus ¹⁄₃₂ in. (1 mm) for wiggle room.

edges aligned to create a single flat surface, you should be able to mark across a set. Mark at ⅜, 1⁹⁄₁₆, 2⁷⁄₁₆, 6⅜ in. (10, 40, 62 and 162 mm) from the face edge.

7 The spline will consist of a piece of ¼ in. (6 mm) thick MDF or plywood, ¹⁵⁄₃₂ in. (12 mm) wide, so the grooves in the miter faces will be ¼ in. (6 mm) wide and ¼ in. (6.5 mm) deep. Make sure your router cutter will make a groove no wider than your spline material; otherwise you may have to make up some solid pieces for the splines.

8 The problem with routing miters is that there is no end for the fence to run against. You will need a jig (see panel, opposite).

9 Use an offcut of the same thickness as the sides to set up the router. Miter the end of the offcut and mark the position of the groove on the face, ⁹⁄₃₂ in. (7 mm) from the inside edge. Clamp the test piece in the jig so that the mitered face is level with the top. With a ¼ in. (6 mm) straight flute cutter in the router, set the fence so that the cutter is aligned with the marked line and adjust the depth stop to give a depth of ¼ in. (6.5 mm). Make a test cut and adjust until the depth and position are correct.

10 Groove the mitered faces of each side within the previously marked lines.

11 Make up some splines to fit the grooves. Hopefully your ¼ in. (6 mm) plywood or MDF is a snug fit in the grooves — do a test with an offcut. It's best to make the splines as a long strip of the correct width — that is, 3¹⁵⁄₁₆ in. (99 mm) and 1³⁄₁₆ in. (29 mm). Plane a rounding on the edge, then cut to length — ½ in. (12 mm).

12 You can now to do a test assembly to check that the joints are okay.

Grooving for top and bottom

The top panel fits in a rabbet in the top, and the bottom is fitted into a groove in the sides. These must be formed before the box is assembled. For a refresher, see Chapter 4, pages 104–108 and 118–20 on grooving and rabbeting.

13 The groove for the bottom is ¼ x ¼ in. (6 x 6 mm), 1 in. (25 mm) from the bottom (non-face edge). Make the groove on the router table with a straight flute or grooving cutter. It can also be done with the hand-held router, but it's easier on the table. Make test cuts to check the fit. Your cutter is not likely to be exactly the correct size, but make sure it's not too big. If it's too small, you will have to groove in two cuts, adjusting in between.

Tip: When making test cuts for grooving or rabbeting, make the first cut quite long and keep the second cut short. If you make the second cut the full length of the first and it's too wide, you have lost the original groove width for further tests.

---

14 While you are in this mode, you can form the rabbet for the top. The top panel is ¼ in. (6 mm) board veneered with two leaves of veneer about 0.02 in. (0.6 mm) thick, so it should be about ⁹⁄₃₂ in. (7.2 mm). Check this with a vernier gauge. You want the rabbet to be ¼ in. (6 mm) wide and 0.01 in. (0.25 mm) deeper than the veneered

panel. This will mean minimal cleaning up after fitting. This is best done on the router table, but can be achieved using a hand-held router — use a ¾ in. (18 mm) cutter. Take test cuts, adjusting the fence and checking with the top panel until you have the desired fit; aim for just a smidgen protruding above the panel surface. When you are ready, make the cut in one pass.

Make a ¼ in. (6 mm) saw cut 2 in. (50 mm) from back edge to prevent breakout.

Make a series of cuts to form the feet.

Creating the "feet"

The bottom of the box sides are profiled to give the appearance of feet. This is most easily done using a stopped cut on the router table. Look at Chapter 4, page 123, for a refresher on this.

15 Fit a 1 in. (25 mm) straight flute cutter. The recess is ¹³⁄₁₆ in. (20 mm) wide, so set the fence to ¹³⁄₁₆ in. (20 mm) from the outside edge of the cutter. The cut will be made between stops. For the front and back, the stops should be 13¾ in. (350 mm) from the far edge of the cutter and 9²⁷⁄₃₂ in. (250 mm) for the sides.

16 Set the router speed a couple of notches below maximum and the cutter height at about ³⁄₁₆ in. (5 mm) and make stopped cuts in the bottom. Repeat, raising the cutter ⁵⁄₃₂–³⁄₁₆ in. (4–5 mm) each time, until the recess is complete. If there is evidence of burning after the first cut, reduce the cutter speed slightly. There is a danger of break-out at the end of the cut. Prevent this by making a slight saw cut about ¼ in. (6 mm) deep at 2 in. (50 mm) from the back end on each cut.

Glue up

Clamp the box by using either a pair of strap clamps or miter clamping blocks as described in Chapter 5, page 78. I prefer to use clamping blocks.

17 Before assembly, clean up and sand all parts, lightly planing or scraping, then sanding to 180 grit. Do not try planing the veneered panel. The panels will be sanded further when the inlay is applied.

18 If using clamping blocks, dry assemble and clamp each joint individually and check for square and that there are no gaps. If using strap clamps, dry clamp the whole assembly with the bottom in (the top will be fitted later), and check all joints and diagonals.

19 When you are ready, apply glue to the spline grooves and miter faces. If using straps, clamp up the whole assembly and check. If using miter clamping blocks, glue and clamp diagonally opposite corners, and check for square on the internal corner with an engineer's square. When the corners have fully set, glue up the other corners with the bottom in place.

Finished back

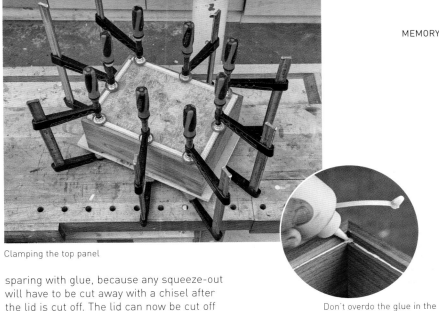

Clamping the top panel

20 Now fit the burl panel. The axes of the quartering need to be square and central in the panel. Hopefully, the alignment will have been correct when the veneer was laid. To centralize the axes, measure the size of the opening the panel will fit into, then halve these dimensions and mark them from the axes to the edge. This should give you lines to cut to, to fit the panel into the recess. Final fitting should be by trimming with a block plane.

21 When the panel is a snug fit into the recess, apply a thin bead of glue to the corner of the rabbet and clamp the top in place with "C," "F" or quick clamps, with narrow clamping strips at the edge. Only light pressure needs to be applied at the very edge of the panel; if you clamp away from the edge, you will dish the top. Be sparing with glue, because any squeeze-out will have to be cut away with a chisel after the lid is cut off. The lid can now be cut off (see panel, below).

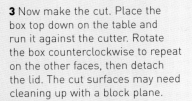

Don't overdo the glue in the rabbet, because squeeze-out will be difficult to remove.

Cutting off the lid

Having made the lid and bottom as one piece, they should be a perfect fit when the lid is removed. The best way of cutting the lid is with a slitting cutter on the router table. You could do it with a rip-sharpened backsaw, but it's tricky and you would have more cleaning up to do afterward.

1 When the top panel is glued, clean up the top — the edges may protrude slightly above the surface. Lightly cut them back with a sharp block plane or scraper.

2 To cut the lid with the slitting cutter, set up the router table with the 1/16 in. (1.5 mm) slitting cutter on a long arbor at a height of 2 1/16 in. (52 mm). Set the fence so that the cutter just fails to cut through the side, leaving a paper-thin wafer. You can check the setting on a suitable thickness offcut. You leave this piece to support the body of the box at the end of the cut, so that it doesn't drop down onto the cutter. A light twist or cutting through with a scalpel will detach the two parts.

3 Now make the cut. Place the box top down on the table and run it against the cutter. Rotate the box counterclockwise to repeat on the other faces, then detach the lid. The cut surfaces may need cleaning up with a block plane.

4 To saw off the lid by hand, use a cutting gauge to mark carefully around the faces of the box 1 31/32 and 2 1/16 in. (50 and 52 mm) from the top. Place the box in the vise, angled so that one corner is uppermost, and saw down between the lines, preferably with a rip-sharpened tenon saw. Turn the box and angle the saw as the cut progresses. When you have to clamp the cut part of the box in the vise, slip a narrow packing piece into the kerf. The cut will require some cleaning up. Mark the lid and box to make sure you offer them up the right way around when checking fit.

You can use a rip-sharpened tenon saw or backsaw to saw off the lid.

End of first cut. Now turn the box counterclockwise for the second cut.

Setting the cutter to 2 1/16 in. (52 mm)

THE CUT LID

Make a test cut in some scrap wood before you attempt to fit the inlay.

Rout the inlay groove with end packing to support the router.

Clean up the corners with a wide chisel.

Inlaying the lid

The joint between the burl panel and the solid walnut lid is covered up by ³⁄₃₂ in. (1.8 mm) or less inlayed boxwood stringing. The groove for the stringing is cut with the router.

22 Set up the router with a ³⁄₃₂ in. (1.8 mm) or less straight flute cutter. Set the depth stop to cut slightly shallower than the depth of the stringing. If you have a micro-adjuster on your router, insert the stringing into the gap of the depth stop, then tweak the micro- adjuster to get the final depth. Set the fence so that the cutter straddles the joint between burl and walnut, with a bias to the burl side.

23 Make a test cut in a long piece of scrap wood. Check the groove is not wider than the stringing and a smidgen — ¹⁄₆₄ in. (0.25 mm) — shallower than the thickness of the stringing. Now make the cut. Start and end at the line between burl and walnut — do not overshoot. Carefully position the cutter before plunging at the start of the cut, and take a steady cut to just shy of the joint at the other end. There's a lot invested in this piece and it is possible to go wrong! There can be a problem with the router dropping at the end of the cut as the corner drops into the gap in the base. You could arrange some support packing beyond the end of the box. Check it works with a test run before making the cut. Remember to breathe when making these cuts. Repeat the cut on all four edges. Adjust the fence slightly to get a snug fit for the stringing. Keep testing with short cuts on the test piece until you are happy with the fit, then repeat the cut on all edges.

24 You now have a groove all around the edge, but the corners will be a bit untidy, especially the outside edges. Use a wide chisel aligned along the groove edge to cut into the corners to define them. I use a small tool made from a sharpened nail to remove the cut waste from the corners and along the groove.

25 Hopefully, your stringing will fit smoothly into the groove. If it's tight in places, you can ease it slightly using a cabinet scraper. The stringing is mitered into the corners. Start by mitering one end of a piece. Cut the stringing with a very sharp, wide chisel.

Miter one end of the stringing. When the stringing and its reflection are at 90°, the miter is true.

Use a chisel to lightly mark the end miter in the groove, lining up the chisel with the miter in the side.

You can make sure that the cut is a true miter by looking at the reflection of the stringing in the back of the chisel. If it's at 90° to the actual stringing, the cut will be at 45°. The chisel is only good for trimming — it does not cut cleanly or square vertically if you cut off more than about ¹⁄₃₂ in. (0.5 mm). With one end mitered, lay the stringing in the groove, with the mitered end butted up to the end, and mark the cut position at the other end with a scalpel or chisel. Cut the piece oversize with the chisel, then miter trim back to the line. Check and repeat for the other pieces. When checking fit, especially if the fit is tight, avoid putting all the inlay in at the same time — it can be difficult getting it out again. Always make sure that one piece is not fully inserted.

26 Once you are happy with the fit, you can glue up. Remove one piece of stringing and

With the first piece ready for gluing, lift the second piece before you press the first piece home.

Scrape back the inlay with a cabinet scraper.

use a narrow-nozzled dispenser to put a very thin bead of glue in the groove. Offer the stringing into the groove with the miter butted up, but before you press it home, lift the next piece. Press the first piece home and then proceed with the next piece in the same way and so on.

27 Press the inlay home fully by rubbing down with a tool handle or similar.

28 Leave overnight for the glue to fully cure, then scrape and sand the stringing back to the veneer surface.

Hinging the lid

The lid is fitted using 2½ in. (62 mm) long solid brass butt hinges. You could use quadrant hinges, but I find them fiddly to fit. Box hinges with an integral stop are stylish and easy to fit with a router table, but they are quite expensive. Badly fitted hinges can spoil the look of a box, so you may want to practice on some scrap before fitting them.

1 Start by fitting the hinges to the box base. With a pencil and square, mark off the position of the hinges 2 in. (50 mm) from the side. Offer the hinges up and mark the length.

2 Set a marking gauge to the width of the hinge — this is from the flap edge to the middle of the hinge pin. Mark the hinge width between the pencil marks, with the gauge stock on the outside face.

3 Now define the hinge length more precisely with a marking knife or scalpel. With square and knife, mark one of the pencil lines, stopping on the gauge line. Offer the hinge precisely on the cut line and mark the length again with the knife point.

4 Square across with a knife. If using a marking knife, arrange for the square to be on the outside of the hinge area so that the flat of the knife is facing out.

5 Mark the hinge length a short way down the outside face with a pencil. Set the marking gauge to very slightly under half the thickness of the hinge knuckle and mark this between the penciled lines. If you have two marking gauges, set one to the width and the other to the thickness. Then you can keep these settings for marking the lid later; this will give greater accuracy.

CONTINUED ▶

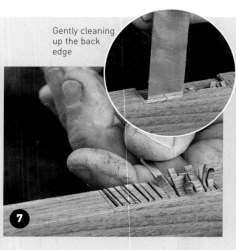

Gently cleaning up the back edge

6 Make light, sloping saw cuts that stop at the gauge lines. Now break up the waste further with chisel chops down at right angles to the gauge lines, stopping short of the knife lines at either end.

7 Pare away the waste, working down to the gauge line. The biggest danger here is overshooting and cutting beyond the width gauge line. Use your index finger against the back to control this.

8 When the waste has been removed, locate the chisel in the knifed lines at either end and chop the length.

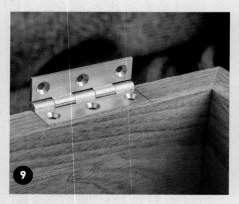

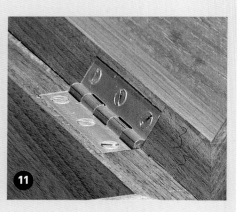

9 Offer the hinge up to check the fit and make adjustments. It should be a press fit, with the top of the flap level with the surface or just below. Fit the hinges into the recesses and mark the center of the middle screw hole with an awl. The mark could be offset very slightly toward the interior so that the screw pulls the hinge into the recess. Drill pilot holes and screw in the hinges with one screw.

10 Now offer the lid up so that it is precisely aligned on the base (make sure it's the right way around!) and mark the hinge position with knife or scalpel. You can now mark up and cut the hinge recesses in the lid in the same way as the base.

11 Fit the hinges initially with single screws and check the alignment of the lid. It may be possible to correct any misalignment by adjusting the recesses. Having just one screw allows slight repositioning using the other screw holes. Check also that the lid sits down on the base easily; if the hinge recesses are too deep, the lid will not come down properly and will leave a slight gap at the front. Correct by planing the areas where the lid is bearing on the base.

Tip: Hinges can be polished using fine abrasive paper and 0000 gauge steel wool. Some people like to have the screw slots aligned when they finally fit the hinges, but I think life is too short for that sort of thing!

Tip: When using brass screws, there is the danger of the screw shearing off just below the shank. To avoid this, drive in a waxed steel screw of the same gauge before using the brass screw.

Finishing

A hard wax oil or Danish oil would be a good finish for this piece. See Chapter 7, page 223, for details on this. The inside can be left unfinished or sealed with shellac sanding sealer.

29 The false base for fitting the suede or fabric bottom should be smaller than the box interior all around by the thickness of the suede. The suede I used was 1/32 in.

(1 mm) thick — yours may be different. Test the fit of the false bottom by pressing it into the box with the suede loosely fitted. Trim the suede so that there is an overhang of about 5/8 in. (15 mm) all around and trim off the corners so there is no overlap when the suede is folded over. Lightly stretch and stick the suede where it folds underneath, using a contact adhesive. Now stick the false bottom in with PVA, weighing it down while it is sticking.

30 Polish up the hinges and fit the lid, avoiding overtightening and breaking the screws. The lid can drop right back when opened. You could fit a light chain to prevent this.

Glossary

Arris A sight chamfering or rounding of edges. This makes for a better finish and shows care in the making.

Back feeding Using the router in the reverse direction to normal to obtain a cleaner cut. Should only be attempted with a very fine cut, 1/32 in. (1 mm) or less.

Bench dog Wooden or metal posts that fit into holes in the vise or bench top to aid work holding.

Book matching A way of jointing boards or veneers by "opening" out previously meeting faces so that a symmetrical figure is achieved down the joint.

Breakout Splitting of grain at an edge, caused by the cutting tool pulling fibers away at the back of a cut.

Bundle A collection of consecutive veneer leaves — 24 or 32 in a full bundle and 12 or 16 in a half bundle.

Burl A decorative veneer cut from the bulbous growth often found on the side of a tree trunk.

BZP Bright zinc plated. A zinc plating used to prevent rust on steel fixings; most common steel screws are BZP.

Cathedral window figure Arched figuring on a board or veneer shaped like a cathedral window.

Concealed hinge The standard kitchen cabinet door-style hinge. Usually sprung and often with a soft-close option.

Cordless Cordless power tools are powered by a rechargeable battery — as opposed to corded, which plug into the mains or a transformer.

Counterboring A method of concealing the screw head in a wider hole at the top of the clearance hole. The head is entirely sunk below the surface, unlike countersinking, where it is level with the surface.

Countersink bit A drill bit with conical shaped end, used for forming countersink holes for screw heads.

Countersunk A screw head is set into a conical hole so that it sits level with the surface.

Crotch veneer Veneer cut from the intersection of the branches and trunk of a tree (the crown). This often gives an attractive chaotic figure.

Dado joint A joint formed by grooving a surface to receive another piece; also known as a housing joint.

Datum A line or surface that you know is true, which is used as a reference for marking and measurement.

De-nibbing Rubbing down a finish between coats to remove dust inclusions in the surface, usually done with very fine-grit abrasive paper.

Earth pigments Natural pigments that can be used for coloring fillers and finishes to achieve color matches when touching up a finish.

Edge tools Tools whose cutting action is from a single sharp edge acting on the wood surface.

Effective pitch Angle of the cutting edge of a plane blade in relation to the cut surface. In a bevel down plane, this will be the angle of the blade. For bevel up, it will be the blade angle plus the honing angle.

EMC Equilibrium saturation point; the moisture content of wood that is in equilibrium with the surrounding air. In normal centrally heated situations, this is about 10–12% EMC.

Euro screw A parallel-sided thick-threaded screw used for fixing fittings such as concealed hinges.

FFP ratings Filtering facepiece ratings specify the level of protection provided by a dust mask. FFPC is acceptable for most woodwork.

Figure Pattern created by the intersection of the annual rings with the cut surface.

FSP Fiber-saturation point; the moisture content of drying wood where all the free water between the cells has been evaporated and the remaining water is in the cell walls. FSP is usually 28–30%.

Gang saw Series of circular or band saws used in a wood mill to cut a number of planks from a log in one pass.

Glue line A slight gap between two glued parts, usually caused by bad jointing or clamping technique.

Grain direction The direction of the wood fibers in relation to the worked surface; not to be confused with figure.

Guide bush A collar fitted under the base of the router that is concentric with the cutter. The collar follows an edge or template to guide the cut.

Kerf The groove left by the action of the saw teeth.

MC Moisture content; the moisture content of wood as a percentage by weight.

OSB Oriented strand board. Man-made board used in the building industry.

Particle board Man-made board formed from particles or flakes of wood formed by compression with adhesive in a heated press. Includes chipboard, oriented strand board (OSB), flake or wafer board.

Patina The aged look to the finish on antique furniture produced by years of polishing and wear and tear.

PIR Polyisocyanurate insulation. The cream-colored insulation that is standard use in most building work.

Pith The center of the trunk around which the annual rings are concentric, often weak and prone to splitting and insect attack when converted.

Plug cutter A hollow cutter that can drill circular plugs. Useful for filling drilled screw clearance holes or drilled-out surface defects.

Plunge cut Some router bits have a plunge cut facility; others do not. You can tell by looking at the end of the cutter. If there is a flat spot in the middle, it is not plunge cut; if there is a cutting edge in the middle, it is.

Posidrive A system for driving screws into a substrate. The screw head has a cross-shaped slot pattern in the head, the screw being driven by a posidrive screwdriver with a cross-shaped end.

PSA Pressure-sensitive adhesive; commonly found as "sticky-back plastic."

RCD Residual current device; a safety device that protects against electrocution and electrical fires by cutting the power if it detects exceptional electrical flow.

RH Relative humidity; the amount of water in the air at a given temperature as a percentage of the total amount that could be held at that temperature.

Ripping Cutting wood in the direction of the grain.

Riving knife A thin metal plate positioned behind a circular saw blade about the thickness of the blade. Its function is to prevent the wood from pinching the blade should it distort while cutting.

Rod A full-size workshop drawing, sometimes reduced to three strips on a board, showing the measurements for height, depth and width.

ROS Random orbital sander. A sander with two orbiting motions, one a very narrow orbit of around $\frac{1}{8}$–$\frac{3}{16}$ in. (2.5–5 mm), the other a rotation of the complete disk. Random orbital sanders are good for fine finishing work.

piece A piece used in a cutting process to prevent damage to the workpiece (often breakout). The sacrifice piece is later discarded.

Sanding block A block around which abrasive paper is wrapped to aid flat sanding. Usually cork.

Sawhorse A trestle or stand for supporting wood while making rough cuts.

Scary sharp A sharpening system using abrasive stuck to float glass. The abrasive is usually 3M microfinishing film on a PSA backing, but can be wet-and-dry silicon carbide paper spray-mounted on glass.

Shim Thin pieces of material used to accurately space parts of an assembly. Shims are often thin metal washers of varying thickness.

Shoulder The stepped part of a joint that bears on the surface of the fitted piece.

Sketchup A popular free 3D design tool. Fairly intuitive to learn, but takes longer to master.

Slip matching A method of jointing veneers by moving them sideways so that a repeated figure is achieved.

Slitting cutter A very thin side-cutting router cutter useful for parting the tops on boxes.

Smidgen A term for a small amount, maybe around 0.01 in. (0.25 mm).

Squeeze-out Glue that squeezes out as a joint is clamped up; should be kept to a minimum.

Straight edge A reference tool to check for flatness; could be a steel rule or the edge of a plane or chisel.

Tack cloth A fine cloth, usually cotton gauze, impregnated with a tacky resin. Used to wipe down surfaces to remove dust particles prior to finish application.

Thou Can be a rough term of measurement for a very, very small amount, or more specifically one thousandth of an inch.

Toggle clamps Lever-activated hold-down clamps, usually fixed to a baseboard. They come in various configurations and are very useful for holding the workpiece to jigs and templates.

Tooth set The bend in a saw's teeth either side of the center line. The greater the TPI, the finer the set.

TPI Teeth per inch; a measure of the coarseness of a saw.

Trammel A method of fixing a marking or cutting tool at a central point, then rotating the tool around that point to form an arc or circle. Specifically used with the router.

Triple chip A tooth configuration for circular saws, with alternate teeth being trapezoidal in shape. Triple-chip blades are very good for cutting veneered and laminated boards.

Vernier gauge A very accurate caliper-style gauge for precise measurement.

Webrax An abrasive nylon pad useful as a substitute for sandpaper or steel wool, particularly when sanding moldings in oak or other tannin-rich woods where ferrous contamination may be a problem. It's color coded for coarseness; the commonly used grade is fine/gray. Also sold as Scotch-Brite.

Index

Credits

All step-by-step and other images are the copyright of Quarto Publishing plc. While every effort has been made to credit contributors, Quarto would like to apologize should there have been any omissions or errors — and would be pleased to make the appropriate correction for future editions of the book.

John Garon, for the author portrait on page 6
GTS Productions/Shutterstock p.7
Gucio_55/Shutterstock p.11
Mahey/Shutterstock p.12
Russell Kord/Alamy p.13
Fekete Tibor/Shutterstock p.10

We would like to thank Axminster for kindly supplying images: Axminster Tools & Machinery, www.axminster.co.uk

We would like to thank Workshop Heaven for kindly supplying tools: Workshop Heaven Ltd, www.workshopheaven.com

WORKSHOP HEAVEN
Fine Tools

We would like to thank Brandon Tool Hire for kindly supplying tools: Workshop Heaven Ltd, www.brandontoolhire.co.uk

With special thanks to Castle Gibson, MC Motors, for use of their location.

Author acknowledgments
I would like to thank Quarto for giving me the opportunity to write this book, and also the excellent furniture maker Neal Crampton who shares my workshop. Neal tolerated being excluded from the workshop during photoshoots with great stoicism. Also, I should mention all the students I have taught over the years. Teaching is not a one-way street — often I learn as much from them as they do from me. Finally, I would like to thank my wife, Alison, for putting up with my grumpiness when things were not quite going to plan.

Updates and resources
Updates and resources to supplement this book are available at:
www.christribefurniturecourses.com/complete-woodworking